CUSTOMS AND FASHIONS

IN

OLD NEW ENGLAND

BY

ALICE MORSE EARLE

" Let us thank God for having given us such ancestors; and
let each successive generation thank him not less fervently,
for being one step further from them in the march of ages."

CORNER HOUSE PUBLISHERS
WILLIAMSTOWN, MASSACHUSETTS 01267
1974

FIRST PUBLISHED 1893

REPRINTED 1969

BY

CORNER HOUSE PUBLISHERS

2nd reprinting 1974

Standard Book Number: 0-87928-007-7

Printed in the United States of America

To the Memory of my Father

CONTENTS

CUSTOMS AND FASHIONS

IN

OLD NEW ENGLAND

I

CHILD LIFE

FROM the hour when the Puritan baby opened his eyes in bleak New England he had a Spartan struggle for life. In summer-time he fared comparatively well, but in winter the ill-heated houses of the colonists gave to him a most chilling and benumbing welcome. Within the great open fireplace, when fairly scorched in the face by the glowing flames of the roaring wood fire, he might be bathed and dressed, and he might be cuddled and nursed in warmth and comfort; but all his baby hours could not be spent in the ingleside, and were he carried four feet away from the chimney on a raw winter's day he found in his new home a temperature that would make a modern infant scream with indignant discomfort or lie stupefied with cold.

Nor was he permitted even in the first dismal days of his life to stay peacefully within-doors. On the Sunday following his birth he was carried to the meeting-house to be baptized. When we consider the chill and gloom of those unheated, freezing

churches, growing colder and damper and deadlier
with every wintry blast — we wonder that grown
persons even could bear the exposure. Still more do
we marvel that tender babes ever lived through their
cruel winter christenings when it is recorded that the
ice had to be broken in the christening bowl. In
villages and towns where the houses were all clustered around the meeting-house the baby Puritans
did not have to be carried far to be baptized; but in
country parishes, where the dwelling-houses were
widely scattered, it might be truthfully recorded of
many a chrisom-child: "Died of being baptized."
One cruel parson believed in and practised infant
immersion, fairly a Puritan torture, until his own
child nearly lost its life thereby.

Dressed in fine linen and wrapped in a hand-woven
christening blanket—a " bearing-cloth "—the unfortunate young Puritan was carried to church in the
arms of the midwife, who was a person of vast importance and dignity as well as of service in early
colonial days, when families of from fifteen to twenty
children were quite the common quota. At the altar
the baby was placed in his proud father's arms, and
received his first cold and disheartening reception
into the Puritan Church. In the pages of Judge
Samuel Sewall's diary, to which alone we can turn
for any definite or extended contemporary picture
of colonial life in Puritan New England, as for
knowledge of England of that date we turn to the
diaries of Evelyn and Pepys, we find abundant proof
that inclemency of weather was little heeded when

religious customs and duties were in question. On January 22d, 1694, Judge Sewall thus records:

"A very extraordinary Storm by reason of the falling and driving of the Snow. Few women could get to Meeting. A child named Alexander was baptized in the afternoon."

He does not record Alexander's death in sequence. He writes thus of the baptism of a four days' old child of his own on February 6th, 1656:

"Between 3 & 4 P.M. Mr. Willard baptizeth my Son whom I named Stephen. Day was louring after the storm but not freezing. Child shrank at the water but Cry'd not. His brother Sam shew'd the Midwife who carried him the way to the Pew. I held him up."

And still again on April 8th, 1677, of another of his children when but six days old:

"Sabbath day, rainy and stormy in the morning but in the afternoon fair and sunshine though with a Blustering Wind. So Eliz. Weeden the Midwife brought the Infant to the Third Church when Sermon was about half done in the Afternoon."

Poor little Stephen and Hull and Joseph, shrinking away from the icy water, but too benumbed to cry! Small wonder that they quickly yielded up their souls after the short struggle for life so gloomily and so coldly begun. Of Judge Sewall's fourteen children but three survived him, a majority dying in infancy; and of fifteen children of his friend Cotton Mather but two survived their father.

This religious ordeal was but the initial step in the rigid system of selection enforced by every detail of the manner of life in early New England. The mortality among infants was appallingly large; and the natural result—the survival of the fittest— may account for the present tough endurance of the New England people.

Nor was the christening day the only Lord's Day when the baby graced the meeting-house. Puritan mothers were all church lovers and strict church-goers, and all the members of the household were equally church-attending; and if the mother went to meeting the baby had to go also. I have heard of a little wooden cage or frame in the meeting-house to hold Puritan babies who were too young, or feeble, or sleepy to sit upright.

Of the dress of these Puritan infants we know but little. Linen formed the chilling substructure of their attire—little, thin, linen, short-sleeved, low-necked shirts. Some of them have been preserved, and with their tiny rows of hemstitching and drawn work and the narrow edges of thread-lace are pretty and dainty even at the present day. At the rooms of the Essex Institute in Salem may be seen the shirt and mittens of Governor Bradford's infancy. The ends of the stiff, little, linen mittens have evidently been worn off by the active friction of baby fingers and then been replaced by patches of red and white cheney or calico. The gowns are generally rather shapeless, large-necked sacks of linen or dimity, made and embroidered, of course, entirely by hand, and drawn into shape by narrow, cotton ferret or linen bobbin. In summer and winter the baby's head was always closely covered with a cap, or "biggin" often warmly wadded, which was more comforting in winter than comfortable in summer.

The seventeenth century baby slept, as does his nineteenth century descendant, in a cradle, frequently made of heavy panelled or carved wood, and always deeply hooded to protect him from the constant drafts. Twins had cradles with hoods at both ends. Judge Sewall paid sixteen shillings for a wicker cradle for one of his many children. The baby was carried upstairs, when first moved, with silver and gold in his hand to bring him wealth and cause him always to rise in the world, just as babies are carried upstairs by superstitious nurses nowadays, and he had "scarlet laid on his head to keep him from harm." He was dosed with various nostrums that held full sway in the nursery even until Federal days, "Daffy's Elixir" being perhaps the most widely known, and hence the most widely harmful. It was valuable enough (in one sense of the word) to be sharply fought over in old England in Queen Anne's time, and to have its disputed ownership the cause of many lawsuits. Advertisements of it frequently appear in the *Boston News Letter* and other New England newspapers of early date.

The most common and largely dosed diseases of

early infancy were, I judge from contemporary records, to use the plain terms of the times, worms, rickets, and fits. Curiously enough, Sir Thomas Browne, in the latter part of the eighteenth century, wrote of the rickets as a new disease, scarce so old as to afford good observation, and wondered whether it existed in the American plantations. In old medical books which were used by the New England colonists I find manifold receipts for the cure of these infan- tile diseases. Snails form the basis, or rather the chief ingredient, of many of these medicines. Indeed, I should fancy that snails must have been almost exterminated in the near vicinity of towns, so largely were they sought for and employed medicinally. There are several receipts for making snail-water, or snail-pottage ; here is one of the most pleasing ones :

"The admirable and most famous Snail water.—Take a peck of garden Shel Snails, wash them well in Small Beer, and put them in an oven till they have done mak- ing a Noise, then take them out and wipe them well from the green froth that is upon them, and bruise them shels and all in a Stone Mortar, then take a Quart of Earthworms, scowre them with salt, slit them, and wash well with water from their filth, and in a stone Mortar beat them in pieces, then lay in the bottom of your distilled pot Angelica two handfuls, and two handfuls of Celandine upon them, to which put two quarts of Rosemary flowers, Bearsfoot, Agrimony, red Dock roots, Bark of Barberries, Betony wood Sorrel of each two handfuls, Rue one hand- ful ; then lay the Snails and Worms on top of the hearbs and flowers, then pour on three Gallons of the Strongest Ale,

and let it stand all night, in the morning put in three
ounces of Cloves beaten, sixpennyworth of beaten Saffron,
and on the top of them six ounces of shaved Hartshorne,
then set on the Limbeck, and close it with paste and so
receive the water by pintes, which will be nine in all, the
first is the strongest, whereof take in the morning two
spoonfuls in four spoonfuls of small Beer, the like in the
Afternoon."

Truly, the poor rickety child deserved to be cured.
Snails also were used externally :

" To anoint the Ricketed Childs Limbs and to recover
it in a short time, though the child be so lame as to go
upon crutches :

" Take a peck of Garden Snailes and bruse them, put
them into a course Canvass bagg, and hang it up, and set
a dish under to receive the liquor that droppeth from
them, wherewith anoint the Childe in every Joynt which
you perceive to be weak before the fire every morning
and evening. This I have known make a Patient Childe
that was extream weak to go alone using it only a week
time."

There were also " unguents to anoynt the Ricketted
Childs breast," and various drinks to be given " to
the patient childe fasting," as they termed him in
what appears to us a half-comic, though wholly truthful appellation.

For worms and fits there were some frightful doses
of senna and rhubarb and snails, with a slight redeeming admixture of prunes ; and as for " Collick "

and "Stomack-Ach," I feel sure every respectable Puritan patient child died rather than swallow the disgusting and nauseous compounds that were offered to him for his relief.

Puritan babies also wore medical ornaments, "anodyne necklaces." I find them advertised in the *Boston Evening Post* as late as 1771—"Anodine Necklaces for the Easy breeding of Childrens Teeth," worn as nowadays children wear strings of amber beads to avert croup.

Another medicine "to make childrens teeth come without paine" was this: "Take the head of a Hare boyled a walm or two or roahed; and with the braine thereof mingle Honey and butter and therewith anoynt the Childes gums as often as you please." Still further advice was to scratch the child's gums with an osprey bone, or to hang fawn's teeth or wolf's fangs around his neck—an ugly necklace.

The first scene of gayety upon which the chilled baby opened his sad eyes was when his mother was taken from her great bed and "laid on a pallat," and the heavy curtains and valances of harrateen or serge were hung within and freshened with "curteyns and vallants of cheney or calico." Then, or a day or two later, the midwife, the nurses, and all the neighboring women who had helped with advice or work in the household during the first week or two of the child's life, were bidden to a dinner. This was also a French fashion, as "*Les Caquets de l'Accouchée*," the popular book of the time of Louis XIII., proves.

Doubtless at this New England amphidromia the
"groaning beer" was drunk, though Sewall "brewed
my Wives Groaning Beer" two months before the
child was born. By tradition, "groaning cake," to be
used at the time of the birth of the child, and given
to visitors for a week or two later, also was made; but
I find no allusion to it under that name in any of the
diaries of the times. At this women's dinner good
substantial viands were served. "Women din'd with
rost Beef and minc'd Pyes, good Cheese and Tarts."
When another Sewall baby was scarcely two weeks
old, seventeen women were dined at Judge Sewall's
on equally solid meats, "Boil'd Pork, Beef, Fowls,
very good Rost Beef, Turkey, Pye and Tarts."
Madam Downing gave her women "plenty of sack
and claret." A survival of this custom existed for
many years in the fashion of drinking caudle at the
bedside of the mother.

As might be expected of a man who diverted
himself in attending the dissection of an Indian,
which gruesome gayety exhilarated him into spend-
ing a tidy sum—for him — on drinks and feeing
"the maid;" and in visiting his family tomb; and
who, when he took his wife on a pleasure trip to Dorchester "to eat cherries and rasberries," spent his
entire day within-doors reading that cheerful book,
Calvin on Psalms;—in the house of such a pleasure-
seeker but small provision was made for the entertainment or amusement of his children. They were
sometimes led solemnly to the house of some old,
influential, or pious person, who formally gave them

his blessing. He took them also to some of the funerals of the endless procession of dead Bostonians that files sombrely through the pages of his diary, to the funeral of their baby brother, little Stephen Sewall, when "Sam and his sisters (who were about five and six years old) cryed much coming home and at home, so that I could hardly quiet them. It seems they looked into Tomb, and Sam said he saw a great Coffin there, his Grandfathers." These were not the only tears that Sam and Betty and Hannah shed through fear of death. When Betty was a year older her father wrote:

"It falls to my daughter Elizabeths Share to read the 24 of Isaiah which she doth with many Tears not being very well, and the Contents of the Chapter and Sympathy with her draw Tears from me also."

Two days later, Sam, who was then about ten years old, also showed evidence of the dejection of soul around him.

"Richard Dumer, a flourishing youth of 9 years old dies of the Small Pocks. I tell Sam of it and what need he had to prepare for Death, and therefore to endeavor really to pray, when he said over the Lord's Prayer: He seemed not much to mind, eating an Aple ; but when he came to say Our Father he burst out into a bitter Cry and said he was afraid he should die. I pray'd with him and read Scriptures comforting against Death, as O death where is thy sting. &c. All things yours. Life and Immortality brought to light by Christ."

In January, 1695, Judge Sewall writes :

"When I came in, past 7 at night, my wife met me in the Entry and told me Betty had surprised them. I was surprised with the Abruptness of the Relation. It seems Betty Sewall had given some signs of dejection and sorrow ; but a little while after dinner she burst out into an amazing cry, which caus'd all the family to cry too ; Her Mother ask'd the reason, she gave none ; at last said she was afraid she should goe to Hell, her Sins were not pardon'd. She was first wounded by my reading a sermon of Mr. Norton's, Text, Ye shall seek me and shall not find me. And those words in the sermon, Ye shall seek me and die in your Sins ran in her mind and terrified her greatly. And staying at home she read out of Mr. Cotton Mather—Why hath Satan filled thy Heart, which increased her Fear. Her Mother asked her whether she pray'd. She answered yes but fear'd her prayers were not heard because her sins were not pardon'd."

A fortnight later he writes :

"Betty comes into me as soon as I was up and tells me the disquiet she had when wak'd ; told me she was afraid she should go to Hell, was like Spira, not Elected. Ask'd her what I should pray for, she said that God would pardon her Sin and give her a new heart. I answer'd her Fears as well as I could and pray'd with many Tears on either part. Hope God heard us."

Three months later still he makes this entry :

"Betty can hardly read her chapter for weeping, tells me she is afraid she is gon back, does not taste that sweet-

ness in reading the Word which once she did ; fears that
what was once upon her is worn off. I said what I could
to her and in the evening pray'd with her alone."

Poor little " wounded " Betty ! She did not die in
childhood as she feared, but lived to pass through
many gloomy hours of morbid introspection and of
overwhelming fear of death, to marry and become the
mother of eight children ; but was always buffeted
with fears and tormented with doubts, which she
despairingly communicated to her solemn and far
from comforting father ; and at last she faced the
dread foe Death at the age of thirty-five. Judge
Sewall wrote sadly the day of her funeral : "I hope
God has delivered her now from all her fears ;" every
one reading of her bewildered and depressed spiritual
life must sincerely hope so with him. In truth, the
Puritan children were, as Judge Sewall said, " stirred
up dreadfully to seek God."

Here is the way that one of Sewall's neighbors
taught his little daughter when she was four years
old :

"I took my little daughter Katy into my Study and
there I told my child That I am to Dy Shortly and Shee
must, when I am Dead, Remember every Thing, that I
now said unto her. I sett before her the sinful condition
of her Nature and I charged her to pray in secret places
every day. That God for the sake of Jesus Christ would
give her a New Heart. I gave her to understand that
when I am taken from her she must look to meet with

more Humbling Afflictions than she does now she has a Tender Father to provide for her."

I hardly understand why Cotton Mather, who was really very gentle to his children, should have taken upon himself to trouble this tender little blossom with dread of his death. He lived thirty years longer, and, indeed, survived sinful little Katy. Another child of his died when two years and seven months old, and made a most edifying end in prayer and praise. His pious and incessant teachings did not, however, prove wholly satisfactory in their results, especially as shown in the career of his son Increase, or " Cressy."

No age appeared to be too young for these remarkable exhibitions of religious feeling. Phebe Bartlett was barely four years old when she passed through her amazing ordeal of conversion, a painful example of religious precocity. The " pious and ingenious Jane Turell " could relate many stories out of the Scriptures before she was two years old, and was set upon a table " to show off," in quite the modern fashion. "Before she was four years old she could say the greater part of the Assembly's Catechism, many of the Psalms, read distinctly, and make pertinent remarks on many things she read. She asked many astonishing questions about divine mysteries." It is a truly comic anticlimax in her father's stilted letters to her to have him end his pious instructions with this advice : " And as you love me do not eat green apples."

Of the demeanor of children to their parents naught can be said but praise. Respectful in word and deed, every letter, every record shows that the young Puritans truly honored their fathers and mothers. It were well for them to thus obey the law of God, for by the law of the land high-handed disobedience of parents was punishable by death. I do not find this penalty ever was paid, as it was under the sway of grim Calvin, a fact which redounds to the credit both of justice and youth in colonial days.

It was not strange that Judge Sewall, always finding in natural events and appearances symbols of spiritual and religious signification, should find in his children painful types of original sin.

"Nov. 6, 1692.—Joseph threw a knop of Brass and hit his Sister Betty on the forehead so as to make it bleed ; and upon which, and for his playing at Prayer-time and eating when Return Thanks, I whip'd him pretty smartly. When I first went in (call'd by his Grandmother) he sought to shadow and hide himself from me behind the head of the Cradle ; which gave me the sorrowful remembrance of Adam's carriage."

It was natural, too, that Judge Sewall's children should be timid; they ran in terror to their father's chamber at the approach of a thunderstorm ; and, living in mysterious witchcraft days, they fled screaming through the hall, and their mother with them, at the sudden entrance of a neighbor with a rug over her head.

All youthful Puritans were not as godly as the

young Sewalls. Nathaniel Mather wrote thus in his diary:

" When very young I went astray from God and my mind was altogether taken with vanities and follies : such as the remembrance of them doth greatly abase my soul within me. Of the manifold sins which then I was guilty of, none so sticks upon me as that, being very young, I was *whitling* on the Sabbath-day ; and for fear of being seen, I did it behind the *door*. A great *reproach* of God ! a specimen of that *atheism* I brought into the world with me ! "

It is satisfactory to add that this young prig of a Mather died when nineteen years of age. Except in Jonathan Edwards's " Narratives of Surprising Conversions," no more painful examples of the Puritanical religious teaching of the young can be found than the account given in the *Magnalia* of various young souls in whom the love of God was remarkably budding, especially this same unwholesome Nathaniel Mather. His diary redounded in dismal groans and self-abasement : he wrote out in detail his covenants with God. He laid out his minute rules and directions in his various religious duties. He lived in prayer thrice a day, and " did not slubber over his prayers with hasty amputations, but wrestled in them for a good part of an hour." He prayed in his sleep. He fasted. He made long lists of sins, long catalogues of things forbidden, " and then fell a-stoning them." He " chewed much on excellent sermons." He not only read the Bible, but " obliged himself to fetch a note and prayer out of each verse," as he read. In spite of all these preparations for a joyous hope and faith, he lived in the deepest despair; was full of blasphemous imaginations, horrible conceptions of God, was dejected, self-loathing, and wretched. Indeed, as Lowell said, soul-saving was to such a Christian the dreariest, not the cheerfullest of businesses.

That the welfare, if not the pleasure, of their children lay very close to the hearts of the Pilgrims, we cannot doubt. Governor Bradford left an account of the motives for the emigration from Holland to the new world, and in a few sentences therein he gives one of the deepest reasons of all—the intense yearning for the true well-being of the children; we can read between the lines the stern and silent love of those noble men, love seldom expressed but ever present, and the rigid sense of duty, duty to be fulfilled as well as exacted. Bradford wrote thus of the Pilgrims:

"As necessitie was a taskmaster over them, so they were forced to be such, not only to their servants, but in a sorte, to their dearest children; the which, as it did not a little wound ye tender harts of many a loving father and mother, so it produced likewise sundrie sad and sorrowful effects. For many of their children, that were of best dispositions and gracious inclinations, haveing lernde to bear ye yoake in their youth, and willing to bear parte of their parents burden, were, often times so oppressed with their hevie labours, that though their minds were free and willing, yet their bodies bowed under ye weight of ye same, and become decreped in their early youth;

the vigor of nature being consumed in ye very budd as it were. But that which was more lamentable and of all sorrowes most heavie to be borne, was, that many of their children, by these occasions, and ye great licentiousness of youth in ye countrie, and ye manifold temptations of the place, were drawn away by evill examples into extravagante and dangerous courses, getting ye raines off their neks and departing from their parents. Some became souldiers, others took upon them for viages by sea, and other some worse courses, tending to disolutenes and the danger of their soules, to ye great greef of their parents and dishonor of God. So that they saw their posteritie would be in danger to degenerate and be corrupted."

Though Judge Sewall could control and restrain his children, his power waxed weak over his backsliding and pleasure-seeking grandchildren, and they annoyed him sorely. Sam Hirst, the son of poor timid Betty, lived with his grandfather for a time, and on April 1st, 1719, the Judge wrote:

"In the morning I dehorted Sam Hirst and Grindall Rawson from playing Idle tricks because 'twas first of April: They were the greatest fools that did so. N. E. Men came hither to avoid anniversary days, the keeping of them such as the 25th of Decr. How displeasing must it be to God the giver of our Time to keep anniversary days to play the fool with ourselves and others."

Ten years earlier the Judge had written to the Boston schoolmaster, begging him to " insinuate into the Scholars the Defiling and Provoking nature of

such a Foolish Practice" as playing tricks on April
first.

Sam was but a sad losel, and vexed him in other
and more serious matters.   On March 15th, 1725, the
Judge wrote :

"Sam Hirst got up betime in the morning, and took
Ben Swett with him and went into the Comon to play
Wicket.   Went before anybody was up, left the door
open : Sam came not to prayer at which I was much dis-
pleased."

Two days later he writes thus peremptorily of his
grandson :

"Did the like again, but took not Ben with him.   I
told him he could not lodge here practicing thus.   So he
log'd elsewhere."

Though Boston boys played " wicket " on Boston
Common, I fancy the young Puritans had, as a rule,
few games, and were allowed few amusements.   They
apparently brought over some English pastimes with
them, for in 1657 it was found necessary to pass this
law in Boston :

"Forasmuch as sundry complaints are made that several persons have received hurt by boys and young men
playing at football in the streets, these therefore are to
enjoin that none be found at that game in any of the
streets, lanes or enclosures of this town under the penalty
of twenty shillings for every such offence."

One needless piece of cruelty which was exercised toward boys by Puritan lawgivers is shown by one of the enjoined duties of the tithingman. He was ordered to keep all boys from swimming in the water. I do not doubt that the boys swam, since each tithingman had ten families under his charge; but of course they could not swim as often nor as long as they wished. From the brother sport of winter, skating, they were not debarred; and they went on thin ice, and fell through and were drowned, just as country boys are nowadays. Judge Sewall wrote on November 30th, 1696:

"Many scholars go in the afternoon to Scate on Fresh Pond. Wm. Maxwell and John Eyre fall in, are drowned."

In the *New England Weekly Journal* of January 15th, 1728, we read:

"On Monday last Two Young Persons who were Brothers, viz Mr. George and Nathan Howell diverting themselves by Skating at the bottom of the Common, the Ice breaking under them they were both drowned;"

and in the same journal of two weeks later date we find record of another death by drowning.

"A young man, viz, Mr. Comfort Foster, skating on the ice from Squantum Point to Dorchester, fell into the Water & was drown'd. He was about 16 or 18 years of age."

Advertisements of "Mens and Boys Scates" appear in the *Boston Gazette*, of 1749, and the *Boston*

Evening Post, of 1758. The February *News Letter*, of 1769, has a notice of the sale of "Best Holland Scates of Different Sizes."

In the list of goods on board a prize taken by a privateersman in 1712 were "Boxes of Toys." Higginson, writing to his brother in 1695, told him that "toys would sell if in small quantity." In exceeding small quantity one would fancy. In 1743 the *Boston News Letter* advertised "English and Dutch Toys for Children." Not until October, 1771, on the lists of the Boston shop-keepers, who seemed to advertise and to sell every known article of dry goods, hardware, house furnishing, ornament, dress and food, came that single but pleasure - filled item "Boys Marbles." "Battledores and Shuttles" appeared in 1761. I know that no little maids could ever have lived without dolls, not even the serious - minded daughters of the Pilgrims; but the only dolls that were advertised in colonial newspapers were the "London drest babys" of milliners and mantua-makers, that were sent over to serve as fashion plates for modish New England dames. A few century - old dolls still survive Revolutionary times, wooden-faced monstrosities, shapeless and mean, but doubtless well-beloved and cherished in the days of their youth.

As years rolled by and eighteenth century frivolity and worldliness took the place of Puritan sobriety and religion, New England children shared with their elders in that growing love of amusement, which found but few and inadequate methods of expression in the lives of either old or young. In the year 1771 there was sent from Nova Scotia a young miss of New England parentage—Anna Green Winslow— to live with her aunt and receive a "finishing" in Boston schools. For the edification of her parents and her own practice in penmanship, this bright little maid kept a diary, of which portions have been preserved, and which I do not hesitate to say is the most sprightly record of the daily life of a girl of her age that I have ever read. There is not a dull word in it, and every page has some statement of historical value. She was twelve years old shortly after the diary was begun, and she then had a "coming-out party"—she became a "miss in her teens." To this rout only young ladies of her own age and in the most elegant Boston society were invited—no rough Boston boys. Miss Anna has written for us more than one prim and quaint little picture of similar parties—here is one of her clear and stiff little descriptions; and a graphic account also of the evening dress of a young girl at that time.

"I have now the pleasure to give you the result Viz; a very genteel well regulated assembly which we had at Mr. Soleys last evening, Miss Soley being mistress of the ceremony. Miss Soley desired me to assist Miss Hannah in making out a list of guests which I did. Sometime since I wrote all the invitation cards. There was a large company assembled in a large handsome upper room in the new end of the house. We had two fiddles and I had the honor to open the diversion of the evening in a minuet with Miss Soley. Here follows a list of the company as we form'd for country-dancing. Miss Soley and Miss Anna Green Winslow; Miss Calif and Miss Scott; Miss Williams and Miss McLarth; Miss Codman and Miss Winslow; Miss Ives and Miss Coffin; Miss Scollay and Miss Bella Coffin; Miss Waldo and Miss Quinsey; Miss Glover and Miss Draper; Miss Hubbard and Miss Cregur (usually pronounced Kicker) and two Miss Sheafs were invited but were sick or sorry and beg'd to be excused.

"There was a little Miss Russel and little ones of the family present who could not dance. As spectators there were Mr. & Mrs. Deming, Mr. & Mrs. Sweetser, Mr. and Mrs. Soley, Mr. & Mrs. Claney, Mrs. Draper, Miss Orice, Miss Hannah—our treat was nuts, raisins, cakes, Wine, punch hot and cold all in great plenty. We had a very agreeable evening from 5 to 10 o'clock. For variety we woo'd a widow, hunted the whistle, threaded the needle, & while the company was collecting we diverted ourselves with playing of pawns —*no rudeness* Mamma I assure you. Aunt Deming desires you would particularly observe that the elderly part of the Company were *Spectators only*, that they mixed not in either of the above-described scenes.

"I was dressed in my yelloe coat, black bib and apron, black feathers on my head, my paste comb and all my paste garnet marquasett & jet pins, together with my silver plume—my locket, rings, black collar round my neck, black mitts and yards of blue ribbon (black and blue is high tast) striped tucker & ruffles (not my best) and my silk shoes completed my dress."

How clear the picture: can you not see it—the low raftered chamber softly alight with candles on mantel-tree and in sconces; the two fiddles soberly squeaking : the rows of demure little Boston maids, all of New England Brahmin blood, in high rolls, with nodding plumes and sparkling combs, with ruffles and mitts, little miniatures of their elegant mammas, soberly walking and curtseying through the stately minuet "with no rudeness I can assure you;" and discreetly partaking of hot and cold punch afterward.

There came at this time to another lady in this Boston court circle a grandchild eight years of age, from the Barbadoes, to also attend Boston schools. Missy left her grandmother's house in high dudgeon because she could not have wine at all her meals. And her parents upheld her, saying she had been brought up a lady and must have wine when she wished it. Evidently Cobbett's statement of the free drinking of wine, cider, and beer by American children was true—as Anna Green Winslow's "treat" would also show.

Though Puritan children had few recreations and amusements, they must have enjoyed a very cheerful, happy home life. Large families abounded. Cotton Mather says :

"One woman had not less than twenty-two children, and another had no less than twenty-three children by one husband whereof nineteen lived to mans estate, and a third who was mother to seven and twenty children."

Sir William Phips was one of twenty-six children, all with the same mother. Printer Green had thirty children. The Rev. John Sherman, of Watertown, had twenty-six children by two wives—twenty by his last wife. The Rev. Samuel Willard, first minister to Groton, had twenty children, and his father had seventeen children. Benjamin Franklin was one of a family of seventeen. Charles Francis Adams has told us of the fruitful vines of old Braintree.

The little Puritans rejoiced in some very singular names, the offspring of Roger Clap being good examples: Experience, Waitstill, Preserved, Hopestill, Wait, Thanks, Desire, Unite, and Supply.

Of the food given Puritan children we know but little. In an old almanac of the eighteenth century I find a few sentences of advice as to the "Easy Rearing of Children." The writer urges that boys as soon as they can run alone go without hats to harden them, and if possible sleep without nightcaps, as soon as they have any hair. He advises always to wet children's feet in cold water and thus make them (the feet) tough, and also to have children wear thin-soled shoes "that the wet may come freely in." He says young children should never be allowed to drink cold drinks, but should always have their beer a little heated; that it is "best to feed them on Milk, Pottage, Flummery, Bread, and Cheese, and not let them drink their beer till they have first eaten a piece of Brown Bread." Fancy a young child nowadays making a meal of brown bread and cheese with warm beer! He suggests that they drink but little wine or liquor, and sleep on quilts instead of feathers. In such ways were reared our Revolutionary heroes.

Of the dazzling and beautiful array in our modern confectioners' shops little Priscilla and Hate-Evil could never have dreamed, even in visions. A few comfit-makers made "Lemon Pil Candy, Angelica Candy, Candy'd Eryngo Root & Carroway Comfits;" and a few sweetmeats came to port in foreign vessels, "Sugar'd Corrinder Seeds," "Glaz'd Almonds," and strings of rock-candy. Whole jars of the latter adamantine, crystalline, saccharine delight graced the shelves of many a colonial cupboard. And I suppose favored Salem children, the happy sons and daughters of opulent epicurean Salem shipowners, had even in colonial days Black Jacks and Salem Gibraltars. The first-named dainties, though dearly loved by Salem lads and lasses, always bore—indeed, do still bear—too strong a flavor of liquorice, too haunting a medicinal suggestion to be loved by other children of the Puritans. As an instance, on a large scale, of the retributive fate that always pursues the candy-eating wight, I state that the good ship Ann and Hope brought into Providence one hundred years ago, as part of her cargo, eight boxes of sweetmeats and twenty tubs of sugar candy, and on the succeeding voyage sternly fetched no sweets, but brought instead forty-eight boxes of rhubarb.

The children doubtless had prunes, figs, "courance," and I know they had "Raisins of the Sun" and "Bloom Raisins" galore. Advertisements of all these fruits appear in the earliest newspapers. Though "China Oranges" were frequently given to and by Judge Sewall, I have not found them adver-

tised for sale till Revolutionary times, and I fancy
few children had then tasted them. The native and
domestic fruits were plentiful, but many of them were
poor. The apples and pears and Kentish cherries
were better than the peaches and grapes. The children gathered the summer berries in season, and the
autumn's plentiful and spicy store of boxberries,
checkerberries, teaberries or gingerbread berries with
October's brown nuts. There were gingerbread and
" cacks " even in the earliest days ; but they were not
sold in unlimited numbers. The omnipotent hand of
Puritan law laid its firm hold on their manufacture.
Judge Sewall often speaks, however, of Banbury
cakes and Meers cakes ; Meer was a celebrated Boston baker and confectioner. The colonists had also
egg cakes and marchepanes and maccaroons.

There were children's books in those early days ;
not numerous, however, nor varied was the assort-
ment from which Puritan youth in New England
could choose. Here is the advertisement of one :

" Small book in easey verse Very Suitable for children,
entitled The Prodigal Daughter or the Disobedient Lady
Reclaimed : adorned with curious cuts, Price Sixpence."

Somehow, from the suggestion of the title we should
hardly fancy this to be an edifying book for children.
John Cotton supplied them with

"Spiritual Milk for Boston Babes in Either England :
Drawn out of the Breasts of both Testaments for their

Souls Nourishment. But may be of like Use to Any
Children."

Another book was published in many editions and
sold in large numbers, and much extolled by contemporary ministers. It was entitled :

" A Token for Children. Being the exact account of
the Conversion & Holy & Exemplary Lives of several
Young Children by James Janeway."

To it was added by Cotton Mather :

"Some examples of Children in whom the fear of God
was remarkably Budding before they died ; in several
parts of New England."

Cotton Mather also wrote: " Good Lessons for
Children, in Verse." Other books were, " A Looking
Glasse for Children," " The life of Elizabeth Butcher,
in the Early Piety series;" " The life of Mary Paddock,
who died at the age of nine ;" " The Childs new Play-
thing" (which was a primer); " Divine Songs in Easy
Language ;" and " Praise out of the Mouth of
Babes ;" " A Particular Account of some Extraordinary Pious Motions and devout Exercises observed of
late in many Children in Siberia." Also accounts of
pious motions of children in Silesia and of Jewish
children in Berlin. One oasis appeared in the desert
waste—after the first quarter of the eighteenth century Puritan children had Mother Goose.

By 1787, in Isaiah Thomas' list of " books Suitable
for Children of all ages," we find less serious books.

" Tom   Jones   Abridged,"   " Peregrine   Pickle
Abridged," "Vice in its Proper Shape," " The Sugar
Plumb," " Bag of Nuts Ready Crack'd," " Jacky
Dandy," " History of Billy and Polly Friendly. "
Among the " Chapman's Books for the Edification
and Amusement of young Men and Women who are
not able to Purchase those of a Higher Price " are,
" The Amours and Adventures of Two English
Gentlemen in Italy," "Fifteen Comforts of Matrimony,"   " The Lovers Secretary," and " Laugh and
be Fat."   Another advertisement of about the same
date contained, among the books for misses, " The
Masqued Wedding," " The Elopement," " The Pas-
sionate Lovers," "Sketches of the History and
Importance of the Fair Sex," " Original Love Letters," and " Six Dialogues of Young Misses Relating
to Matrimony ; " thus showing that love-stories were
not abhorred by the descendants of the Puritans.

In such an exceptional plantation as New England,
a colony peopled not by the commonplace and average Englishmen of the day, but by men of special
intelligence, and almost universally of good education, it was inevitable that early and profound attention should be paid to the establishment of schools.
Cotton Mather said in 1685, in his sermon before the
Governor and his Council, " the Youth in this country
are verie Sharp and early Ripe in their Capacities."
So quickly had New England air developed the typical New England traits. And the early schoolmasters, too, may be thanked for their scholars' early ripe-
ness and sharpness.

At an early age both girls and boys were sent to dame-schools, where, if girls were not taught much book-learning, they were carefully instructed in all housewifely arts. They learned to cook; and to spin and weave and knit, not only for home wear but for the shops; even little children could spin coarse tow string and knit coarse socks for shop-keepers. Fine knitting was well paid for, and was a matter of much pride to the knitter, and many curious and elaborate stitches were known; the herring-bone and the fox-and geese-patterns being prime favorites. Initials were knit into mittens and stockings; one clever young miss of Shelburne, N. H., could knit the alphabet and a verse of poetry into a single pair of mittens. Fine embroidery was to New England women and girls a delight. The Indians at an early day called the English women "lazie Squaes" when they saw the latter embroidering coifs instead of digging in the fields. Mr. Brownell, the Boston school-master in 1716, taught "Young Gentle Women and Children all sorts of Fine Works as Feather works, Filigree, and Painting on Glass, Embroidering a new Way, Turkey-work for Handkerchiefs two new Ways, fine new Fashion purses, flourishing and plain Work." We find a Newport dame teaching "Sewing, Mark-ing, Queen Stitch and Knitting," and a Boston shop-keeper taking children and young ladies to board and be taught "Dresden and Embroidery on gauze, Tent Stitch and all sorts of Colour'd Work." Crewels, embroidery, silks, and chenilles appear frequently in early newspapers. Many of the fruits of these careful lessons of colonial childhood remain to us; quaint samplers, bed hangings, petticoats and pockets, and frail lace veils and scarfs. Miss Susan Hayes Ward has resuscitated from these old embroideries a curious stitch used to great effect on many of them, and employed also on ancient Persian embroideries, and she points out that the designs are Persian also. This stitch was not known in the modern English needlework schools; but just as good old Elizabethan words and phrases are still used in New England, though obsolete in England, so this curious old stitch has lived in the colony when lost in the mother country; or, it may be possible, since it is found so frequently in the vicinity of Plymouth, that the Pilgrims obtained both stitch and designs in Holland, whose greater commerce with the Orient may have supplied to deft English fingers the Persian pattern.

Other accomplishments were taught to girls; "cutting of Escutcheons" and paper flowers—"Papyrotamia" it was ambitiously called—and painting on velvet; and quilt-piecing in a hundred different and difficult designs. They also learned to make bone lace with pillow and bobbins.

The boys were thrust at once into that iron-handed but wholly wise grasp—the Latin Grammar. The minds trained in earliest youth in that study, as it was then taught, have made their deep and noble impress on this nation. The study of mathematics was, until well into this century, a hopeless maze to many youthful minds. Doubtless the Puritans learned mul-

tiplication tables and may have found them, as did
Marjorie Fleming, "a horrible and wretched plaege,"
though no pious little New Englanders would have
dared to say as she did, "You cant conceive it the
most Devilish thing is 8 times 8 and 7 times 7, it is
what nature itself can't endure."

Great attention was paid to penmanship. Spelling
was nought if the "wrighting" were only fair and
flowing. I have never read any criticism of teach-
ers by either parents or town officers save on the one
question of writing. How deeply children were versed
or grounded in the knowledge of the proper use of
"Simme colings nots of interiogations peorids and
commoes," I do not know. A boundless freedom apparently was given, as was also in orthography—if we
judge from the letters of the times, where "horrid
false spells," as Cotton Mather called them, abound.

It is natural to dwell on the religious teaching of
Puritan children, because so much of their education
had a religious element in it. They must have felt,
like Tony Lumpkin, "tired of having good dinged
into 'em." Their primers taught religious rhymes;
they read from the Bible, the Catechism, the Psalm
Book, and that lurid rhymed horror "The Day of
Doom;" they parsed, too, from these universal books.
How did they parse these lines from the Bay Psalm
Book?

> "And sayd He would not them waste; had not
> Moses stood (whom he chose)
> 'fore him i' th' breach; to turn his wrath
> lest that he should waste those."

Their "horn books "—

> " books of stature small
> Which with pellucid horn secured are
> To save from fingers wet the letters fair,"

those framed and behandled sheets of semi-transparent horn, which were worn hanging at the side and were studied, as late certainly as the year 1715 by children of the Pilgrims, also managed to instil with the alphabet some religious words or principles. Usually the Lord's Prayer formed part of the printed text.   Though horn-books are referred to in Sewall's diary and in the letters of Wait Still Winthrop, and appear on stationers' and booksellers' lists at the beginning of the eighteenth century, I do not know of the preservation of a single specimen to our own day.

The schoolhouses were simple dwellings, often tumbling down and out of repair. The Roxbury teacher wrote in 1681 :

"Of inconveniences [in the schoolhouse] I shall mention no other but the confused and shattered and nastie posture that it is in, not fitting for to reside in, the glass broke, and thereupon very raw and cold ; the floor very much broken and torn up to kindle fires, the hearth spoiled, the seats some burned and others out of kilter, that one had well-nigh as goods keep school in a hog stie as in it."

This schoolhouse had been built and furnished

with some care in 1652, as this entry in the town records shows :

" The feoffes agreed with Daniel Welde that he provide convenient benches with forms, with tables for the scholars, and a conveniente seate for the scholmaster, a Deske to put the Dictionary on and shelves to lay up bookes."

The schoolmaster " promised and engaged to use his best endeavour both by precept and example to instruct in all Scholasticall morall and Theologicall discipline the children so far as they be capable, all A. B. C. Darians excepted." He was paid in corn, barley or peas, the value of £25 per annum, and each child, through his parents or guardians, supplied half a cord of wood for the schoolhouse fire. If this load of wood were not promptly furnished the child suffered, for the master did not allow him the benefit of the fire ; that is, to go near enough the fireplace to feel the warmth.

The children of wise parents like Cotton Mather, were also taught " opificial and beneficial sciences," such as the mystery of medicine—a mystery indeed in colonial times.

Puritan schoolmasters believed, as did Puritan parents, that sparing the rod spoiled the child, and great latitude was given in punishment ; the rod and ferule were fiercely and frequently plied " with lamming and with whipping, and such benefits of nature " as in English schools of the same date. When young men were publicly whipped in colleges, children were sure

to be well trained in smaller schools. Every grada-
tion of chastisement was known and every instrument
from

> "A beesome of byrche for babes verye fit
> To a long lastinge lybbet for lubbers as meete,"

from the "thimell-pie" of the dame's school—a
smart tapping on the head with a heavy thimble—to
belaboring with a heavy walnut stick or oaken ruler.
Master Lovell, that tigerish Boston teacher, whipped
the culprit with birch rods and forced another scholar
to hold the sufferer on his back. Other schoolmasters
whipped on the soles of the feet, and one teacher
roared out, "Oh the Caitiffs! it is good for them."
Not only were children whipped, but many ingenious
instruments of torture were invented. One instructor
made his scholars sit on a "bark seat turned upside
down with his thumb on the knot of a floor." Another master of the inquisition invented a unipod—a
stool with one leg—sometimes placed in the middle
of the seat, sometimes on the edge, on which the unfortunate scholar tiresomely balanced. Others sent
out the suffering pupil to cut a branch of a tree, and,
making a split in the large end of the branch, sprung
it on the culprit's nose, and he stood painfully
pinched, an object of ridicule with his spreading
branch of leaves. One cruel master invented an instrument of torture which he called a flapper. It was
a heavy piece of leather six inches in diameter with a
hole in the middle, and was fastened at the edge to a
pliable handle. The blistering pain inflicted by this

brutal instrument can well be imagined. At another school, whipping of unlucky wights was done "upon a peaked block with a tattling stick;" and this expression of colonial severity seems to take on additional force and cruelty in our minds that we do not at all know what a tattling stick was, nor understand what was meant by a peaked block.

I often fancy I should have enjoyed living in the good old times, but I am glad I never was a child in colonial New England—to have been baptized in ice water, fed on brown bread and warm beer, to have had to learn the Assembly's Catechism and " explain all the Quaestions with conferring Texts," to have been constantly threatened with fear of death and terror of God, to have been forced to commit Wigglesworth's " Day of Doom " to memory, and, after all, to have been whipped with a tattling stick.

II

COURTSHIP AND MARRIAGE CUSTOMS

In the early days of the New England colonies no more embarrassing or hampering condition, no greater temporal ill could befall any adult Puritan than to be unmarried. What could he do, how could he live in that new land without a wife? There were no house-keepers—and he would scarcely have been allowed to have one if there were. What could a woman do in that new settlement among unbroken forests, un-cultivated lands, without a husband? The colonists married early, and they married often. Widowers and widows hastened to join their fortunes and sor-rows. The father and mother of Governor Winslow had been widow and widower seven and twelve weeks, respectively, when they joined their families and themselves in mutual benefit, if not in mutual love. At a later day the impatient Governor of New Hamp-shire married a lady but ten days widowed. Bache-lors were rare indeed, and were regarded askance and with intense disfavor by the entire community, were almost in the position of suspected criminals. They were seldom permitted to live alone, or even to choose their residence, but had to find a domicile

wherever and with whomsoever the Court assigned.
In Hartford lone-men, as Shakespeare called them,
had to pay twenty shillings a week to the town for
the selfish luxury of solitary living.   No colonial law
seems to me more arbitrary or more comic than this
order issued in the town of Eastham, Mass., in 1695,
namely :

"Every unmarried man in the township shall kill six
blackbirds or three crows while he remains single ; as a
penalty for not doing it, shall not be married until he
obey this order."

Bachelors were under the special spying and tattling supervision of the constable, the watchman, and
the tithingman, who, like Pliable in Pilgrim's Progress, sat sneaking among his neighbors and reported
their "scirscumstances and conuersation."   In those
days a man gained instead of losing his freedom by
marrying.   "Incurridgement" to wedlock was given
bachelors in many towns by the assignment to them
upon marriage of home-lots to build upon.   In Med-
field there was a so-called Bachelor's Row, which had
been thus assigned.   In the early days of Salem "maid
lotts" were also granted ; but Endicott wrote in the
town records that it was best to abandon the custom
and thus "avoid all presedents & evil events of grant-
ing lotts vnto single maidens not disposed of."   This
line he crossed out and wrote instead, "for avoiding
of absurdities."   He kindly, but rather disappoint-
ingly, gave one maid a bushel of corn when she came
to ask for a house and lot, and told her it would be a

"bad president" for her to keep house alone. A maid had, indeed, a hard time to live in colonial days, did she persevere in her singular choice of remaining single. Perhaps the colonists "proverb'd with the grandsire phrase," that women dying maids lead apes in hell. Maidens "withering on the virgin thorn," in single blessedness, were hard to find. One Mistress Poole lived unmarried to great old age, and helped to found the town of Taunton under most discouraging rebuffs; and in the Plymouth church record of March 19, 1667, is a record of a death which reads thus :—

"Mary Carpenter sister of Mrs. Alice Bradford wife of Governor Bradford being newly entered into the 91st year of her age. She was a godly old maid never married."

The state of old maidism was reached at a very early age in those early days; Higginson wrote of an "antient maid" of twenty-five years. John Dunton in his "Life and Errors" wrote eulogistically of one such ideal "Virgin" who attracted his special attention.

"It is true an *old* (or superanuated) Maid in Boston is thought such a curse, as nothing can exceed it (and looked on as a *dismal* spectacle) yet she by her good nature, gravity, and strict virtue convinces all (so much as the fleering Beaus) that it is not her necessity but her choice that keeps her a Virgin. She is now about thirty years (the age which they call a *Thornback*) yet she never disguises herself, and talks as little as she thinks, of Love. She never reads any Plays or Romances, goes to no Balls or Dancing-match (as they do who go to such Fairs) to meet with Chapmen. Her looks, her speech, her whole behavior are so very chaste, that but once (at Govenor's Island, where we went to be merry at roasting a hog) going to kiss her, I thought she would have blushed to death.

" Our *Damsel* knowing this, her conversation is generally amongst the women (as there is least danger from that sex) so that I found it no easy matter to enjoy her company, for most of her time (save what was taken up in needle work and learning French &c.) was spent in Religious Worship. She knew time was a dressing-room for Eternity, and therefore reserves most of her hours for better uses than those of the Comb, the Toilet and the Glass.

" And as I am sure this is most agreeable to the Virgin modesty, which should make Marriage an act rather of their obedience than their choice. And they that think their Friends too slowpaced in the matter give certain proof that lust is their sole motive. But as the Damsel I have been describing would neither anticipate nor contradict the will of her Parents, so do I assure you she is against Forcing her own, by marrying where she cannot love ; and that is the reason she is still a Virgin."

Hence it may be seen that though there was not in Boston the "glorious phalanx of old maids" of Theodore Parker's description, yet the Boston old maid was lovely even in colonial days, though she did bear the odious name of thornback.

An English traveller, Josselyn, gives a glimpse of Boston love-making in the year 1663.

"On the South there is a small but pleasant Common, where the Gallants, a little before sunset, walk with their Marmalet-Madams till the nine o'clock bell rings them home to their respective habitations."

This simple and quaint picture of youthful love in the soft summer twilight, at that ever beautiful trysting-place, gives an unwonted touch of sentiment to the austere daily life of colonial New England. The omnipotent Puritan law-giver, who meddled and interfered in every detail, small and great, of the public and private life of the citizen, could not leave untouched, in fancy free, these soberly promenading Puritan sweethearts. A Boston gallant must choose well his marmalet-madam, must proceed cautiously in his love-making in the gloaming, obtaining first the formal permission of parents or guardians ere he take any step in courtship. Fines, imprisonment, or the whipping-post awaited him, did he "inveigle the affections of any maide or maide servant" by making love to her without proper authority. Numberless examples might be given to prove that this law was no dead letter. In 1647, in Stratford, Will Colefoxe was fined £5 for "laboring to invegle the affection of Write his daughter." In 1672 Jonathan Coventry, of Plymouth town, was indicted for "making a motion of marriage" to Katharine Dudley without obtaining formal consent. The sensible reason for these courtship regulations was "to prevent young folk from intangling themselves by rash and inconsiderate contracts of maridge." The Governor of Plymouth colony, Thomas Prence, did not hesitate to drag his daughter's love affairs before the public, in 1660, by prosecuting Arthur Hubbard for "disorderly and unrighteously endeavouring to gain the affections of Mistress Elizabeth Prence." The unrighteous lover was fined £5. Seven years later, patient Arthur, who would not "refrain and desist," was again fined the same amount; but love prevailed over law, and he triumphantly married his fair Elizabeth a few months later. The marriage of a daughter with an unwelcome swain was also often prohibited by will, "not to suffer her to be circumvented and cast away upon a swaggering gentleman."

On the other hand, an engagement of marriage once having been permitted, the father could not recklessly or unreasonably interfere to break off the contract. Many court records prove that colonial lovers promptly resented by legal action any attempt of parents to bring to an end a sanctioned love affair. Richard Taylor so sued, and for such cause, Ruth Whieldon's father in Plymouth in 1661; while another ungallant swain is said to have sued the maid's father for the loss of time spent in courting. Breach of promise cases were brought against women by disappointed men who had been "shabbed" (as jilting was called in some parts of New England), as well as by deserted women against men.

But sly Puritan maids found a way to circumvent and outwit Puritan law makers, and to prevent their unsanctioned lovers from being punished, too. Hear the craft of Sarah Tuttle. On May day in New Haven, in 1660, she went to the house of a neighbor, Dame Murline, to get some thread. Some very loud jokes were exchanged between Sarah and her friends Maria and Susan Murline — so loud, in fact, that Dame Murline testified in court that it "much distressed her and put her in a sore strait." In the midst of all this doubtful fun Jacob Murline entered, and seizing Sarah's gloves, demanded the centuries old forfeit of a kiss. "Wherupon," writes the scandalized Puritan chronicler, "they sat down together; his arm being about her; and her arm upon his shoulder or about his neck; and hee kissed her, and shee kissed him, or they kissed one another, continuing in this posture about half an hour, as Maria and Susan testified." Goodman Tuttle, who was a man of dignity and importance, angrily brought suit against Jacob for inveigling his daughter's affections; "but Sarah being asked in court if Jacob inveagled her, said No." This of course prevented any rendering of judgment against the unauthorized kissing by Jacob, and he escaped the severe punishment of his offence. But the outraged and baffled court fined Sarah, and gave her a severe lecture, calling her with justice a "Bould Virgin." She at the end, demurely and piously answered that "She hoped God would help her to carry it Better for time to come." And doubtless she did carry it better; for at the end of two years, this bold virgin's fine for unruly behavior being still unpaid, half of it was remitted.

Of the etiquette, the pleasures, the exigencies of colonial "courtship in high life," let one of the actors speak for himself through the pages of his diary. Judge Sewall's first wife was Hannah Hull, the only daughter of Captain Hull of Pine Tree Shilling fame. She received as her dowry her weight in silver shillings. Of her wooing we know naught save the charming imaginary story told us by Hawthorne. The Judge's only record is this:

"Mrs. Hannah Hull saw me when I took my Degree and set her affection on me though I knew nothing of it till after our Marriage."

She lived with him forty-three years, bore him seven sons and seven daughters, and died on the 19th day of October, 1717.

Of course, though the Judge was sixty-six years old, he would marry again. Like a true Puritan he despised an unmarried life, and on the 6th day of February he made this naive entry in his diary: "Wandering in my mind whether to live a Married or a Single Life." Ere that date he had begun to take notice. He had called more than once on Widow Ruggles, and had had Widow Gill to dine with him; had looked critically at Widow Emery, and noted that Widow Tilley was absent from meeting; and he had gazed admiringly at Widow Winthrop in "her

sley," and he had visited and counseled and consoled
her ere his wife had been two months dead, and had
given her a few suitable tokens of his awakening
affection such as "Smoking Flax Inflamed," "The
Jewish Children of Berlin," and "My Small Vial of
Tears;" so he had "wandered" in the flesh as well
as in the mind.

Such an array of widows! Boston fairly blossomed
with widows, the widows of all the "true New England men" whose wills Sewall had drawn up, whose
dying bedsides he had blessed and harassed with his
prayers, whose bodies he had borne to the grave,
whose funeral gloves and scarves and rings he had
received and apprized, and whose estates he had
settled. Over this sombre flower-bed of black
garbed widows, these hardy perennials, did this aged
Puritan butterfly amorously hover, loth to settle,
tasting each solemn sweet, calculating the richness of
the soil in which each was planted, gauging the
golden promise of fruit, and perhaps longing for the
whole garden of full-blown blossoms. "Antient
maides" were held in little esteem by him; not one
thornback is on his list.

Not only did he look and wander, but all his
friends and neighbors arose and began to suggest
and search for a suitable wife for him, with as officious
alacrity as if he needed help, which he certainly did
not. In March Madam Henchman strongly recommended to him "Madam Winthrop, the Major
General's widow." This recommendation was very
sweet to the widower, who had turned his eyes with

such special approval on this special widow, and further and warm encouragement came quickly.

"Deacon Marion comes to me, sits with me a great while in the evening ; after a great deal of Discourse about his Courtship He told me the Olivers said they wish'd I would court their Aunt. I said little, but said 'twas not five Moneths since I buried my dear Wife. Had said before 'twas hard to know whether to marry again or no or whom to marry."

The Olivers' aunt was Madam Winthrop. It would seem somewhat presumptuous and officious for nieces and nephews to suggest courtship, when there were grown up Winthrop children who might dislike the marriage, but in those days everyone meddled in love affairs ; to quote Pope : " Marriage was the theme on which they all declaimed." The Judge gossiped publicly about his intentions. He writes : " They had laid one out for me, and Governor Dudley told me 'twas Madam Winthrop. I told him I had been there but thrice and twice upon business. He said *cave tertium.*" Even solemn Cotton Mather proffered counsel in a letter on " paying regards to the Widow."

In spite of all these hints and commendations, and the Judge's evident pleasure in receiving them, the Winthrop agitation all came to naught, for about this time he was called to make a will for a Mr. Denison, of Roxbury, who died on March 22d. Though the Judge was too upright and too pious to let even his thoughts wander to a wife, the amazing rapidity with which he turned his longing eyes on the newly-made widow (cruelly forsaking Madam Winthrop) is only equalled by the act of the famous Irish lover who proposed to a widow at the open grave of her husband.

Judge Sewall went home with widow Denison from her husband's funeral and "prayed God to keep house with her." The very next day he writes, "Mr. Danforth gives the Widow Denison a high commendation for her Piety, Goodness, Diligence and Humility." On April 7th she came to the widower to prove her husband's will; and another match-making friend, Mr. Dow, "took occasion to say in her absence that she was one of the most Dutiful Wives in the World." A few days later the Judge made her a gift, "a Widow's book having writ her name in it."

At last, after talking the matter over with all his friends, he decided positively to go a-courting. Widow Denison came to his house and he says:

"I took her up into my chamber and discoursed Thorowly with her: told her I intended to visit her next Lecture Day. She said 'twould be talk'd of, I answered: In such Cases persons must run the Gantlet. Gave her an Oration."

He visited her as he had promised and gave her "Dr. Mathers Sermons neatly bound and told her in it we were invited to a wedding. She gave me very good Curds." Other love gifts followed: "K. Georges Effigies in Copper and an English Crown of

K. Charles II. 1677." "A pound of Reasons and Proportionate Almonds," "A Psalmbook elegantly bound in Turkey leather," "A pair of Shoe Buckles cost five shillings three pence." "Two Cases with a knife and fork in each; one Turtle Shell Tackling; the other long with Ivory Handles squar'd cost four shillings sixpence."

In the meantime he read with Cousin Moodey the history of Rebekah's courtship, and then prayed over it, and over his own wooing. Madam Rogers and Madam Leverett much congratulated him, and his daughter Judith visited her prospective stepmother. But alas! the lady was coy and averse to a decision:

"She mentions her Discouragement by reason of Discourse she had heard. Ask't what I should allow her, she not speaking I told her I was willing to allow her two hundred and fifty pounds per annum if it should please God to take me out of the world before her. She answered she had better keep as she was than give up a certainty for an uncertainty. She would pay dear for her living in Boston. I desired her to make Proposals but she made none. I had thought of Publishment next Thursday. But I now seem far from it. My God who has the pity of a Father Direct and help me."

Mr. Denison's will left his widow a portion of his estate to dispose of as she wished if she did not marry again. Judge Sewall was unwilling to make equal provision for her, hence the stumbling block in their courtship

After consulting with a friend, the Judge made a final visit to her on November 28th.

"She said she thought it was hard to part with all and having nothing to bestow on her Kindred. I had ask'd her to give me proposals in Writing and she upbraided me That I who had never written her a Letter should ask her to write. She asked me if I would drink, I told her yes. She gave me Cider Aples and a Glass of Wine, gathered together the little things I had given her and offered them to me, but I would none of them. Told her I wish'd her well and should be glad of her welfare. She seem'd to say she should not again take in hand a thing of this nature. Thank'd me for what I had given her and Desir'd my Prayers. My bowels yern towards Mrs. Denison but I think God directs me in his Providence to desist."

This love affair was not, however, quite ended, for the following Lord's Day "after dark" Widow Denison came "very privat" to his house. This Sunday visit betokened great anxiety on her part. She had walked in from Roxbury in the cold, and when we remember how wolves and bears abounded in the vicinity we comprehend still further her solicitude.

"She ask'd pardon if she had affronted me . . . . Mr. Denison spake to her after signing his will that he would not make her put all out of her Hand and power but reserve something to bestow on her friends that might want . . . . I could not observe that she made me any offer all the while. She mentioned two

Glass Bottles she had. I told her they were hers and the other small things I had given her only now they had not the same signification as before, I was much concerned for her being in the cold, would fetch her a plate of something warm ; she refused. However I fetched a Tankard of Cider and drank to her. She desired that nobody might know of her being here. I told her they should not. She went away in the bitter Cold, no moon being up, to my great pain. I Saluted her at Parting."

With that parting kiss on that dark cold night, in "great pain," ended the Judge's second wooing.

That he was sincerely in love with Widow Denison one cannot doubt, though he loved his money more. Disappointed, he did not again turn to courting until the following August — much longer than he had waited after the death of his wife. He then proceeded in a matter-of-fact way to visit Widow Tilley, whom he had early noted in meeting. He asked her, at his third visit, to "come and live in his house." "She expressed her unworthiness with much respect," and both agreed to consider it. He gave her a little book called "Ornaments of Sion ; " Mr. Pemberton applauded his courtship ; Mrs. Armitage said that Mrs. Tilley had been a great blessing to them ; the banns were published ; and the Judge's third wooing ended in a marriage on October 24th.

But the bride was very ill on her wedding night, and after several slight sicknesses through the winter, died on May 20th, to her husband's "great amazement." Again he was a-seeking a "dear Yoke fellow," and on September 30th, "Daughter Sewall acquainted Madam Winthrop that if she pleased to be within at 3 P.M. I would wait on her." This was the same Madam Winthrop whose attractions had been so completely obscured by the bright halo which encircled the much-longed-for Widow Denison.

"Madam Winthrop returning answer that she would be at home, I went to her house and spake to her saying my loving wife died so soon and suddenly 'twas hardly convenient for me to think of Marrying again, however I came to this Resolution that I would not make my Court to any person without first consulting with her. Had a pleasant Discourse about Seven Single persons sitting in the Fore-Seat. She propounded one after another to me but none would do."

Now, I think the Judge was very graceful in approaching a proposal to this widow, for on his next visit he asked to see her alone, and he resumed the pleasant discourse about the seven widows on the fore seat, and said :

"At last I pray'd Katharine might be the person assigned for me. She evidently took it up in the way of denial as if she had catched at an opportunity to do it, saying she could not do it, could not leave her children."

The Judge begged her not to be so speedy in decision, and brought her gifts, "pieces of Mr. Belchar's cake and gingerbread wrapped in a clean sheet of paper ; " China oranges ; the *News Letter ;* Preston's " Church Marriage ; " sugared almonds (of which she inquired the price). He wrote her a stilted letter with an allusion in it to Christopher Columbus, and he had to explain it to her afterward.   He gave money to her servants and "penys" to her grand-children, and heard them "say their catechise;" and he had interviews and consultations with her rela-tives—her children, her sister—who agreed not to oppose the marriage.

Still the progress of the courtship was not encour-aging.   Katharine went to her neighbors' houses when she knew her suitor was coming to visit her, and left him to read "Dr. Sibbs Bowels" for scant comfort.   She "look'd dark and lowering" at him and coldly placed tables or her grandchild's cradle between her chair and his as they sat together.   She avoided seeing him alone.   She "let the fire come to one short Brand beside the Block and fall in pieces and make no recruit"—a broad hint to leave.   She "would not help him on with his coat"—a cutting blow.   She would not let her servant accompany him home with a lantern, but heartlessly permitted her elderly lover to stumble home alone in the dark. She spoke to him of his luckless courtship of Widow Denison (a most unpleasant topic), thus giving a clue to the whole situation, in showing that Madam Win-throp resented his desertion of her in his first widow-erhood, and like Falstaff, would not "undergo a sneap without reply."   He said, in apologetic answer:

"If after a first and second Vagary she would Accept of me returning her Victorious Kindness and Good Will would be very Obliging."

Undeterred by these many rebuffs, as she grew cold he waxed warm, and a most lover-like and gallant scene ensued which would have done credit to a younger man than the Judge. Here it is in his own words :

"I asked her to Acquit me of Rudeness if I drew off her Glove. Enquiring the reason I told her 'twas great odds between handling a dead Goat and a Living Lady. Got it off . . .   Told her the reason why I came every other night was lest I should drink too Deep draughts of Pleasure. She had talked of Canary, her Kisses were to me better than the best Canary."

Naturally these warm words had a marked effect ; she relaxed, drank a glass of wine with him, and I trust gave him a Canary-sweet kiss, and sent a servant home with him with a lantern.

The next visit the wind blew cold again. He had had one experience with a short-lived wife, and he had determined that should his next wife die he would still have some positive benefit from having married her. Hence he kept pressing Madam Winthrop in a most unpleasant and ghoulish manner to know what she would give him in case she died. He would allow her but one hundred pounds per annum. She in turn persisted in questioning him about the property he had given to his children ; and she wished him to agree to keep a coach (which he could well afford to do), and she wanted it set on springs too. He said he could not do it while he paid his debts. She also suggested that he should wear a wig. This annoyed him beyond measure, for he hated with extreme Puritan intenseness those "horrid Bushes of Vanity," and the suggestion from his would-be bride was irritating in the extreme.   He answered her with much self-control :

" As to a Periwigg my best and Greatest Friend begun to find me with Hair before I was born and has continued to do so ever since and I could not find it in my heart to go to another."

Still, when nearly all the men of dignity and position in the colony wore imposing stately wigs, no woman would be pleased to have a lover come a-courting in a *hood*.

So, though she gave him " drams of Black Cherry Brandy " and Canary to drink and comfits and lump sugar to eat, while he so pressed her to name her settlement on him, and while the wig and coach questions were so adversely met, she would not answer yes, and he regretted making more haste than good speed.   At last the lover of the " kisses sweeter than Canary " critically notes that his mistress has not on " Clean Linen ;" and the next day he writes rather sourly, " I did not bid her draw off her Glove as sometime I had done.   Her dress was not so clean as sometime it had been ; " the beginning of the end was plainly come.   That week he forbade her being invited to a family dinner, and she in turn gave a " treat " from which he was excluded.   Thus ended his fourth wooing.

The next widow on whom he called was Widow

Belknap, but eftsoons he transferred his attention to
Widow Ruggles and wrote thus sentimentally to her
brother:

"I remember when I was going from school at Newbury to have sometime met your sisters Martha and
Mary in Hanging Sleeves coming home from their school
in Chandlers Lane, and have had the pleasure of speaking
to them. And I could find it in my heart to speak to Mrs.
Martha again, now I myself am reduc'd to my Hanging
Sleeves. The truth is, I have little occasion for a Wife
but for the sake of Modesty, and to lay my Weary Head
in Her Lap, if it might be brought to pass upon Honest
Conditions. You know your sisters Age and Disposition
and Circumstances. I should like your advice in my
Fluctuations."

The Judge called on Mrs. Martha, probably after learning with precision her circumstances. "I
showed my willingness to renew my old acquaintance.
She expressed her inability to be serviceable." Even
after the Denison and Winthrop fluctuations he was
not abashed by refusal, and he must have been (to
quote Mrs. Peachum's words) "a bitter bad judge 'o
women," for he called again and again.

"She seemed resolved not to move out of the house ;
made some Difficulties to accept an Election Sermon lest
it should be an obligation to her. The coach staying
long, I made some excuse for my stay. She said she
would be glad to wait on me till midnight provided I
should solicit her no more to that effect."

This decision he accepted.

Poor old wife-seeking Judge, with your hanging sleeves, your broken and drooping wings, feebly did you still flutter around for a resting-place to "lay your Weary Head in modesty." You fluctuated to a new widow, Madam Harris, and she gave you "a nutmeg as it grew," ever a true lover's gift in Shakespeare's day. On January 11th, 1722, this letter was sent to "Mrs. Mary Gibbs, widow, at Newton."

"Madam, your removal out of town and the Severity of the Weather are the Reason of my making you this Epistolary Visit. In times past (as I remember) you were minded that I should marry you by giving you to your desirable Bridegroom. Some sense of this intended Respect abides with me still and puts me upon enquiring whether you be willing I should marry you now by becoming your Husband. Aged feeble and exhausted as I am your favourable Answer to this Enquiry in a few lines, the Candour of it will much oblige, Madam, your humble serv't Samuel Sewall."

This not-too-alluring love-letter brought a favorable answer, for the Judge assured her she "writ incomparably well," and he accompanied this praise with a suitable and useful gift, "A Quire of Paper, a good Leathern Ink Horn, a stick of Sealing Wax and 200 Wafers in a little Box."

He was even sharper in bargaining with Widow Gibbs than he had been with other matrimonial candidates. She had no property to leave him by will,

but he astutely stipulated that her children sign a contract that, should she die before him, they would pay
him £100.   She thought him " hard," and so did her
sons and her son-in-law, and so he was—hard even
for those times of hard bargains and hard marriage
contracts in hard New England.   He would agree to
give her but £50 a year in case of his death.   The
value of wives had depreciated in his eyes since the
£250 a year Widow Denison.   His gifts too were
not as rich as those bestowed on that yearned-for
widow.   He had seen too many tokens go for naught.
Glazed almonds, Meers cakes, an orange, were good
enough for so cheap a sweetheart.   He remained very
stiff and peremptory about the marriage contract, the
£100, and wrote her one very unpleasant letter about
it ; and he feared lest she being so attached to her
children might not be tender to him " when there
soon would be an end of the old man."   At last she
yielded to his sharp bargain and they were married.
He lived eight years, so I doubt not Mary was tender to him and mourned him when he died, hard
though he was and wigless withal.

  We gather from the pages of Judge Sewall's
diary many hints about the method of conducting
other courtships.   We discover the Judge craftily
and slyly inquiring whether his daughter Mary's
lover-apparent had previously courted another Boston maid ; we see him conferring with lover Gerrish's
father ; and after a letter from the latter we see the
lover " at Super and drank to Mary in the third
place."   He called again when it was too cold to sit

downstairs, and was told he would be " wellcomm to come Friday night." We read on Saturday :

" In the evening Sam Gerrish comes not ; we expected him ; Mary dress'd herself ; it was a painfull disgracefull disapointment."

A month later the recreant lover reappeared and finally married poor disappointed Mary, who died very complaisantly in a short time and left him free to marry his first love, which he quickly did. We find the Judge after his daughter's death higgling over her marriage portion with Mr. Gerrish, Sr., and see that grief for her did not prevent him from showing as much shrewdness in that matter as he had displayed in his own courtships.

Timid Betty Sewall was as much harassed in love as in religion. We find her father, when she was but seventeen years old, making frequent investigation about the estate of one Captain Tuthill, a prospective suitor who had visited Betty and " wished to speak with her." The Judge had his hesitating daughter read aloud to him of the mating of Adam and Eve, as a soothing and alluring preparation for the thought of matrimony, with, however, this most unexpected result :

" At night Capt. Tuthill comes to speak with Betty, who hid herself all alone in the coach for several hours till he was gone, so that we sought her at several houses, till at last came in of herself and look'd very wild."

This action of pure maidenly terror elicited sympathy even in the Judge's match-making heart, and he told the lover he was willing to know his daughter's mind better. This was on January 10th, 1698. Ten days later we find wild-eyed Betty going out of her way to avoid drinking wine with one Captain Turner, much to her father's annoyance. By September she had refused another suitor.

Her father wrote thus:

"Got home [from Rhode Island] by seven, in good health, though the day was hot, find my family in health, only disturbed at Betty's denying Mr. Hirst, and my wife hath a cold. The Lord sanctify Mercyes and Afflictions."

And again, a month later:

"Mr. Wm. Hirst comes and thanks my wife and me for our kindness to his Son, in giving him the liberty of our house. Seems to do it in the way of taking leave. I thank'd him, and for his countenance to Hannah at the Wedding. Told him that the well wisher's of my daughter and his son had persuaded him to go to Brantry and visit her there, &c.; and said if there were hopes would readily do it. But as things were twould make persons think he was so involved that he was not fit to go any wether else. He has I suppose taken his final leave. I gave him Mr. Oakes Sermon, and my Father Hulls Funeral Sermon."

Two days later, Judge Sewall writes to Betty, who has gone to "Brantry" on a visit.

BOSTON, October 26, 1699.

"ELIZABETH : Mr. Hirst waits on you once more to see if you can bid him welcome. It ought to be seriously considered, that your drawing back from him after all that has passed between you, will be to your Prejudice ; and will tend to discourage persons of worth from making their Court to you. And you had need well consider whether you will be able to bear his final leaving of you, howsoever it may seem grateful to you at present. When persons come toward us we are apt to look upon their undesirable Circumstances mostly : and thereupon to shun them. But when persons retire from us for good and all, we are in danger of looking only on that which is desirable in them, to our wofull disquiet. Whereas 'tis the property of a good Ballance to turn where the most weight is, though there be some also in the other Scale. I do not see but the match is well liked by judicious persons, and such as are your Cordial friends, and mine also.

"Yet notwithstanding, if you find in yourself an unmovable, incurable Aversion from him and cannot love and honor and obey him, I shall say no more, nor give you any further trouble in this matter. It had better off than on. So praying God to pardon us and pitty our Undeserving, and to direct and strengthen and settle you in making a right judgment, and giving a right Answer, I take leave, who am, Dear Child,   Your loving father.

"Your mother remembers to you."

Even this very proper and fatherly advice did not have an immediate effect upon the shy and vacillating young girl, for not until a year later did she become the wife of persistent Grove Hirst.

One of the most typical stories of colonial methods of "matching" among fine gentlefolk is found in the worry of Emanuel Downing, a man of dignity in the commonwealth, and of his wife, Lucy (who was Gov. Winthrop's sister), in regard to the settlement of their children. Downing begins with anxious overtures to Endicott in regard to "matching his sonne" to an orphan maid living in Endicott's family, a maid who it is needless to state had a very pretty fortune. Downing states that he has been blamed for not marrying off his children earlier, "that none are disposed of," and deplores his ill-luck in having them so long on his hands, and he recounts pathetically his own and his son's good points. He also got Governor Winthrop to write to Endicott pleading the match. Endicott answered both letters in a most dignified manner, stating his objections to furthering Downing's wishes, giving a succession of reasons, such as the maid's unwillingness to marry, being but fifteen years of age, his own awkward position in seeming to crowd marriage upon her when she was so rich, etc., etc. The Downings had hoped to have thriftily two marriages in the family in one day, but the daughter Luce's affairs also halted. She had been enamoured of a Mr. Eyer, an unsuitable match. He had put out to sea, to the Downings' delight, but had returned at an unlucky time when she was on with a fresh suitor. Her mother was much distressed because, though Luce

declared she much liked Mr. Norton, she still showed
to all around her that " she hath not yet forgotten
Mr. Eyer his fresh Red."

But Mistress Luce, by a telling statement of pecun-
iary benefits, was brought to a proper mind and
became " verie sensible of loseing fair opportunities,"
and consented speedily to wed Norton, to her father's
abounding joy, who wrote, " shee may stay long ere
she meet with a better vnless I had more monie for
her than I now can spare." The betrothal was
formally announced, when shortly a distressed letter
from Madam Downing shows foul weather ahead.
Luce had been talking among her friends, giving to
them " unjust suspicions of the enforcement to her of
Mr. Norton," and while she had seemed to love Mr.
Eyer, and her family had eagerly striven to win her
regard from him, " we now suspect by her late words
her affections to be now inclininge at Jhon Harrold."
It was found that Jhon had " practised upon her and
disturbed her," and that while she was " free and
cheerful " with Lover Norton, " passing conversation "
with him, she was really conspiring to jilt him.   The
mother wrote sadly : " I am sorrie my daughter Luce
hath caryed things thus vnwisely and vnreputably
both to herselfe and our friends ; " and the whole
family were evidently sorely afraid that the " perverse
Puritan jade " would be left on their hands, when
suddenly came the news of her marriage to Norton,
owing perhaps to a very decided and sharp letter
from Norton's brother to the Governor about Mistress
Luce's vagaries, and also to some more satisfactory

and liberal marriage settlements. She probably made as devoted a wife to him as if she had never longed for Eyer his fresh red, nor Jhon his disturbments.

Nor were these upright and pious Puritan magistrates and these gentlewomen of Boston and Salem the only colonists who displayed such sordid and mercenary bargaining and stipulating in matrimonial ventures: numberless letters and records throughout New England prove the unvarying spirit of calculation that pervaded fashionable courtship. A bride's portion was openly discussed, her marriage settlement carefully decided upon, and even agreements for bequests were arranged as " incurredgment to marriage." Nor did happy husbands hesitate to sue for settlement too tardy or too remiss fathers-in-law who failed to keep their word about the bride's portion : Edward Palmes for years harassed the Winthrops about their sister's (his first wife's) portion, long after he had married a second partner.

Though the tender passion walked thus ceremoniously and coldly in narrow and carefully selected paths in town, in the country it regarded little the bounds of reserve or regard for appearances. Much comparative grossness prevailed. The mode of courting, known as " bundling " or " tarrying " was too prevalent in colonial times to be ignored. A full description of its extent, and an attempt to trace its origin, have been given in a book on the subject prepared by Dr. H. R. Stiles, and with much fairness in a pamphlet by Charles Francis Adams on " Some

Phases of Sexual Morality and Church Discipline in Colonial New England."

Its existence has been a standing taunt for years against New England, and its prevalence has. been held up as a proof of a low state of morality in early New England society. Indeed, it was strange it could so long exist in so austere and virtuous a colony; that it did, to a startling extent, must be conceded; much proof is found in the books of contemporary writers. Rev. Andrew Burnaby, who travelled in New England in 1759–1760, says that though it may "at first appear to be the effects of grossness of character, it will upon deeper research be found to proceed from simplicity and innocence." To this assertion, after some research, I can give—to use Sir Thomas Browne's words — " a staggering assent to the affirmative, not without some fear of the negative." Rev. Samuel Peters, in his General History of Connecticut, speaks at length upon the custom, and apparently endeavors to prove that it was a very prudent and Christian fashion. Jonathan Edwards raised his powerful voice against it. It prevailed apparently to its fullest extent on Cape Cod, and longest in the Connecticut valley, where many Dutch customs were introduced and much intercourse with the Dutch was carried on. In Pennsylvania, among the Dutch and German settlers and their descendants, it lingered long; it was a matter of Court record as late as 1845. Yet the custom of bundling has never been held to be a result of copying the similar Dutch "queesting," which in

Holland met with the sanction of the most circumspect Dutch parents; and tergiversating Diedrich Knickerbocker even asserted the contrary assumption, that the Dutch learned of it from the Yankees. In Holland, as now in Wales and then in New England, the custom arose not from a low state of morals, nor from a disregard of moral appearances, but from the social and industrial conditions under which such courting was done. The small size and crowded occupancy of the houses, the alternative waste of lights and fuel, the hours at which the hurried courtship must be carried on, all led to the recognition and endurance of the custom; and in its open recognition lay its redeeming feature. There was no secrecy, no thought of concealment; the bundling was done under the supervision of mother and sisters.

As a contrast to all this laxity of behaviour, let me state that in the very locality where it obtained—the Connecticut Valley—other sweethearts are said to have been forced to a most ceremonious courtship, to whisper their tender nothings through a " courting-stick," a hollow stick about an inch in diameter and six or eight feet long, fitted with mouth- and ear-pieces. In the presence of the entire family, lovers, seated formally on either side of the great fireplace, carried on this chilly telephonic love-making. One of these bâtons of propriety still is preserved in Longmeadow, Mass.

Of this primitive colony with primitive manners some very extraordinary cases of bucolic love at first sight are recorded—love that did not follow the law of pounds, shillings, and pence. At an ordination in Hopkinton, New Hampshire, a country bumpkin forgot the place, the preacher, and the preaching, in the ravishing sight of an unknown damsel whom he saw for the first time within the meeting-house. He sat entranced through the long sermon, the tedious psalm-singings, the endless prayers, until at last the services were over. In an ecstasy of uncouth and unreasoning passion he rushed out of church, forced his way through the departing congregation, seized the unknown fair one in his arms crying out, "Now I have got ye, you jade, I have! I have!" And from so startling and unalluring a beginning, a marriage followed. In a neighboring community a dignified officer of the law went to "warn out of town" a strange "transient woman" who might become a pauper, and would then have to be kept at the town's expense, were this ceremony omitted. Terrified at the majesty of the law and its grand though incomprehensible wording, the young warned one burst into tears, which so worked upon the tender-hearted officer that he (being conveniently a widower) proposed to her offhand, was called in meeting, married her, and thus took her under his own and the town's protection. More than one case of "marriage at first sight" is recounted, of bold Puritan wooers riding up to the door of a fair one whom they had never seen, telling their story of a lonely home, forlorn housekeeping, and desired marriage, giving their credentials, obtaining a hasty consent, and sending in their "publishings" to the town clerk, all within a day's time.

The "matrimonial" advertisement did not appear till 1759. In the *Boston Evening Post* of February 23d of that year, this notice, for its novelty and boldness, must have caused quite a heart-fluttering among Boston " thornbacks " who would try to pass for the desired age:

"To the Ladies. Any young Lady between the Age of Eighteen and twenty three of a Midling Stature ; brown Hair, regular Features and a Lively Brisk Eye : Of Good Morals & not Tinctured with anything that may Sully so Distinguishable a Form possessed of 3 or 400£ entirely her own Disposal and where there will be no necessity of going Through the tiresome Talk of addressing Parents or Guardians for their consent : Such a one by leaving a Line directed for A. W. at the British Coffee House in King Street appointing where an Interview may be had will meet with a Person who flatters himself he shall not be thought Disagreeable by any Lady answering the above description. N. B. Profound Secrecy will be observ'd. No Trifling Answers will be regarded."

Hawthorne says: " Now this was great condescension towards the ladies of Massachusetts Bay in a threadbare lieutenant of foot."

Other matrimonial advertisements, those of recreant and disobedient wives, appear in considerable number, especially in Connecticut papers. They were sometimes prefaced by the solemn warning : " Cursed be he that parteth man & wife & all the people shall say Amen." Some very disagreeable allegations were made against these Connecticut wives—that they were rude, gay, light-carriaged girls, poor and lazy housewives, ill cooks, fond of dancing, and talking balderdash talk, and far from being loving consorts. The wives had something to say from their point of view. One, owing to her spouse's stinginess, had to use "Indian branne for Jonne bred," and never tasted good food ; another stated that her loving husband "cruelly pulled my hair, pinched my flesh, kicked me out of bed, drag'd me by my arms & heels, flung ashes upon me to smother me, flung water from the well till I had not a dry thread on me." All these notices were apparently printed in the advertiser's own language and individual manner of spelling, some even in rhyme. "Timothy hubbard" thus ventilated his domestic infelicities and his spelling in the *Connecticut Courant* of January 30th, 1776 :

"Whearis my Wife Abigiel hes under Rote me by saying it is veri Disagria bell to Hur to Expose to the World the miseris & Calamatis of a Distractid famely, and I think as much for hur Father & mother to Witt Stephen deming & his wife acts very much like Distractid or BeWicht & I believe both, for the truth of this I will apell to the Nabors. When I first Married I had land of my one and lived at my one hous but Stephen deming & his Wife cept coming down & hanting of me til they got me up to thare house but presently I was deceived by them as Bad as Adam & Eve was by the Divel though not in the Same Shape for they got a bill of

Sail of a most all by thare Sutilly & still hold the Same. perhaps the Jentlemen will say it is to pay my debt. Queri. Wherino a man that ows one pound to my shiling. I dont want it to pay his one, I believe he dos. My wife pretends to say I abus'd her for the truth of this I will apiel to all thare nabors."

Anenst this I am glad to add that I have found repentant sequels to the mortifying story, in the form of humble retractions of the husband's allegations. Wives were, on the whole, marvellously well protected by early laws. A husband could not keep his consort on outlying and danger-filled plantations, but must "bring her in, else the town will pull his house down." Nor could a man leave his wife for any length of time, nor "marrie too wifes which were both alive for anything that can appear otherwise at one time," nor beat his wife (as he could to his heart's content in old England); he could not even use "hard words" to her. Nor could she raise her hand or use "a curst and shrewish tongue" to him without fear of public punishment in the stocks or pillory.

In the first years of the colonies there existed a formal ceremony of betrothal called in Plymouth a pre - contract. This semi - binding ceremony had hardly a favorable influence upon the morals of the times. Cotton Mather states:

"There was maintained a Solemnity called a Contraction a little before the Consummation of a marriage was allowed of. A Pastor was usually employed and a sermon also preached on this occasion."

If the prospective marriage were an important or a genteel one, an applicable sermon was often preached in church at the time of the "contraction." One minister took the text, Ephesians vi. 10, 11, in order "to teach that marriage is a state of warfaring condition." It was also the custom to allow the bride to choose the text for the sermon to be delivered on the Sunday when she "came out bride." Much ingenuity was exercised by these Puritan brides in finding appropriate and interesting texts for these wedding sermons. Here are some of the verses selected:

2 Chronicles xiv. 2: "And Asa did that which was good and right in the eyes of the Lord"—Asa and his bride Hepzibah sitting up proudly in the congregation to listen.

Proverbs xxiv. 23: "Her husband is known in the gates when he sitteth among the elders of the land."

Ecclesiastes iv. 9, 10: "Two are better than one; because they have a good reward for their labour. For if they fall the one will lift up his fellow."

I can imagine the staid New England lover and his shy sweetheart anxiously and solemnly searching for many hours through the great leather-bound family Bible for a specially appropriate text, turning over the leaves and slowing scanning the pages, skipping over tedious Leviticus and Numbers, and finding always in the Song of Solomon " in almost every verse " a sentiment appealing to all lovers, and worthy a selection for a wedding sermon.

The "coming out," or, as it was called in Newburyport, " walking out " of the bride was an important

event in the little community.   Cotton Mather wrote
in 1713 that he thought it expedient for the bridal
couple to appear as such publicly, with some dignity.
We see in the pages of Sewall's diary one of his
daughters with her new-made husband leading the
orderly bridal procession of six couples on the way
to church, observed of all in the narrow Boston street
and in the Puritan meeting-house.   In some communities the bride and groom took a prominent seat in
the gallery, and in the midst of the sermon rose to
their feet and turned around several times slowly, in
order to show from every point of view their bridal
finery to the admiring eyes of their assembled friends
and neighbors in the congregation.

Throughout New England, except in New Hampshire, the law was enforced for nearly two centuries,
of publishing the wedding banns three times in the
meeting-house, at either town meeting, lecture, or
Sunday service.   Intention of marriage and the
names of the contracting parties were read by
the town clerk, the deacon, or the minister, at
any of these forgatherings, and a notice of the
same placed on the church door, or on a "publishing post"—in short, they were "valled." Yet in
the early days of the colonies the all-powerful
minister could not perform the marriage ceremony—
a magistrate, a captain, any man of dignity in the
community could be authorized to marry Puritan
lovers, save the parson.   Not till the beginning of the
eighteenth century did the Puritan minister assume
the function of solemnizing marriages.   Gov. Bel-

lingham married himself to Penelope Pelham when he was a short time a widower and forty-nine years old, and his bride but twenty-two. When he was "brought up" for this irregularity he arrogantly and monopolizingly persisted in remaining on the bench to try his own case. "Disorderly marriages" were punished in many towns; doubtless many of them were between Quakers. Some couples were fined every month until they were properly married. A very trying and unregenerate reprobate in New London persisted that he would "take up" with a woman in the town and make her his wife without any legal or religious ceremony. This was a great scandal to the whole community. A pious magistrate met the ungodly couple on the street and sternly reproved them thus: "John Rogers, do you persist in calling this woman, a servant, so much younger than yourself, your wife?"

"Yes, I do," violently answered John.

"And do you, Mary, wish such an old man as this to be your husband?"

"Indeed I do," she answered.

"Then," said the governor, coldly, "by the laws of God and this commonwealth, I as a magistrate pronounce you man and wife."

"Ah! Gurdon, Gurdon," said the groom, married legally in spite of himself, "thee's a cunning fellow."

There is one peculiarity of the marriages of the first century and a half of colonial and provincial life which should be noted—the vast number of unions between the members of the families of Puritan ministers. It seemed to be a law of social ethics that the sons of ministers should marry the daughters of ministers. The new pastor frequently married the the daughter of his predecessor in the parish, sometimes the widow—a most thrifty settling of pastoral affairs. A study of the Cotton, Stoddard, Eliot, Williams, Edwards, Chauncey, Bulkeley, and Wigglesworth families, and, above all, of the Mather family, will show mutual kinship among the ministers, as well as mutual religious thought.

Richard Mather took for his second wife the widow of John Cotton. Their children, Increase Mather and Mary Cotton, grew up as brother and sister, but were married and became the parents of Cotton Mather. The sons and grandsons and great-grandsons of Richard Mather were ministers. His daughters, granddaughters, and great-granddaughters became the wives of ministers. Thus was the name of "Mather Dynasty" well given. The Mather blood and the Mather traits of character were felt in the most remote parishes of New England. The Mather expressions of religious thought were long heard from the pulpit, and long taught in ministerial homes; and to that Mather blood and that upright Mather character and God-fearing Mather faith and teaching, we of New England owe more gratitude than can ever find expression.

We have several meagre pictures of weddings in early days. One runs thus :

"There was a pretty deal of company present . . . Many young gentlemen and gentlewomen. Mr. Noyes made a speech, said love was the sugar to sweeten every condition in the marriage state. Prayed once. Did all very well. After the Sack-posset sung 45th Psalm from 8th verse to end, five staves. I set it to Windsor tune. I had a very good Turkey Leather Psalm book which I looked in while Mr. Noyes read; then I gave it to the bridegroom saying I give you this Psalm book in order to your perpetuating this song and I would have you pray that it may be an introduction to our singing with the quire above."

For many years sack-posset was drunk at weddings, sometimes within the bridal chamber; but not with noisy revelry, as in old England. A psalm preceding and a prayer following a Puritan posset-pot made a satisfactorily solemn wassail. Bride-cake and bride-gloves were sent as gifts to the friends and relatives of the contracting parties. Other and ruder English fashions obtained. The garter of the bride was sometimes scrambled for to bring luck and speedy marriage to the garter-winner. In Marblehead the brides-maids and groomsmen put the wedded couple to bed.

It is said that along the New Hampshire and upper Massachusetts coast, the groom was led to the bridal chamber clad in a brocaded night-gown. This may have occasionally taken place among the gentry, but I fancy brocaded night-gowns were not common wear among New England country folk. I have also seen it stated that the bridal chamber was invaded, and healths there were drunk and prayers offered. The only proof of this custom which I have found is the negative one which Judge Sewall gives when he states

of his own wedding that "none came to us," after he
and his elderly bride had retired. When the weddings
of English noblemen of that period were attended
by most indecorous observances, there is no reason
to suppose that provincial and colonial weddings
were entirely free from similar rude customs.

It was found necessary in 1651 to forbid all "mixt
and unmixt" dancing at taverns on the occasion of
weddings, abuses and disorders having arisen. But
I fancy a people who would give an "ordination ball"
would not long sit still at a wedding ; and by the year
1769, at a wedding in New London, ninety-two jigs,
fifty contra-dances, forty-three minuets, and seventeen hornpipes were danced, and the party broke up
at quarter of one in the morning—at what time could
it have begun ?

Isolated communities retained for many years marriage customs derived or copied from similar customs
in the "old country." Thus the settlers of Londonderry, New Hampshire—Scotch-Irish Presbyterians—
celebrated a marriage with much noisy firing of guns,
just as their ancestors in Ireland, when the Catholics
had been forbidden the use of firearms, had ostenta-
tiously paraded their privileged Protestant condition
by firing off their guns and muskets at every celebration. A Londonderry wedding made a big noise in
the world. After the formal publishing of the banns,
guests were invited with much punctiliousness. The
wedding day was suitably welcomed at daybreak by
a discharge of musketry at both the bride's and the
groom's house. At a given hour the bridegroom,

accompanied by his male friends, started for the bride's home. Salutes were fired at every house passed on the road, and from each house pistols and guns gave an answering "God speed." Half way on the journey the noisy bridal party was met by the male friends of the bride, and another discharge of firearms rent the air. Each group of men then named a champion to "run for the bottle"—a direct survival of the ancient wedding sport known among the Scotch as "running for the bride-door," or "riding for the kail" or "for the broose"—a pot of spiced broth. The two New Hampshire champions ran at full speed or rode a dare-devil race over dangerous roads to the bride's house, the winner seized the beribboned bottle of rum provided for the contest, returned to the advancing bridal group, drank the bride's health, and passed the bottle. On reaching the bride's house an extra salute was fired, and the bridegroom with his party entered a room set aside for them. It was a matter of strict etiquette that none of the bride's friends should enter this room until the bride, led by the best man, advanced and stationed herself with her bridesmaid before the minister, while the best man stood behind the groom. When the time arrived for the marrying pair to join hands, each put the right hand behind the back, and the bridesmaid and the best man pulled off the wedding-gloves, taking care to finish their duty at precisely the same moment. At the end of the ceremony everyone kissed the bride, and more noisy firing of guns and drinking of New England rum ended the day.

In some communities still rougher horse-play than unexpected volleys of musketry was shown to the bridal party or to wedding guests. Great trees were felled across the bridle-paths, or grapevines were stretched across to hinder the free passage, and thus delay the bridal festivities.

Occasionally the wedding-bells did not ring smoothly. One Scotch-Irish lassie seized the convenient opportunity, when the rollicking company of her male friends had set out to meet the bridegroom, to mount a-pillion behind a young New Hampshire Lochinvar, and ride boldly off to a neighboring parson and marry the man of her choice. Such an unpublished marriage was known in New Hampshire as a "Flagg marriage," from one Parson Flagg, of some notoriety, of Chester, Vermont, whose house was a sort of Yankee Gretna Green; and such a marriage was made possible by the action of the government of New Hampshire in issuing marriage licenses at the price of two guineas each, as a means of increasing its income. Sometimes easygoing parsons kept a stock of these licenses on hand, ready for issue to eloping couples at a slightly advanced price. Such a marriage, without proper " publishing " in meeting, was not, however, deemed very reputable.

Madam Knight, travelling through Connecticut in 1704, wrote thus in her diary of Connecticut youth :

"They generally marry very young; the males oftener as I am told under twenty years than above; they generally make public weddings and have a way something singular in some of them ; viz. just before joining hands the bridegroom quits the place, who is soon followed by the Bridesmen and, as it were, dragged back to duty, being the °reverse to the former practice among us to steal Mistress Bride."

Poor-spirited creatures Connecticut maids must have been to endure meekly such an ungallant custom and such ungallant lovers.

The sport of stealing " Mistress Bride," a curious survival of the old savage bridals of many peoples, lingered long in the Connecticut valley. A company of young men, usually composed of slighted ones who had not been invited to the wedding, rushed in after the marriage ceremony, seized the bride, carried her to a waiting carriage, or lifted her up on a pillion, and rode to the country tavern. The groom with his friends followed, and usually redeemed the bride by furnishing a supper to the stealers. The last bride stolen in Hadley was Mrs. Job Marsh, in the year 1783. To this day, however, in certain localities in Rhode Island, the young men of the neighborhood invade the bridal chamber and pull the bride downstairs, and even out-of-doors, thus forcing the husband to follow to her rescue. If the room or house-door be locked against their invasion, the rough visitors break the lock.

In England throughout the eighteenth century the grotesque belief prevailed that if a widow were " married in Her Smock without any Clothes or

Head Gier on," the husband would be exempt from paying any of his new wife's ante-nuptial debts; and many records of such debt-evading marriages appear. In New England, it was thought if the bride were married "in her shift on the king's highway," a creditor could follow her person no farther in pursuit of his debt. Many such eccentric "smock-marriages" took place, generally (with some regard for modesty) occurring in the evening. Later the bride was permitted to stand in a closet.

Mr. William C. Prime, in his delightful book, "Along New England Roads," gives an account of such a marriage. In Newfane, Vt., in February, 1789, Major Moses Joy married Widow Hannah Ward; the bride stood, with no clothing on, within a closet, and held out her hand to the major through a diamond-shaped hole in the door, and the ceremony was thus performed. She then appeared resplendent in wedding attire, which the gallant major had thoughtfully deposited in the closet for her assumption. Mr. Prime tells also of a marriage in which the bride, entirely unclad, left her room by a window at night, and standing on the top round of a high ladder donned her wedding garments, and thus put off the obligations of the old life.

In Hall's "History of Eastern Vermont," we read of a marriage in Westminster, Vt., in which the Widow Lovejoy, while nude and hidden in a chimney recess behind a curtain, wedded Asa Averill. Smock-marriages on the public highway are recorded in York, Me., in 1774, as shown in the History of

Wells and Kennebunkport. It is said that in one case the pitying minister threw his coat over the shivering bride, Widow Mary Bradley, who in February, clad only in a shift, met the bridegroom half way from her home to his.

The traveller Kalm, writing in 1748, says that one Pennsylvania bridegroom saved appearances by meeting the scantily-clad widow-bride half way from her house to his, and announcing formally, in the presence of witnesses, that the wedding clothes which he then put on her were only lent to her for the occasion. This is curiously suggestive of the marriage investiture of Eastern Hindostan.

In Westerly, R. I., in 1724, other smock-marriages were recorded, and in Lincoln County, Me., in 1767, between John Gatchell and Sarah Cloutman, showing that the belief in this vulgar error was widespread. The most curious variation of this custom is told in the "Life of Gustavus Vassa," wherein that traveller records that a smock-marriage took place in New York in 1784 on a gallows. A malefactor condemned to death, and about to undergo his execution, was reprieved and liberated through his marriage to a woman clad only in a shift.

In spite of the hardness and narrowness of their daily life, and the cold calculation, the lack of sentiment displayed in wooing, I think Puritan husbands and wives were happy in their marriages, though their love was shy, almost sombre, and "flowered out of sight like the fern." A few love-letters still remain to prove their affection : letters of sweethearts and letters of married lovers, such as Governor Winthrop and his wife Margaret; letters like the words of another Margaret—a queen—to her "alderliefest;" letters so simple and tender that truth and love shine round them like a halo :

" MY OWN DEAR HUSBAND : How dearly welcome thy kind letter was to me, I am not able to express. The sweetness of it did much refresh me. What can be more pleasing to a wife than to hear of the welfare of her best beloved and how he is pleased with her poor endeavors! I blush to hear myself commended, knowing my own wants. But it is your love that conceives the best and makes all things seem better than they are. I wish that I may always be pleasing to thee, and that these comforts we have in each other may be daily increased so far as they be pleasing to God. I will use that speech to thee that Abigail did to David, I will be a servant to wash the feet of my lord ; I will do any service wherein I may please my good husband. I confess I cannot do enough for thee ; but thou art pleased to accept the will for the deed and rest contented. I have many reasons to make me love thee, whereof I shall name two : First, because thou lovest God, and secondly, because thou lovest me. If these two were wanting all the rest would be eclipsed. But I must leave this discourse and go about my household affairs. I am a bad housewife to be so long from them ; but I must needs borrow a little time to talk with thee, my sweetheart It will be but two or three weeks before I see thee, though they be long ones. God will bring us together in good time, for which time I shall pray. And thus with my mother's and my own best love to yourself I shall leave scribbling. Farewell my good husband, the Lord keep thee.

"Your obedient wife,

"MARGARET WINTHROP."

Who can read the beautiful words without feeling for that sweet Margaret, who died two centuries ago, a thrill of the affection that must have glowed for her in John Winthrop's heart, when, far away from her, he first opened and read this tender letter.

Warm eulogies did many a staid New Englander write of his loving consort, eulogies in rhyme, and epitaphs, elegies, threnodies, epicediums, anagrams, acrostics, and pindarics, all speaking loudly of loving, "painful" care, if not of a spirit of poesy. And the even, virtuous tenor of the life in New England proved too a happiness and contentment equal to the marital results of more emotional and romantic love-making. There were some divorces. Madam Knight found that they were plentiful in Connecticut in 1704, as they are in that State nowadays. She writes :

"These uncomely Stand-aways are too much in vogue among the English in this indulgent colony, as their records plentifully prove ; and that on very trivial matters of which some have been told me, but are not Proper to be Related by a Female Pen."

In town records we find that divorces, though infrequent, still were occasionally given in other New England States ; but the causes assigned therefor, to follow Madam Knight's example, need not be "Related by a Female Pen."

III

DOMESTIC SERVICE

It is plainly evident that in a country where land was to be had for the asking, fuel for the cutting, corn for the planting and harvesting, and game and fish for the least expenditure of labor, no man would long serve for another, and any system of reliable service indoors or afield must fail. Whether the colonists came to work or not, they had to in order to live, for domestic service was soon in the most chaotic state. Women were forced to be notable housekeepers ; men were compelled to attend to every detail of masculine labor in their households and on their farms, thus acquiring and developing a "handiness" at all trades, which has become a Yankee trait.

The question of adequate and proper household service soon became a question of importance and of painful consideration in the new land. Rev. Ezekiel Rogers wrote most feelingly in 1656 on this subject :

"Much ado have I with my own family, hard to get a servant glad of catechizing or family duties. I had a rare blessing of servants in Yorkshire, and those I brought over were a blessing, but the young brood doth much afflict me."

The Massachusetts colonists had attempted even before starting, to meet and simplify the servant question by rigidly excluding any corrupt element. They even sent back to England boys who had been unruly on shipboard. But the number of penalties imposed on servants during the early years are a lasting record of the affliction caused by the young brood.

All the early travellers speak of the lack of good servants in the new land. The " Diary of a French Refugee in Boston," in 1687, says: " There is an absolute Need of Hired help;" and that savages were employed in the fields at eighteen-pence a day. This latter form of service was naturally the first way of solving the vexed question. The captives in war were divided in lots and assigned to housekeepers. We find even gentle Roger Williams asking for " one of the drove of Adam's degenerate seed " as a slave. Hugh Peters, of Salem, wrote to a Boston friend: " Wee haue heard of a diuidence of women & children in the baye & would bee glad of a share viz.: a young woman or girle & a boy if you thinke good." Two years later he wrote: " My wife desires my daughter to send to Hanna that was her maid now at Charlestowne to know if she would dwell with us, for truly wee are now so destitute (having now but an Indian) that wee know not what to do." Lowell thus comments on such savage ministrations:

" Let any housewife of our day who does not find the Keltic element in domestic life so refreshing as to Mr.

Arnold in literature, imagine a household with one wild Pequot woman, communicated with by signs, for its maid-of-all-work, and take courage. Those were serious times indeed when your cook might give warning by taking your scalp or chignon, as the case might be, and making off with it into the woods."

We frequently glean from diaries of the times hints of the pleasures of having a wild Nipmuck or Narragansett Indian as "help." Rev. Peter Thatcher, of Milton, Mass., bought an Indian in 1674 for £5 down and £5 more at the end of the year—a high-priced servant for the times. One of her duties was, apparently, the care of a young Thatcher infant. Shortly after the purchase, the reverend gentleman makes this entry in his diary: "Came home and found my Indian girl had liked to have knocked my Theodorah on the head by letting her fall. Whereupon I took a good walnut stick and beat the Indian to purpose till she promised to do so no more." Mr. Thatcher was really a very kindly gentleman and a good Christian, but the natural solicitude of a young father over his firstborn provoked him to the telling use of the walnut stick as a civilizing influence.

When we reach newspaper days we find Indian servants frequently among the runaways; as Mather said, they could not endure the yoke; and, indeed, it would seem natural enough that any such wild child of the forests should flee away from the cramped atmosphere of a Puritan household and house. We read pathetic accounts of the desertion of aged colonists by their Indian servants. One writes that he took his " Pecod girle " as a " chilld of death " when but two years old, had reared her kindly, nursed her in sickness, and now she had run away from him when he sorely needed her, and he wished to buy a blackamoor in her place. Sometimes the description of the costumes in which these savages took their flitting, is extremely picturesque. This is from the *Boston News Letter* of October, 1707 :

" Run away from her master Baker. A tall Lusty Carolina Indian woman named Keziah Wampum, having long straight Black Hair tyed up with a red Hair Lace, very much marked in the hands and face. Had on a strip'd red blue & white Homespun Jacket & a Red one. A Black & White Silk Crape Petticoat, A White Shift, as Also a blue one with her, and a mixt Blue and White Linsey Woolsey Apron."

A reward of four pounds was offered for this barbaric creature.

Another Indian runaway in 1728 was thus bedizened, showing a startling progress in adornment from the apron of skins and blanket of her wildwood home.

" She wore off a Narrow Stript pinck Cherredary Goun turn'd up with a little flour'd red & white Callico. A Stript Homespun Quilted Petticoat, a plain muslin Apron, a suit of plain Pinners & a red & white flower'd knot, also a pair of green Stone Earrings with White Cotton Stockings & Leather heel'd Wooden Shoes."

Indian men often left their masters dishonestly dressed in their masters' fine apparel, and even wearing beribboned flaxen wigs, which must have been comic to a degree over their harsh, saturnine countenances—" as brown as any bun."

A limited substitute for Indian housemaids was found at an early day in "help," as it was called even then. Roger Williams, writing of his daughter, said : " She desires to spend some time in service & liked much Mrs. Brenton who wanted." John Tinker, who himself was help, wrote thus to John Winthrop ; " Help is scarce, hard to get, difficult to please, uncertain, &c. Means runneth out and wages on & I cannot make choice of my help." Children of well-to-do citizens thus worked in domestic service. Members of the family of the rich Judge Sewall lived out as help. The sons of Downing and of Hooke went with their kinsman, Governor Winthrop, as servants. Sir Robert Crane also sent his cousin to the governor as a farm-servant. In Andover an Abbott maiden lived as help for years in the house of a Phillips. Children were bound out when but eight years old. These neighborly forms of domestic assistance were necessarily slow of growth and limited in extent, and negro slavery appeared to the colonists a much more effectual and speedy way of solving the difficulty ; and the Indian war-prisoners, who proved such poor and dangerous house-servants, seemed a convenient, cheap, and God-sent means of exchange for " Moores," as they were called, who were far better servants. Emanuel Downing wrote in 1645 that he thought it "synne in us having power in our hand to suffer them (the Indians) to mayntayne the worship of the devill," that they should be removed from their pow-wows, and suggests the exchange for negroes, saying: "I doe not see how wee can thrive vntill wee into gett a stock of slaves sufficient to doe all our business."

Downing had a personal interest in the gaining of Moors; for he had had almost as much trouble in obtaining servants as he did in marrying off his children. We find him and his wife writing to Winthrop for help, buying Indians, sending home more than once to England for "godlye skylful paynstakeing girles," beseeching their neighbors to send them servants " of good caridg and godly conuersation ; " and at last buying negroes, to try in every way to solve the vexed question.

Though the early planters came to New England to obtain and maintain liberty, and " bond slaverie, villinage," and other feudal servitudes were prohibited under the ninety-first article of the Body of Liberties, still they needed but this suggestion of Downing's to adopt quickly what was then the universal and unquestioned practice of all Christian nations—slavery. Josselyn found slaves on Noddle's Island in Boston Harbor at his first visit, though they were not held in a Puritan family. By 1687 a French refugee wrote home :

" You may also here own Negroes and Negresses, there is not a house in Boston however small may be its means, that has not one or two. . . . Negroes cost from twenty to forty Pistoles."

In Connecticut the crime of man-stealing was made punishable by death; and in 1646 the Massachusetts General Court awoke to the growing condition of affairs and bore witness " by the first Optunity, ag't the hainous & crying sinn of man-stealing," and undertook to send back to " Gynny " negroes who had been kidnapped by a slaver and brought to New England, and to send a letter of explanation and apology with them.

Though in the beginning he refused to harbor or tolerate negro-stealers, the Massachusetts Puritan of that day, enraged at the cruelty of the savage red men, did not hesitate to sell Indian captives as slaves to the West Indies. King Philip's wife and child were thus sold and there died. Their story was told in scathing language by Edward Everett. In 1703 it was made legal to transport and sell in the Barbadoes all Indian male captives under ten, and Indian women captives. Perhaps these transactions quickly blunted whatever early feeling may have existed against negro slavery, for soon the African slave-trade flourished in New England as in Virginia, Newport being the New England centre of the Guinea Trade. From 1707 to 1732 a tax of three guineas a head was imposed in Rhode Island on each negro imported—on " Guinea blackbirds." It would be idle to dwell now on the cruelty of that horrid traffic, the sufferings on board the slavers from lack of room, of food, of water, of air. But three feet three inches was allowed between decks for the poor negro, who, accustomed to a free, out-of-door life, thus crouched and sat through the passage. No wonder the loss of life was great. It was chronicled in the newspapers and letters of the day in cold, heartless language that plainly spoke the indifference of the public to the trade and its awful consequences. I have never seen in any Southern newspapers advertisements of negro sales that surpass in heartlessness and viciousness the advertisements of our New England newspapers of the eighteenth century. Negro children were advertised to be given away in Boston, and were sold by the pound as was other merchandise. Samuel Pewter advertised in the *Weekly Rehearsal* in 1737 that he would sell horses for ten shillings pay if the horse sale were accomplished, and five shillings if he endeavored to sell and could not ; and for negroes " *sixpence a pound* on all he sells, and a reasonable price if he does not sell."

Many letters still exist of advices from shipowners to ship-captains, advice as to the purchase, care, and choice of captives, " to get one old man for a Lingister; to worter ye Rum & sell by short mesuer &c. &c." Negro-stealing by Americans continued till 1864, when a brig sailing westward from Africa on that iniquitous errand, was lost at sea—a grim ending to three centuries of incredible and unchristian cruelty.

The first anti-slavery tract published in America was written by Judge Sewall in the year 1700—" The

Selling of Joseph." His timid protest but little availed, though he persevered in his belief and his opposition to the day of his death. Other colonists who were opposed to the traffic were willing to buy slaves, that the poor heathen might be brought up in a Christian land, be led away from their idols—Abraham and the patriarchs were given as authorities in justification of thus doing. One respectable Newport elder, who sent many a profitable venture to the Gold Coast for "black ivory," always gave pious thanks in meeting on the Sunday after the safe arrival of a slaver, "that a gracious overruling Providence had been pleased to bring to this land of Freedom another cargo of benighted heathen to enjoy the blessing of a Gospel dispensation," and I suppose he fancied he had cheated his Maker, his congregation, and himself into believing that there was some truth and decency in the specious words that framed a lie in every clause. Many ministers were slave owners ; Daille—the French Huguenot, Dr. Hopkins, Dr. Williams, Ezra Stiles, and Jonathan Edwards being noted examples. The ministers from Eliot down were kind to the blacks, preaching special sermons to them, and forming religious associations for them. A negro school for reading, writing, and catechizing was established in Boston in 1728.

Cotton Mather had a negro worth fifty pounds given him by his congregation, and that "most notorious benefactor," with his never-ceasing "essay to doe good," at once, in gratitude for the gift, devoted the negro to God's service, and made many a noble resolve to save, through God's grace, his bondsman's soul. It is painful to read at a later date that he found his unregenerate slave " horribly arrested by spirits," by which he did not mean captured by the dreaded emissaries of the devil who pervaded the air of Boston and Salem at that time, but simply very drunk.

Slaves were more plentiful in Connecticut and Rhode Island than in Massachusetts. Madam Knight gives a glimpse of Connecticut slave life in 1704, and of awkward table traits in both master and slave as well, when she says that the negroes were too familiar, were permitted to sit at the table with the master, and " into the Dish goes the black Hoof as freely as the white Hand." Hawthorne says of New England slaves :

" They were not excluded from the domestic affections ; in families of middling rank, they had their places at the board ; and when the circle closed around the evening hearth its blaze glowed on their dark shining faces, intermixed familiarly with their master's children. It must have contributed to reconcile them to their lot, that they saw white men and women imported from Europe as they had been from Africa, and sold, though only for a term of years, yet as actual slaves to the highest bidder."

In the main, New England slaves were not unhappy, for they were well treated, and the race has the gift to be merry in the worst of circumstances. Occasionally one would be brought to the northern land, one of higher sensibilities, more sensitive affections, greater pride ; one who could not live a slave. Such a one was the haughty Congo Pomp, who escaped to a swamp near Truro on Cape Cod—a swamp now called by his name—and placing at the foot of a tree a jug of water and loaf of bread to sustain him on his last long journey, hanged himself from the low-hanging limbs, and thus obtained freedom. Such also was Parson Williams's slave Cato in Longmeadow, Mass. He bore repeated whippings for his high-spirited disobedience, "for speaking out loud in meeting, drinking too much cider, going on a rampage," and finally drowned himself in a well.

Waitstill Winthrop wrote thus of one suicidal Moor to Fitz John Winthrop in 1682.

"I fear Black Tom will do but little seruis. He usued to make a show of hangeing himselfe before folkes, but I believe he is not very nimble about it when he is alone. Tis good to have an eye to him & you think it not worth while to keep him eyether sell him or send him to Virginia or the Barbadoes."

William Pyncheon had also a slave who was "assiduous in hangeing." To be sold to Virginia was a standard threat to New England slaves, as work in Southern tobacco-fields was thought much more severe than in northern cornfields.

Slavery lingered in New England until after Revolutionary days. It is said that its death blow was dealt in Worcester, Mass., in 1783, when a citizen was tried for assaulting and beating his negro servant. The defence was that the black man was a slave, and the beating was but necessary restraint and correction. The master was found guilty in the Worcester County Court and fined forty shillings.

Though there were few slaves who were willing to leave life in order to be free, many were willing to try to leave their masters. The early New England newspapers abound in advertisements of runaway blacks—in gay attire, with fiddles and guns, bewigged and silk-stockinged, well dressed if not well treated.

I know no records that show more fully, though wholly unconsciously, the vast simplicity of our ancestors than these advertisements of runaway servants. Fancy giving as a possible means of identification of any human being such an item of descriptions as this: "When he gets drunk or drinks much he is red in the face"—as if that were an extraordinary or peculiar trait in any drunken man! Another runaway is said to have had "sometimes a sly look in his eye and wears the button of his hat in front;" another to have been a liar; another to have been "somewhat impudent if crossed, and has a leering look under his eyes." Others were "awkward in manners," "somewhat morose in countenance," "had long finger-nails," "had one or two pimples on the face," "is too fond of talking." It seems almost incredible that intelligent persons should have given such childish and easily obliterated or varied particulars of description.

Diverse names were applied to these runaways: "Sirrinam Indianman Slave," "Mustee-fellow," "Molatto," "Moor," "Maddagerscar-boy," "Guinyman," "Congoman," "Coast-fellow," "Tawny," "Black-amoor"—all apparently conveying some distinction of description universally comprehended at the time.

We have a few records of worthy black servants who remind us of the faithful, loving house-servants of old Southern families. Such a one was Judge Sewall's man, Boston—a freeman—to a master who deserved faithful service, if ever master did. The entries in the Judge's diary, meagre as they are, somehow show fully to us that faithful life of service. We see Boston taking the Sewall children out sledding; we see him carrying one of the little daughters out of town in his arms when the neighbors were suddenly smitten with that colonial plague, the small-pox. We find him, in later years, a tender nurse, sleeping by the fire in languishing Hannah Sewall's sick-chamber; and, after her death, we hear him protesting against the removal of her dead form from her chamber; and we can see him weeping as he sat through the lonely nights with his dead and dearly loved mistress, till she was hidden from his view. It is pleasing to know that though he lived a servant, he was buried like a gentleman; he received that token of final respect so highly prized in Boston— a ceremonious funeral, with a good fire, and chairs set in rows, and plenty of wine and cake, and a notice in the *News Letter*, and doubtless gloves in decent numbers.

Other black men led noble lives in service, if we can trust the records on their tombstones.

This elegant epitaph is upon a gravestone in Concord, Mass.:

"GOD WILLS US FREE ; MAN WILLS US SLAVES
I WILL AS GOD WILLS, GODS WILL BE DONE.
HERE LIES THE BODY OF

JOHN JACK

A NATIVE OF AFRICA, WHO DIED
MARCH 1773 AGED ABOUT SIXTY YEARS.
THOUGH BORN IN A LAND OF SLAVERY
HE WAS BORN FREE
THOUGH HE LIVED IN A LAND OF LIBERTY
HE LIVED A SLAVE.
TILL BY HIS HONEST (THOUGH STOLEN) LABORS
HE ACQUIRED THE CAUSE OF SLAVERY
WHICH GAVE HIM FREEDOM
THOUGH NOT LONG BEFORE
DEATH, THE GRAND TYRANT
GAVE HIM HIS FINAL EMANCIPATION
AND PUT HIM ON A FOOTING WITH KINGS.
THOUGH A SLAVE TO VICE
HE PRACTISED THOSE VIRTUES
WITHOUT WHICH KINGS ARE BUT SLAVES."

At Attleborough, Mass., near the old Hatch Tavern, may be seen this epitaph:

"HERE LIES THE BEST OF SLAVES
NOW TURNING INTO DUST,
CÆSAR THE AETHIOPIAN CLAIMS
A PLACE AMONG THE JUST.

HIS FAITHFUL SOUL HAS FLED
TO REALMS OF HEAVENLY LIGHT,

AND BY THE BLOOD THAT JESUS SHED
IS CHANGED FROM BLACK TO WHITE.

JAN. 15TH HE QUITTED THE STAGE
IN THE 77TH YEAR OF HIS AGE.

1781."

Besides slaves, Indians, and help, a species of nexal servitude also existed in all the colonies. At the beginning of colonization bound or indentured white servants were sent in large numbers to the new land. Thirty came to the Bay Colony as early as 1625. Some of the terms of service were very long, even for ten years. These indentured servants were in three classes: " free-willers," or "redemptioners," or voluntary emigrants; "kids," who had been seduced through ignorance or duplicity on board ships that carried them off to America ; and convicts transported for crime. The latter expatriated vagabonds were sent chiefly to Virginia. The "kids" were trapanned, by the fair promises of crimps or "spirits," in Scotland, Ireland, and England, where kidnapping formed an extensive and incredibly bold business. The Scots were brought over and sold at the time of English wars. At one time "Scots, Indians, and Negars" were not allowed to train in the militia in Massachusetts. Many curious and romantic stories are told of these kidnapped servants. One day, in 1730, a number of Boston gentlemen went to the Long Wharf to examine a cargo of Irish transports then offered for sale. Among the lads who ran up and down the wharf to show his strength and condition was one who had gone to sea on another ship. The captain, his uncle, died at sea, and the crew sold the boy to this transport-ship, which chanced to pass them. The boy faithfully served out his time to his purchaser, and became a gallant officer in the wars with the Indians.

These indentured servants were just as trying as the Indians and the negroes, and in particular showed a lawless disregard for their masters' property, an indifference to the authority of the weal-public, and a lazy disinclination to work; one writer describes them as " tender fingered in cold weather." The Mt. Wollaston lot that followed Morton to Merry Mount were but the forerunners of hundreds of others. The Bradstreets' servant, John, may be taken as a type of many refractory bound servants. He was brought to trial in 1661, for " stealing several things as pigges, capons, mault, bacon, butter, eggs, etc., and breaking open a seller door several times." John, when pulled up for trial, affirmed that he had really a very small appetite, but the food furnished by that colonial blue-stocking, Anne Bradstreet, was not fit to eat, the bread being black and heavy and sour, and he only took an occasional surreptitious bite to keep himself from starvation. But it was proved that he had feasted not only himself, but comrades, and that a neighbor, who had a " great fat Turkey against his daughter's marriage " hung up in a locked room, was relieved of it by the hungry and agile John, who got some of his fellows to let him down the chimney to steal the turkey and good store of beer, with which they all caroused; and he was fitly punished.

The laws were strict enough at first as to the behavior of servants, and occasionally a topping young maid felt their force. In Hartford, "Susan Coles for her rebellious cariedge towards her mistris is to be sent to the house of correction and be kept to hard labour and course dyet, to be brought forth the next Lecture Day to be publicquely corrected and so to be corrected weekly until Order be given to the contrary."

In York, Me., in 1645, "Alexander Maxwell for his grosse offence in his exorbitant and abusive carriages towards his master Mr. George Leader shall be publicly brought forth to the Whipping Post, where he shall be fastened till 30 lashes be given him upon his bare skin." Maxwell was ordered to satisfy his master for the money paid for his board in prison, and, if he further misbehaved, Mr. Leader could sell him to Virginia.

In later days New England housewives must have longed for the good old times of the whipping-post and coarse diet and hard work for disorderly and insubordinate redemptioners. Hear what gentle Mary Dudley endured with one of her maids. She had written many pathetic entreaties to her mother, Madam Winthrop, to send her a "good girle, a strong lusty servant," one "vsed to all kind of work who would refuse none," and we learn what she got, from a letter written a few months later, with a newborn babe by her side:

"A great affliction I have met withal by my maide ser-

vant and now I am like through God his mercie to be freed
from it ; at her first coming me she carried her selfe du-
tifully as became a servant; but since through mine and
my husbands forbearance towards her for small faults,
she hath got such a head and is growen so insolent that
her carriage towards vs especialle myselfe is unsufferable.
If I bid her doe a thinge she will bid me to doe it myselfe, and she sayes how she can give content as wel as
any servant but shee will not, and sayes if I love not quiet-
nes I was never so fitted in my life for she would make
mee have enough of it. If I should write to you of all
the reviling speeches and filthie language she hath vsed
towards me I should but grieve you. My husband hath
vsed all meanes for to reforme her, reasons and perswa-
sions, but shee doth profess that her heart and her nature will not suffer her to confesse her faults. If I tell
my husband of her behavior towards me, vpon examination she will denie all she hath done or spoken, so that
we know not how to proceed against her."

We must not forget that the Winthrops had the
best opportunity of any in the land to have good
servants ; for not only were help placed in their
families, but the best of English servants were con-
signed to them ; yet neither the Governor's sister,
Madam Downing, nor his daughter, Madam Dudley,
could be "suited." And hear the plaint of John
Winthrop to his father in 1717:

"It is not convenient now to write the trouble and
plague we have had with this Irish creature the year past.
Lying and unfaithfull; w'd doe things on purpose in con-

tradiction and vexation to her mistress; lye out of the house anights and have contrivances w'th fellows that have been stealing from o'r estate and gett drink out of ye cellar for them; saucy and impudent, as when we have taken her to task for her wickedness she has gone away to complain of cruell usage. I can truly say we have used this base creature w'th a great deal of kindness and lenity. She w'd frequently take her mistresses capps and stockins, hankerchers etc., to dresse herselfe and away without leave among her companions. I may have said some time or other when she has been in fault that she was fitt to live nowhere but in Virginia, and if she w'd not mend her ways I should send her thither tho I am sure nobody w'd give her passage thither to have her service for twenty yeares she is such a high-spirited pirnicious jade. Robin has been run away neare ten dayes as you will see by the inclosed and this creature know of his going and of his carrying out 4 dozen bottles of cyder, metheglin and palme wine out of the cellar among the servants of the town and meat and I know not w't. The bottles they broke and threw away after they had drunk up the liquor, and they got up o'r sheep anight, killed a fatt one, roasted and made merry w'th it before morning."

This wild Irish girl was indentured to the unfortunate Winthrop and his more unfortunate wife for four years, and was to have fifty shillings and some other start in the world when her time was up.

Out-of-the-way plantations fared no better in the question of service. John Wynter, the head agent of the settlement at Richmonds Island in Maine, wrote thus resentfully in 1639, to Mr. Trelawny, of the London company, of his maid, one Priscilla Beckford :

" You write of some yll reports is given of my Wyfe for beatinge the maide : yf a faire waye will not doe yt, beatinge must sometimes vppon such Idlle girrels as she is. Yf you think yt fitte for my Wyfe to do all the work, and the maide sitt still, and she must forbear her hands to strike, then the work will ly vndonn. She hath bin now 2½ yeares in the house & I do not thinke she hath risen 20 tymes before my Wyfe hath bin vp to Call her, and many tymes light the fire before she comes out of her bed. She hath twice gone a mechinge in the woodes which we have bin fain to send all our Company to seek her. We can hardly keep her within doors after we are gonn to bed except we carry the kay of the door to bed with vs. She coulde never milke Cow nor Goate since she came hither. Our men do not desire to have her boyl the kittle for them she is so sluttish. She cannot be trusted to serve a few piggs but my Wyfe must commonly be with her. She hath written home I heare that she was fain to ly vppon goates skinns. She might take some goates skinns to ly in her bedd but not given to her for her lodginge. For a yeare & quarter or more she lay with my daughter vppon a good feather bed ; before my daughter being lacke 3 or 4 days to Sacco the maid goes into bed with her cloths & stockins & would not take the paines to pluck off her Cloths ; her bed after was a doust bedd & shee had 2 Coverletts to ly on her, but Sheets she had none, after that tyme she was found to be so sluttish. Her beatinge that she hath had hath never hurt her body nor limes. She is so fatt & soggy she can hardly do any worke. Yf this maide at her lazy tymes when she hath bin found in her yll accyons do not deserve 2 or 3 blowes I pray you who hath the most reason to complain my Wyfe or maide. My Wyfe hath an Vnthankefull office. Yt does not please me well, being she hath taken so much paines and care to order things as well as she could, and ryse in the morning rath & go to bed soe latte, and have hard speeches for yt."

We can well imagine his exhausted patience, and that of poor overworked Mistress Wynter, at that fat soggy thing, that lag-last, so shiftless and useless about the house, lazing from rath to latte, and then to complete their exasperation, miching off into the woods to shirk her work so that the whole company had to turn out with a mort of trouble to hunt for the leg-trape. We cannot marvel at the beating, but simply wonder at its being remarked in those days of many and hard beatings, when scholars, servants, soldiers, and college students were well whipped, and, in Old England, wives also.

Wynter had no better fortune without doors with his men-servants and workmen; they proved kittle cattle. He found them not "plyable" or "condishionabell," that they "spoke Fair to the Face and Colloged behind the back." Of one malcontent he wrote,

"He is verry vnwilling to do vs servize, he is alwaies too hard labored, he cares not what Spoyle he makes, and will not be commanded but when he list. He is such a talkinge Fellow as makes our company worse than would be."

He says his bound servants ran away at their pleasure, worked when they pleased, and led others off to their lure, and should be punished if they had returned to England. One only was " frace " of his ways and promised to do better. Not only do we gain from Wynter's letters a knowledge of the pains of colonial domestic service, but I know among New England historical collections no other such well of good old English words and phrases.

The Declaration of Independence did not better the aspect of the servant question. The *Providence Gazette* advertised in 1796 that a reward of five hundred dollars and the " warmest blessings of abused householders" would be given to any restoring the conditions of the good old times, or rather what they fancied was

> " The constant service of the antique world
> When service sweat for duty not for need."

The notice opens thus:

" Was mislaid or taken away by mistake, soon after the formation of the abolition society, from the servant girls in this town all inclination to do any kind of work, and left in lieu thereof an independent appearance, a strong and continued thirst for high wages, a gossiping disposition for every sort of amusement, a leering and hankering after persons of the other sex, a desire of finery and fashion, a never-ceasing trot after new places, more advantageous for stealing, with a number of contingent accomplishments that do not suit the wearers."

President Dwight wrote that the servants of that day were " distinguished for vice and profligacy; " so the nineteenth century opened no more promisingly than the eighteenth.

The pious colonists felt that great spiritual, as well as temporal responsibility rested upon them in regard to their bond-servants. We find in contemporary letters frequent reference to the souls of the indentured ones; Englishmen at the old home wrote to the settlers to remember well their religious, their proselyting duties; and they faithfully reminded each other of their accountability for souls. For instance, when a smart young Irishman came over with some Irish hounds, his consigner besought the New Englanders to remember that it was as godly to "winne this fellowes soule out of the subtillest snare of Sathan, Romes pollitick religion, as to winne an Indian soule out of the Dieuells clawes;" and he urged them to watch the Papist narrowly as to his carriage in Puritandom, his attitude toward Protestantism. This was the same religious zeal that led the Boston elders to send missionaries from New England to convert the heathen of the Established Church in Virginia.

The moral and religious condition of these servants was truly of great importance in the preservation of such a theocracy as was New England, since few of them returned to England, but after serving out their time became freemen with homes and land and votes of their own; and the commonwealth could not live as a religious organization unless it thrived through the religious spirit of its citizens.

One other form of domestic service existed until this century. A limited amount of assistance was given in some households by those unhappy wights, the town-poor. These wretched paupers were sold to the lowest bidder. Sometimes the buyer received but a few shillings a year from the town for the " keep " of one of these helpless souls. We may be sure that he got some work out of the pauper to pay for his board. We read of one old Dimbledee, of Widow Bump and Widow Bumpus, degenerate successors in name as well as in estate of the Pilgrim Bompasse, who were sold from year to year from one farm to another and given a grudged existence, till at last we find the town paying for their welcome coffins and winding sheets. Two curious facts are to be noted in the poor accounts : that the women paupers were almost invariably " very comfortable on it for clothes," as were other women of that dress-loving day ; and that liquor was frequently supplied to both male and female paupers by the town. Sometimes ten gallons apiece, a very consoling amount, was given in a year. I have also noted the frequent presence on the poor-list of what are termed " French Neuterls." These were Acadians—the neighbors and compatriots of Evangeline—feeble folk, who, void of romance, succumbed in despair to exile and homesickness, a new language and a new manner of living, and yielded weakly to work as servants when they had no courage to maintain homes. New England paupers lived to a good old age. I have been told that the unhappy fate of one of these town-poor—an Acadian—was traced for over thirty years in the town records of her sale. In 1767 there were twenty-one paupers in Danvers, Mass., and their average age was eighty-four years, thus apparently offering proof of good rum and good usage from the town. There was also an hereditary pauperism. In Salem a certain family always had some of its members on the list of town-poor from the year 1721 to 1848; and perhaps they found better homes through "living around" than in trying to support themselves.

Criminals were also sold into service to work out their sentences. Thus did the practical settlers attempt to carry out one of Sir Thomas More's Utopian notions. Upon the whole, I think I should rather have a Nipmuck squaw cooking in my kitchen, or a Pequot warrior digging in my garden, than to have a white burglar or ruffian in either situation.

It is well to observe in passing that no gingerly nicety of regard in calling those who served by any other name than servant, was shown or heeded in olden times. They believed with St. Paul, " Art thou called being a servant? Care not for it." All hired workers in the house, hired laborers in the field, those contracting to work under a master at any trade for a period of time, apprentices, and many whom we should now term agents or stewards, were then called servants, and signed contracts as servants, and did not appear at all insulted by being termed servants.

IV

HOME INTERIORS

IT is easy to gain a definite notion of the furnishing of colonial houses from a contemporary and reliable source—the inventories of the estates of the colonists. These are, of course, still preserved in court records. As it was customary in early days to enumerate with much minuteness the various articles of furniture contained in each room, instead of classifying or aggregating them, we have the outlines of a clear picture of the household belongings of that day.

The first room beyond the threshold of the door that one finds named in the houses " of the richer sort," is the entry. This was apparently always bare of furniture, and indeed well it might be, for it was seldom aught but a vestibule to the rest of the house, containing, save the staircase, but room enough to swing the front door in opening. Dr. Lyon gives the inventory of John Salmon of Boston in the year 1750 as the earliest record which he has found of the use of the word hall instead of entry, as we now employ it. In the *Boston News Letter*, thirty one years earlier, on August 24th, 1719, I find this advertisement:

" Fine Glass Lamps & Lanthorns well gilt and painted both Convex and Plain. Being suitable for Halls, staircases, or other Passage ways, at the Glass Shop in Queen Street." This advertisement is, however, exceptional. The hall in Puritan houses was not a passageway, it was the living-room, the keeping-room, the dwelling-room, the sitting-room ; in it the family sat and ate their meals—in it they lived. Let us see what was the furniture of a Puritan home-room in early days, and what its value. The inventory of the possessions of Theophilus Eaton, Governor of the New Haven colony, is often quoted. At the time of his death, in 1657, he had in his hall,

" A drawing Table & a round table, £1.18s.
A cubberd & 2 long formes, 14s.
A cubberd cloth & cushions, 13s.; 4 setwork cushions 12s. £1.5.
6 greene cushions, 12s; a greate chaire with needleworke, 13s. £1.5.
2 high chaires set work, 20s ; 4 high stooles set worke, 26s 8d £6.6.8.
4 low chaires set worke, 6s 8d, £1.6.8.
2 low stooles set worke, 10s.
2 Turkey Carpette, £2; 6 high joyne stooles, 6s. £2.6.
A pewter cistern & candlestick, 4s.
A pr of great brass Andirons, 12s.
A pr of small Andirons, 6s 8d.
A pr of doggs, 2s 6d.
A pr of tongues fire pan & bellowes, 7s."

Now, this was a very liberally furnished living-room. There were plenty of seats for diners and loungers, if Puritans ever lounged ; two long forms and a dozen stools of various heights, with green or embroidered cushions, upon which to sit while at the Governor's board; and seven chairs, gay with needlework covers, to draw around his fireplace with its shining paraphernalia of various sized andirons, tongs, and bellows. The low, heavy-raftered room with these plentiful seats, the tables with their Turkey covers, the picturesque cupboard with its rich cloth, and its display of the Governor's silver plate, all aglow with the light of a great wood fire, make a pretty picture of comfortable simplicity, pleasant of contemplation in our bric-a-brac filled days, a fit setting for the figures of the Governor, "New England's glory full of warmth and light," and his dearest, greatest, best of temporal enjoyments, his "vertuous, prudent and prayerful wife."

Contemporary inventories make more clear and more positive still this picture of a planter's home-room, for similar furniture is found in all. All the halls had cisterns for water or for wine (and I fancy they stood on the small table usually mentioned); all had a table for serving meals; a majority had the cupboard; a few had "picktures" or "looke-ing glasses;" very rarely a couch or "day-bed" was seen; some had "lanthorns" as well as candlesticks; others a spinning-wheel for the good wife, when she "keepit close the house and birlit at the wheel."

Chairs were a comparatively rare form of furniture in New England in early colonial days, nor were they frequently seen in humble English homes of that date. Stools and forms were the common seats. Turned, wainscot, and covered chairs are the three distinct types mentioned in the seventeenth century. Turned chairs are shown in good examples in what are known as the Carver and Brewster chairs, now preserved in Pilgrim Hall in Plymouth. The president's chair at Harvard College is another ancient turned chair.

The seats of many of these chairs were of flags and rushes. The bark of the elm and bass trees was also used for bottoming chairs.

The wainscot chairs were all of wood, seats as well as backs, usually of oak. They were frequently carved or panelled. One now in Pilgrim Hall is known as the Winslow chair. Another fine specimen in carved oak is in the Essex Institute in Salem. Carved chairs were owned only by persons of wealth or high standing, and were frequently covered with " redd lether " or " Rusha lether." Sometimes the leather was stamped and different rich fabrics were employed to cover the seats. " Turkey wrought " chairs are frequently mentioned. Velvet " Irish stitch," red cloth, and needlework covers are named. Green appeared to be, however, the favorite color.

Cane chairs appeared in the last quarter of the century. It is said that the use of cane was introduced into furniture with the marriage of Charles II. to Catharine of Braganza.

The bow-legged chair, often with claw and ball foot, came into use in the beginning of the eighteenth century. " Crowfoot " and " eaglesfoot " were named in inventories. These are copies of Dutch shapes.

Easy-chairs also appeared at that date, usually as part of the bedroom furniture, and were covered with the stuffs of which the bed-hangings and window-curtains were made, such as " China," " callico," " camblet," " harrateen."

The three-cornered chair, now known as an "As you like it " chair, appeared in the middle of the century under the names of triangle, round-about, and half-round chair.

The chairs known now as Chippendale may date back to the middle of the century; Windsor chairs, also known and manufactured in Philadelphia at that date, were not common in New England till a score of years later, when they were made and sold in vast numbers, being much more comfortable than the old bannister or slat-backed chairs then in common use.

Another piece of hall furniture deserves special mention. Dr. Lyon gives these names of cupboards found in New England : Cupboard, small cupboard, great cupboard, court cupboard, livery cupboard, side cupboard, hanging cupboard, sideboard cupboard, and cupboard with drawers. To this list might be added corner cupboard. The word court cupboard is found from the years 1647 to 1704. It was a high piece of furniture with an enclosed closet or drawers, originally intended to display plate, and was the highest-priced cupboard found. Upon it were set, in New England, both glass and plate. The livery cupboard, similar in its uses, seldom had an enclosed portion. " Turn pillar cuberds," painted and carved cupboards, were found. The item of cupboard in any inventory was usually accompanied by that of a cupboard cloth. This latter seemed to be the most elegant and luxurious article in the whole house. Cupboard cloths of holland, "laced," "pantado," "cambrick," "kalliko," "green wrought with silk fringe"—all are named. Cushions also, " to set upon a cubberds head," are frequently named. They were made of damask, needlework, velvet or cloth. A corner cupboard was apparently a small affair; a japanned one is named. What we now call a corner cupboard was then known as a beaufet.

The hall was naturally on one side of the entry and opening into it. On the other side, in large houses, was the parlor; this room was sometimes used as a dining-room, sometimes as a state bedroom. It frequently held, in addition to furniture like that of the hall, a chest or chests of drawers to hold the family linen, and also that family idol—the best bed.

Of the exact shape and height of the bedsteads used by the early colonists, I find no accurate nor very suggestive descriptions. The terms used in wills, inventories, and letters seem too vague and curt to give us a correct picture. What was the "half-headed bedstead" left with "Curtaince & Valance of Dornix" by will by Simon Eire in Boston in 1658? Or, to give a fuller description of a similar one in the sale of furniture of the King's Arms in Boston, in 1651, " one half-headed Bedsted with Blew Pillars." I fancy they were bedsteads with moderately high headboards. It is easy enough to obtain full items of the bed itself and the bed-furniture, its coverings and hangings. We read of " ffether beds," " flocke beds," " downe bedds," "wool beds," and even " charf beds," the latter worth but three shillings apiece, all of importance enough to be named in wills and left with as much dignity of bequest as Shakespeare's famous "second-best bed." Even so influential a man as Thomas Dudley did not disdain to leave by specification to his daughter Pacy a "ffeather beed & boulster." In 1666 Nicholas Upsall, of Boston, left a "Bedstead fitted with a Rope Matt & Curtains to it." In March, 1687, Sewall wrote to London for "White Fustian Drawn enough for curtains, vallen counterpaine for a bed & half a duz chaires with four threeded green worsted to work it." In 1691 we find him writing for "Fringe for the Fustian bed & half a duz Chairs. Six yards and a half for the vallons, fifteen yards for 6 chairs two Inches deep; 12 yards half inch deep." This wrought fustian bed was certainly handsome.

By revolutionary times we read such items as these: "Neet sette bed," "Very genteel red and white copperplate Cottonbed with Squab and Window Curtains Fring'd and made in the Newest Taste," "Sacken' & Corded Beds and a Pallat Bed," "Very Handsome Flower'd Crimson worsted damask carv'd and rais'd Teaster Bed & Curtains compleat," "A Four Post Bedstead of Mahogany on Casters with Carved Foot Posts, Callico Curtains to Ditto & Window Curtains to Match, and a Green Harrateen Cornish Bed." Harrateen, a strong, stiff woollen material, formed the most universal bed hanging. Trundle-beds or truckle-beds were used from the earliest days. So there was variety in plenty.

A form of bedstead called a slawbank was common

enough in New York, New Jersey, Delaware, and Pennsylvania until this century. They were more rarely found in Connecticut and Massachusetts, and as I do not know what they were called in New England, we will give them the Dutch name slawbank, from *sloapbancke*, a sleeping-bench. A slawbank was the prototype of our modern folding-bed. It was an oblong frame with a network of rope. This frame was fastened at one end to the wall with heavy hinges, and at night it was lowered to a horizontal position, and the unhinged end was supported on heavy wooden turned legs which fitted into sockets in the frame. When not in use the bed was hooked up against the wall, and doors like closet doors were closed over it, or curtains were drawn over it to conceal it. It was usually placed in the kitchen, and upon it slept goodman and goodwife. I know of several slawbanks still in old Narragansett, and one in a colonial house in Shrewsbury, Mass. A similar one may be seen at Deerfield Memorial Hall. It is hung around with blue serge curtains. I have seen no advertisements of slawbanks under any name in New England newspapers, unless the "bedstead in a painted press" in the *Boston Gazette* of November, 1750, may be one.

The bed furniture was of much importance in olden days, and the coverlet was frequently mentioned separately. Margaret Lake, of Ipswich, in 1662, so named a "Tapestry coverlet" worth £4. Susannah Compton had at about the same date a "Yearne Courlead." "Strieked couerlids" appear, and Adam Hunt, of Ipswich, had in 1671 "an embroadured couerled." "Happgings"—coarse common coverlets —are also named. In 1716, on September 24th, in the *Boston News Letter*, the word counterpane first appears. "India counterpins" often were advertised, and cheney, harrataen, and camlet coverlets or counterpanes were made to match the bed-hangings.

A pair of sheets was furnished in 1628 to each Massachusetts Bay colonist. This was a small allowance, but quite as full as the average possession of sheets by other colonists. Cotton sheets were not plentiful; flaxen or "fleishen" sheets, "canvas" sheets, "noggan" sheets, "towsheets," and "nimming" sheets (mentioned by Lechford in his notebook in 1640) were all of linen. Flannel sheets also were made, and may appear in inventories under the name of rugs, and thus partially explain the untidy absence, even among the possessions of wealthy citizens, of sheets. "Straken" sheets were of kersey. After spinning became fashionable, and flax was raised in more abundance, homespun sheets were made in large quantities, and owned by all respectable householders. "Twenty and one pair" was no unusual number to appear in an inventory.

There were plenty of "ffether boulsters," "shafe boulsters," "wool bolsters;" and John Walker had in 1659 a "Thurlinge Boulster," and each household had many pillows. The word bear was universally used to denote a pillow-case. It was spelled ber, beer, beir, beare and berr. In 1689 the value of a "pelerbeare" in an inventory was given at three shillings. In 1664 Susannah Compton had linen "pillow

coates." Pillow covers also were named, and pillow
clothes, but pillow bear was the term most commonly
applied.

The following list of varieties of chests is given by
Dr. Lyon : Joined chests, wainscot chests, board
chests, spruce chests, oak chests, carved chests,
chests with one or two drawers, cypress chests.
Joined and wainscot chests were framed chests with
panels, distinguished clearly from the board chests,
made of plain boards. The latter were often called
plain chests, the former panel chests. Carved chests
were much rarer. William Bradford, of Plymouth, had one in 1657 worth £1. Dr. Lyon also
gives as possibly being carved these items : " wrought
chest," " ingraved," " settworke," and " inlayed chests."
Chests were also painted, usually on the parts in
relief on the carving, the colors being generally
black and red. Chests with drawers were not rare in
New England. A good specimen may be seen in the
rooms of the Connecticut Historical Society. They
were distinct in shape from what we now call chests
of drawers. Nearly all the oak chests were quartered
to show the grain, and " drop ornaments " and " egg
ornaments " of various woods were applied. Cypress
and cedar chests were used then, as now, to protect
garments from moths. Governor Bellingham had
one of the former worth £5. Ship chests or sea
chests were, of course, plentiful enough. Cristowell
Gallup had in 1655 a " sea chest and a great white
chest." These sea chests being made of cheap
materials, have seldom been preserved. There would

appear to be in addition to the various chests already named, a hanging chest. In 1737 Sir William Pepperell wrote to England for "4 dozen pair Snipe bills to hang small chissts." This may possibly refer to snipe-bill hinges to be placed on chests.

It is safe to infer that almost every emigrant brought to America among his household belongings at least one chest. It was of use as a travelling trunk, a packing-box, and a piece of furniture. Many colonists had several. Jane Humphreys had and named in her will " my little chest, my great old chest, my great new chest, my lesser small box, my biggest small box "—and she needed them all to hold her finery.

Chests also were made in New England. Pine was used in the backs and drawers of chests of New England make. English chests were wholly of oak.

In the Memorial Hall at Deerfield may be seen many fine specimens of old chests, forming, indeed, a complete series, showing the various shapes and ornamentations.

Another furnishing of the parlor was the scrutoire. Under the spellings scritoire, scredoar, screetor, scrittore, scriptore, scrutoir, scritory, scrutore, escrutor, scriptoree, this useful piece of furniture appears constantly in the inventories of men of wealth in the colonies from the year 1669 till a century later. Judge Sewall tells of losing the key of his " scrittoir." The definition of the word in Phillips's " New World of Words," 1696, was " Scrutoire, a sort of large Cabinet with several Boxes, and a place for Pen, Ink

and Paper, the door of which opening downward and
resting upon Frames that are to be drawn out and
put back, serves for a Table to write on." This
description would appear to identify the "scrutoire"
with what we now call a writing-desk ; and it was
called interchangeably by these two names in wills.
They were made with double bow fronts and box
fronts, of oak, pine, mahogany, cherry ; and some
had cases of shelves for books on the top, forming
what we now call a secretary—our modern rendering of the word scrutoire. These book scrutoires
frequently had glass doors.

When Judith Sewall was about to be married, in
1720, her father was much pleased with his prospective
son-in-law and evidently determined to give the pair
a truly elegant wedding outfit. The list of the house-
furnishings which he ordered from England has been
preserved, and may be quoted as showing part of the
"setting-off" in furniture of a rich bride of the day.
It reads thus :

" Curtains & Vallens for a Bed with Counterpane Head
Cloth and Tester made of good yellow waterd worsted
camlet with Triming well made and Bases if it be the
Fashion.   Send also of the Same Camlet & Triming as
may be enough to make Cushions for the Chamber
Chairs.

"A good fine large Chintz Quilt well made.

" A true Looking Glass of Black Walnut Frame of the
Newest Fashion if the Fashion be good, as good as can
be bought for five or six pounds.

"A second Looking Glass as good as can be bought for four or five pounds, same kind of frame.

"A Duzen of good Black Walnut Chairs fine Cane with a Couch.

"A Duzen of Cane Chairs of a Different Figure and a great Chair for a Chamber ; all black Walnut.

"One bell-metal Skillet of two Quarts, one ditto one Quart.

"One good large Warming Pan bottom and cover fit for an Iron handle.

"Four pair of strong Iron Dogs with Brass heads about 5 or 6 shillings a pair.

"A Brass Hearth for a Chamber with Dogs Shovel Tongs & Fender of the newest Fashion (the Fire is to ly upon Iron).

"A strong Brass Mortar That will hold about a Quart with a Pestle.

"Two pair of large Brass sliding Candlesticks about 4 shillings a Pair.

"Two pair of large Brass Candlesticks not sliding of the newest Fashion about 5 or 6 shillings a pair.

"Four Brass Snuffers with stands.

"Six small strong Brass Chafing dishes about 4 shillings apiece.

"One Brass basting Ladle ; one larger Brass Ladle.

"One pair of Chamber Bellows with Brass Noses.

"One small hair Broom sutable to the Bellows.

"One Duzen of large hard-mettal Pewter Plates new fashion, weighing about fourteen pounds.

"One Duzen hard-mettal Pewter Porringers.

"Four Duzen of Small glass Salt Cellars of white glass ; Smooth not wrought, and without a foot.

"A Duzen of good Ivory-hafted Knives and Forks."

The floors of colonial houses were sometimes sanded, but were not carpeted, for a carpet in early days was not a floor covering, but the covering of a table or cupboard. In 1646 an inquiry was made into some losses on the wreck of the " Angel Gabriel." A servant took oath that Mr. John Coggeswell " had a Turky-work'd Carpet in old England which he commonly used to lay on his Parlour Table ; and this Carpet was put aboard among my Maisters goods and came safe ashore to the best of my Remembrance." Another man testified that he did "frequentlie see a Turkey-work Carpet & heard them say it used to lay upon their Parlour Table." Dornix, arras, cloth, calico, and broadcloth carpets are named. Sewall tells of an " Irish stitch't hanging made a carpet of." Samuel Danforth gave, in 1661, a " Convenient Carpet for the table of the meeting house." In 1735, in the advertisement of the estate of Jonathan Barnard, "one handsome Large Carpet 9 Foot 0 inches by 6 foot 6 inches " was named. This was, I fancy, a floor covering. In the *Boston Gazette* of November, 1748, "two large Matts for floors " were advertised—an exceptional instance in the use of the word mat. Large floor-carpets were advertised the following year, and in 1755 a " Variety of List Carpets wide & Narrow," and "Scotch Carpets for Stairs." In 1769 came " Persia Carpets 3 yards Wide." In 1772, in the *Boston Evening Post*, " A very Rich Wilton Carpet 18 ft by 13 " was named. The following year " Painted Canvass Floor Cloth " was named. This was doubtless the " Oyl Cloth for Floors and Tables " of the

year 1762. Oilcloth had been known in England a
century previously. What the "False Carpets" advertised on June 7, 1762, were I do not know.

The walls of the rooms were wainscoted and
painted. Gurdon Saltonstall had on the walls of
some of his state-rooms leathern hangings or tapestries. We find wealthy Sir William Pepperel sending
to England, in 1737, the draught of a chamber he was
furnishing, and writing, "Geet mock Tapestry or
paint'd Canvass lay'd in Oyls for ye same and send
me." In 1734 "Paper for Rooms," and a little later
"Rolled Paper for Hanging of Rooms" were advertised in the *Boston News Letter*. "Statues on Paper"
were soon sold, and "Architraves on Roll Paper" and
"Landscape Paper." These old paper-hangings were
of very heavy and strong materials, close-grained,
firm and durable. The rooms of a few wealthy men
were hung with heavy tapestries. The ceilings usually exposed to view the great summer-tree and cross
rafters, sometimes rough-hewn and still showing the
marks of the woodman's axe. But little decoration
was seen overhead, even in the form of chandeliers;
sometimes a candle beam bore a score of candles, or
in some fine houses, such as the Storer mansion in
Boston, great ornamental globes of glass hung from
the summer-tree.

In the first log cabins oiled paper was placed in
windows. We find more than one colonist writing to
England for that semi-opaque window-setting. Soon
glass windows, framed in lead, were sent from London and Liverpool and Bristol, ready for insertion in

the walls of houses; and at an early day sheets of glass came to Winthrop. We find, by Sewall's time, that the houses of well-to-do folk all had "quarrels of glass" set in windows.

The flight of time in New England houses was marked without doors by sun-dials; within, by noon-marks, hour-glasses, and rarely by clepsydras, or water-clocks.

The first mention, in New England records, of a clock is in Lechford's note-book. He states that in 1628 Joseph Stratton had of his brother a clock and watch, and that Joseph acknowledged this, but refused to pay for them and was sued for payment. Hence Lawyer Lechford's interest in the articles and mention of them. In 1640 Henry Parks, of Hartford, left a clock by will to the church. In the inventory of Thomas Coteymore, made in Charleston, in 1645, his clock is apprized at £1. In 1657 there was a town-clock in Boston and a man appointed to take care of it. In 1677 E. Needham, of Lynn, left a "striking clock, a Larum that does not strike and a watch," valued at £5—this in an estate of £1,117 total. Judge Sewall wrote, in 1687, "Got home rather before 12 Both by my Clock and Dial."

Clocks must have become rather plentiful in the early part of the following century, for in 1707 this advertisement appeared in the *Boston News Letter* :

"To all gentlemen and others : There is lately arrived in Boston by way of Pennsylvania a Clock maker. If any person or persons hath any occasions for new Clocks or to have Old Ones turn'd into Pendulums, or any other thing either in making or mending, they can go to the Sign of the Clock and Dial on the South Side of the Town House."

In 1712, in November, appeared in the *News Letter* the advertisement of a man who "performed all sorts of New Clocks and Watch works, viz: 30 hour Clocks, Week Clocks, Month Clocks, Spring Table Clocks, Chime Clocks, quarter Clocks, quarter Chime Clocks, Church Clocks, Terret Clocks;" and on April 16, 1716, this notice appeared: "Lately come from London. A Parcel of very Fine Clocks. They go a week and repeat the hour when Pull'd. In Japan Cases or Wall Nutt."

By this time, in the inventory or "enroulment" of the estate of any person of note, we always find a clock mentioned. Increase Mather left to his son Cotton "one Pendilum Clock." Soon appear Japann'd clocks and Pullup Clocks. In the *New England Weekly Journal* of October, 1732, the fourth prize in the Newport lottery was announced to be a clock worth £65. "A Handsome new Eight day Clock which shows the Moons Age, Strikes the Quarters on Six very Tunable Bells & is in a Good Japann'd Case in Imitation of Tortoise Shell & Gold."

This advertisement of Edmund Entwisle, in the *Boston News Letter* of November 18, 1742, proves, I think, that they had some very handsome clocks in those days:

"A Fine Clock. It goes 8 or 9 days with once winding up. And repeats the Hour it struck last when you pull it. The Dial is 13 inches on the Square & Arched with a SemiCircle on the Top round which is a strong Plate with this Motto (Time shews the Way of Lifes Decay) well engraved & silver'd, within the Motto Ring it shews from behind two Semispheres the Moons Increase & Decrease by two curious Painted Faces ornamented with Golden Stars between on a Blue Ground, and a white Circle on the Outside divided into Days figured at every Third, in which Divisions is shewn the Age by a fix't Index from the Top, as they pass by the great Circle is divided into three Concentrick Collums on the outmost of which it shews the Minute of each Hour and the Middlemost the Hours &c. the innermost is divided into 31 equal parts figur'd at every other on which is shewn the Day of the Month by a Hand from the Dial Plate as the Hour & Minute is, it also shews the Seconds as common & is ornamented with curious Engravings in a Most Fashionable Manner. The case is made of very Good Mohogony with Quarter Collums in the Body, broke in the Surface with Raised Pannels with Quarter Rounds burs Bands & Strings. The head is ornamented with Gilded Capitalls Bases & Frise with New fashion'd Balls compos'd of Mohogony with Gilt Leaves & Flowers."

I do not quite understand this description, and I know I could never have told the correct time by this clock, but surely it must have been very elegant and costly.

The earliest and most natural, as well as most plentiful, illuminating medium for the colonists was found in pine-knots. Wood says:

"Out of these Pines is gotten the Candlewood that is so much spoke of which may serve as a shift among poore folks but I cannot commend it for Singular good because it is something sluttish dropping a pitchy kind of substance where it stands."

Higginson wrote in 1630, "Though New England has no tallow to make candles of yet by abundance of fish thereof it can afford oil for lamps."

Though lamps and "lamp yearne," or wicks, appear in many an early invoice, I cannot think that they were extensively used. Betty lamps were the earliest form. They were a shallow receptacle, usually of pewter, iron, or brass, circular or oval in shape, and occasionally triangular, and about two or three inches in diameter, with a projecting nose an inch or two long. When in use they were filled with tallow or grease, and a wick or piece of twisted rag was placed so that the lighted end could hang on the nose. Specimens can be seen at Deerfield Memorial Hall. I have one with a hook and chain by which to hang it up, and a handled hook attached with which to clean out the grease. These lamps were sometimes called " brown-bettys," or " kials," or " cruiseys." A phœbe lamp resembled a betty lamp, but had a shallow cup underneath to catch the dripping grease.

Soon candles were made by being run in moulds, or by a tedious process of dipping. The fragrant bayberry furnished a pale green wax, which Robert Beverly thus described in 1705:

" A pale brittle wax of a curious green color, which by refining becomes almost transparent. Of this they

make candles which are never greasy to the touch, nor
melt with lying in the hottest weather ; neither does the
snuff of these ever offend the smell, like that of a tallow
candle ; but, instead of being disagreeable, if an accident puts a candle out, it yields a pleasant fragrancy
to all that are in the room; insomuch that nice people
often put them out on purpose to have the incense of the
expiring snuff."

The Abbé Robin and other travellers gave similar
testimony.   Bayberry wax was a standard farm production wherever bayberries grew, and was advertised
in New England papers until this century.   I entered
within a year a single-storied house a few miles from
Plymouth Rock, where an aged descendant of the
Pilgrims earns her scanty spending-money by making
"bayberry taller," and bought a cake and candles of
the wax, made in precisely the method of her ancestors ; and I too can add my evidence as to the
pure, spicy perfume of this New England incense.

The growth of the whaling trade, and consequent
use of spermaceti, of course increased the facilities for,
and the possibilities of, house illumination.   In 1686
Governor Andros petitioned for a commission for a
voyage after "Sperma-Coeti Whales," but not till
the middle of the following century did spermaceti
become of common enough use to bring forth such
notices as this, in the *Boston Independent Advertiser*
of January, 1749 :

"Sperma-Ceti Candles, exceeding all others for Beauty
Sweetness of Scent when Extinguished.   Duration being

more than Double with Tallow Candles of Equal Size.
Dimensions of Flame near 4 Times more. Emitting a
Soft easy Expanding Light, bringing the object close to
the Sight, rather than causing the Eye to trace after
them, as all Tallow Candles do, from a Constant Dimnes
which they produce. One of these Candles serves the
use and purpose of 3 Tallow Candles, and upon the
Whole are much pleasanter and cheaper."

These candles were placed in candle-beams—rude
chandeliers of crossed sticks of wood or strips of
metal with sockets ; in sliding stands, in sconces,
which were also called prongs or candle-arms. The
latter appeared in the inventories of all genteel folk,
and decorated the walls of all genteel parlors.

Candlesticks and snuffers were found in every
house ; the latter were called by various names, the
word snit or snite being the most curious. It is from
the old English snyten, to blow, and was originally a
verb—to snite the candle, or put it out. In the inventory of property of John Gager, of Norwich, in
1703, appears " One Snit."

Snuffer-boats or slices were snuffer-trays. Another
curious illuminating appurtenance was called a save-
all or candle-wedge. It was a little frame of rings or
cups with pins, by which our frugal ancestors held
up the last dying bit of burning candle. They were
sometimes of pewter with iron pins, sometimes wholly
of brass or iron. They have nearly all disappeared
since new and more extravagant methods of illumination prevail.

The argand lamps of Jefferson's invention and the various illuminating and heating contrivances of Count Rumford must have been welcome to the colonists.

The discomfort of a colonial house in winter-time has been ably set forth by Charles Francis Adams in his "Three Episodes of Massachusetts History." Down the great chimneys blew the icy blasts so fiercely that Cotton Mather noted on a January Sabbath, in 1697, as he shivered before "a great Fire, that the Juices forced out at the end of short billets of wood by the heat of the flame on which they were laid, yett froze into Ice on their coming out." Judge Sewall wrote, twenty years later, "An Extraordinary Cold Storm of Wind and Snow. Bread was frozen at Lords Table. . . . Though 'twas so Cold yet John Tuckerman was baptized. At six oclock my ink freezes so that I can hardly write by a good fire in my Wives Chamber"—and the pious man adds (we hope with truth) "Yet was very Comfortable at Meeting." Cotton Mather tells, in his pompous fashion, of a cold winter's day four years later. "Tis Dreadful cold, my ink glass in my standish is froze and splitt in my very stove. My ink in my pen suffers a congelation." If sitting-rooms were such refrigerators, we cannot wonder that the chilled colonists wished to sleep in beds close curtained with heavy woollen stuffs, or in slaw-bank beds by the kitchen fire.

The settlers builded as well as they knew to keep their houses warm; and while the vast and virgin forests supplied abundant and accessible wood for fuel, Governor Eaton's nineteen great fireplaces and Parson Davenport's thirteen, could be well filled; but by 1744 Franklin could write of these big chimneys as the "fireplace of our fathers;" for the forests had all disappeared in the vicinity of the towns, and the chimneys had shrunk in size. Sadly did the early settlers need warmer houses, for, as all antiquarian students have noted, in olden days the cold was more piercing, began to nip and pinch earlier in November, and lingered further into spring; winter rushed upon the settlers with heavier blasts and fiercer storms than we now have to endure. And, above all, they felt with sadder force "the dreary monotony of a New England winter, which leaves so large a blank, so melancholy a death-spot, in lives so brief that they ought to be all summertime." Even John Adams in his day so dreaded the tedious bitter New England winter that he longed to hibernate like a dormouse from autumn to spring.

As the forests disappeared, sea-coal was brought over in small quantities, and stoves appeared for town use. By 1695 and 1700 we find Cotton Mather and Judge Sewall speaking of stoves and stove-rooms, and of chambers warmed by stoves. Ere that one John Clark had patented an invention for "saving and warming rooms," but we know nothing definite of its shape.

Dutch stoves and china stoves were the first to be advertised in New England papers; then "Philadelphia Fire Stoves" — what we now term Franklin grates. Wood was burned in these grates. We find

clergymen, until after Revolutionary times, having
sixty or eighty cords of hardwood given to them annually by the parish.

Around the great glowing fireplace in an old New
England kitchen centred all of homeliness and comfort that could be found in a New England home.
The very aspect of the domestic hearth was picturesque, and must have had a beneficent influence.
In earlier days the great lug-pole, or, as it was called
in England, the back-bar, stretched from ledge to
ledge, or lug to lug, high up the yawning chimney,
and held a motley collection of pot-hooks and tram-
mels, of gib-crokes, twicrokes, and hakes, which in
turn suspended at various heights over the fire, pots,
and kettles and other cooking utensils.   In the
hearth-corners were displayed skillets and trivets,
peels and slices, and on either side were chimney-
seats and settles.   Above—on the clavel-piece—were
festooned strings of dried apples, pumpkins, and
peppers.

The lug-pole, though made of green wood, sometimes became brittle or charred by too long use over
the fire and careless neglect of replacement, and
broke under its weighty burden of food and metal;
hence accidents became so frequent, to the detriment of precious cooking utensils, and even to the
destruction of human safety and life, that a Yankee
invention of an iron crane brought convenience and
simplicity, and added a new grace to the kitchen
hearth.

The andirons added to the fireplace their homely

charm. Fire-dogs appear in the earliest inventories under many names of various spelling, and were of many metals—copper, steel, iron, and brass. Sometimes a fireplace had three sets of andirons of different sizes, to hold logs at different heights. Cob irons had hooks to hold a spit and dripping-pan. Sometimes the " Handirons " also had brackets. Creepers were low irons placed between the great fire-dogs. They are mentioned in many early wills and lists of possessions among items of fireplace furnishings, as, for instance, the list of Captain Tyng's furniture, made in Boston in 1653. The andirons were sometimes very elaborate, with claw feet, or cast in the figure of a negro, a soldier, or a dog.

In the Deerfield Memorial Hall there lives in perfection of detail one of these old fireplaces—a delight to the soul of the antiquary. Every homely utensil and piece of furniture, every domestic convenience and inconvenience, every home-made makeshift, every cumbrous and clumsy contrivance of the old-time kitchen here may be found, and they show to us, as in a living photograph, the home life of those olden days.

V

TABLE PLENISHINGS

In the early days of the colonies doubtless the old
Anglo-Saxon board laid on trestles was used for a
dining-table instead of a table with a stationary top.
"Table bords" appear in early New England wills,
and "trestles" also. "Long tables" and "drawing
tables" were next named. A "long table" was used
as a dining-table, and, from the frequent appearance
of two forms with it, was evidently used from both
sides, and not in the ancient fashion of the diners
sitting at one side only. A drawing-table was an ex-
tension-table; it could by an arrangement of drop
leaves be doubled in length. A fine one can be seen
in the rooms of the Connecticut Historical Society.
Chair tables were the earliest example, in fact the
prototype, of some of our modern extraordinary "com-
bination" furniture. The tops were usually round,
and occasionally large enough to be used as a dining-table, and when turned over by a hinge arrangement formed the back of the chair. "Hundred legged"
tables had flaps at either end which turned down or
were held up in place by a bracket composed of a number of turned perpendicular supports which gave to it

the name of "hundred legs." These tables were frequently very large; a portion of the top of one in the
Connecticut Historical Society is seven feet four
inches wide. Tea-tables came with tea; they were advertised in the *Boston News Letter* in 1712. Occasionally we find mention of a curious and unusual
table, such as the one named in the effects of Sir
Francis Bernard, which were sold September 11,
1770: "Three tables forming a horseshoe for the
benefit of the Fire."

As a table was in early days a board, so a tablecloth was a board-cloth; and ere it was a tablecloth
it was table-clothes. Cristowell Gallup, in 1655, had
"1 Holland board-cloth;" and William Metcalf, in
1644, had a "diaper board-cloth." Another Boston
citizen had "broad-clothes." Henry Webb, of Boston, named in his will, in 1660, his "beste Suite of
Damask Table-cloath, Napkins & cupboard-cloath."
Others had holland tablecloths and holland square
cloths with lace on them. Arras tablecloths are also
named in 1654, and cloths enriched with embroidery
in colors. The witch Ann Hibbins had "1 Holland
table cloth edged with blewe," worth twelve shillings;
and a Hartford gentleman had, in 1689, a "table Cloth
wrought with red." In 1728 "Hukkbuk Tabling"
was advertised in the *New England Weekly Journal*,
but the older materials—damask, holland, and diaper—were universally used then, as now.

The colonists had plenty of napkins, as had all
well-to-do and well-bred Englishmen at that date.
Napkins appear in all the early inventories. In 1668

the opulent Jane Humphreys, of Dorchester, left "two wrought Napkins with no lace around it," "half a duzzen of napkins," and "napkins wrought about and laced." In 1680 Robert Adams had six "diaper knapkins." Captain Tyng had in 1653 four dozen and a half of napkins, of which two dozen were of "layd worke." It has been said that these napkins were handkerchiefs, not table napkins ; but I think the way they are classed in inventories does not so indicate. For instance, in the estate of Captain Corwin, a wealthy man, who died in Salem in 1685, was a "suit of Damask 1 Table cloth, 18 napkins, 1 Towel," valued at £8. Occasionally, however, they are specially designated as "pocket napkins," as in the estate of Elizabeth Cutter in 1663, where four are valued at one shilling.

Early English books on table manners, such as "The Babees Boke" and "The Boke of Nurture," though minute in detail, yet name no other table-furniture than cups, chafing-dishes, chargers, trenchers, salt-cellars, knives, and spoons. The table plenishings of the planters were somewhat more varied, but still simple ; when our Pilgrim fathers landed at Plymouth, the collection of table-ware owned by the entire band was very meagre. With the exception of a few plate-silver tankards and drinking-cups, it was also very inexpensive. The silver was handsome and heavy, but items of silver in the earliest inventories are rare. By the beginning of the eighteenth century silver became plentiful, and the wills even of humble folk contain frequent mentions of it. Ministers, doctors, and magistrates had many handsome pieces. By the middle of the century a climax was reached, as in the possessions of Peter Faneuil, when pieces of furniture were of solid silver.

The salt-cellar was the focus of the old-time board. In earlier days, in England, to be seated above or below the salt plainly spoke the social standing of a guest. The " standing salt " was often the handsomest furnishing of the table, the richest piece of family plate. Comfort Starr, of Boston, had, in 1659, a "greate Siluer-gilt double Saltceller." Isaac Addington bequeathed by will his "Bigges Siluer Sewer & Salt." A sewer was a salver. As we note by the list of Judith Sewall's wedding furniture in 1720, standing salts were out of date, and " trencher salt-cellars " were in fashion. Four dozen was a goodly number, and evinced an intent of bounteous hospitality. These trencher-salts were of various shapes and materials : " round and oval pillar-cut Salts, Bonnet Salts, 3 Leg'd Salts," were all of glass ; others were of pewter, china, hard metal, and silver.

The greater number of spoons owned by the colonists were of pewter or of alchymy—or alcamyne, ocamy, ocany, orkanie, alcamy, or occonie—a metal composed of pan-brass and arsenicum. The reference in inventories, enrolments, and wills, to spoons of these materials are so frequent, so ever-present, as to make citation superfluous. An evil reputation of poisonous unhealthfulness hung around the vari-spelled alchymy (perhaps it is only a gross libel of succeeding generations) ; but, harmful or harmless, alchymy, no matter how spelt, disappears from use before Revolutionary times. Wooden spoons also are named. Silver spoons were not very plentiful. John Oxenbridge bequeathed thirteen spoons in 1673, and " one sweetmeat spoon," and " 1 childs spoon which was mine in my infancy." Other pap-spoons and caudle-spoons are named in wills ; marrow-spoons also, long and slender of bowl. The value of a dozen silver spoons was given in 1689 as £5 13s. 6d. In succeeding years each genteel family owned silver spoons, frequently in large number ; while one Boston physician, Dr. Cutter, had, in 1761, half a dozen gold teaspoons.

Forks, or "tines," for cooking purposes, and " prongs " or "grains " or "evils " for agricultural purposes, were imported at early dates; but I think Governor Winthrop had the first table-fork ever brought to America. In 1633, when forks were rare in England, he received a letter from E. Howes, saying that the latter had sent to him a "case containing an Irish skeayne or knife, a bodekyn & a forke for the useful applycation of which I leave to your discretion." I am strongly suspicious that Winthrop's discretion may not have been educated up to usefully applying the fork for feeding purposes at the table. In the inventory of the possessions of Antipas Boyes (made in 1669) a silver spoon, fork, and knife are mentioned. Dr. Lyon gives the names of seven New Englanders whose inventories date from 1671 to 1693, and who owned forks. In 1673 Parson Oxenbridge had " one forked spoon," and his widow had two silver forks. Iron forks were used in the kitchen, as is shown in the inventory of Zerubbabel Endicott in 1683. And three-tined iron forks were stuck into poor witch-ridden souls in Salem by William Morse— his Dæmon.

In 1718 Judge Sewall gave Widow Denison two cases with a knife and fork in each, " one Turtleshell tackling the other long with Ivory handles squar'd cost 4s. 6d." In 1738 Peter Fanueil ordered one dozen silver forks from England, " with three prongs, with my arms cut upon them, made very neat and handsome." One Boston citizen had in 1719 six four-pronged forks, an early example of that fashion. In 1737 shagreen cases with ivory-handled forks were advertised ; bone, japanned metal, wood, and horn handles also appeared—all, of course, with metal prongs. Sir Francis Bernard had in 1770 three cases of china-handled knives and forks, "with spoons to each," which must have formed a pretty table furnishing.

In many New England inventories of the seventeenth century, among personal belongings, appears the word taster. Thus in 1659 Richard Webb, of Boston, left by will "1 Silver Wine Taster;" and in 1673 John Oxenbridge had "1 Siluer Taster with a funnel." A taster was apparently a small cup. Larger drinking-cups of silver were called beakers, or tankards, beer-bowls, or wine-bowls. These latter vessels were made also of humbler metal. A sneaker was a small drinking-glass, used by moderate drinkers—sneak-cups they were called.

The Pilgrims may have had a few mugs and jugs

of coarse earthen ware. A large invoice of Portu-
guese " road ware " was sent to the Maine settlers in
1634, and proved thoroughly unsuitable and undur-
able ; but probably no china—not even Delft ware—
came over on the Mayflower. For when the Pilgrims
made their night trip through the Delft-producing
cities, no such wares were seen on the tables of plebeian persons. Early mentions of china are in the
estate of President John Davenport in 1648—" Cheney £5," and of Martha Coteymore in 1647.

Earthen ware, Green ware, Lisbon ware, Spanish
platters, are mentioned in early inventories ; but I am
sure neither china ware nor earthen ware was plentiful in early days ; nor was china much known till
Revolutionary times.

The table furnishings of the New England planters
consisted largely of wooden trenchers, and these
trenchers were employed for many years. Sometimes they were simply square blocks of wood whit-
tled out by hand. From a single trencher two persons—two children, or a man and wife—ate their
meals. It was a really elegant household that furnished a trencher apiece for each diner. Trenchers
were of quite enough account to be left by name in
early wills, even in those of wealthy colonists. In
1689 "2 Spoons and 2 Trenchers " were appraised
at six shillings. Miles Standish left twelve wooden
trenchers when he died. Many gross of them were
purchased for use at Harvard College. As late as
May, 1775, I find " Wooden Trenchers " advertised
among table furnishings, in the *Connecticut Courant*.

It was the same in Old England. J. Ward, writing in 1828 of the " Potter's Art," spoke thus of the humble boards of his youth :

> "And there the trencher commonly was seen
> With its attendant ample platter treen."

Until almost our own time trenchers were made in Vermont of the white, clean, hard wood of the poplar-tree, and were sold and used in country homes. Old wooden trenchers may be seen in Deerfield Memorial Hall. Bottles, noggins, cups, and lossets (flat dishes) of wood were also used at colonial boards.

The time when America was settled was the era when pewter ware had begun to take the place of wooden ware, just as the time of the Revolutionary War may be assigned to mark the victory of porcelain over pewter.

A set of pewter platters, or chargers and dishes, made what was called a " garnish " of pewter, and were a source of great pride to every colonial housewife, and much time and labor were devoted to polishing them until they shone like silver. Dingy pewter was fairly accounted a disgrace. The most accomplished Virginian gentleman of his day gave as a positive rule, in 1728, that " Pewter Bright " was the sign of a good housekeeper.

The trade of pewterer was a very influential and respectable one in New England as well as Old England. One of Boston's richest merchants, Henry Shrimpton, made large quantities of pewter ware for the Massachusetts colonists. So proud was he of his business that in his later years of opulence he had a great kettle atop of his house, to indicate his past trade and means of wealth. Pewter and pewterers abounded until the vast increase of Oriental commerce brought the influx of Chinese porcelain to drive out the dull metal. Advertisements of pewter table utensils did not disappear, however, in New England newspapers until this century.

A universal table furnishing was—

> " The porringers that in a row
> Hung high and made a glittering show."

When not in use porringers were hung by their pierced handles on hooks on the edge of the dresser-shelf, and, being usually of polished pewter or silver, indeed made a glittering show. Pewter porringers were highly prized. One family, in 1660, had seven, and another housewife boasted of nine. They were bequeathed in nearly all the early colonial wills. In 1673 John Oxenbridge left three silver porringers and his wife one silver pottinger; but pewter was the favorite metal. I do not find porringers ever advertised under that name in New England papers, though many were made as late as this century by New Haven, Providence, and Boston pewterers. Many bearing the stamps of these manufacturers have been preserved until the present day, seeming to have escaped the sentence of destruction apparently passed on other pewter utensils and articles of tableware.

Perhaps they have been saved because the little, shallow, graceful dishes, with flat pierced handle on one side, are really so pretty. The fish-tail handles are found on Dutch pewter. Silver porringers were made by all the silversmiths. Many still exist bearing the stamp of one honored maker, Paul Revere. Little earthen porringers of red pottery and tortoise-shell ware are also found, but are not plentiful.

A similar vessel, frequently handleless, was what was spelt, in various colonial documents, posned, possnet, posnett, porsnet, pocneit, posnert, possenette, postnett, and parsnett. It is derived from the Welsh *posned*, a porringer or little dish. In 1641 Edward Skinner left a "Postnett" by will; this was apparently of pewter. In 1653 Governor Haynes, of Hartford, left an "Iron Posnet" by will. In the inventory of the estate of Robert Daniel, of Cambridge, in 1655, we learn that "a Little Porsenett" of his was worth five shillings. In 1693 Governor Caleb Carr, of Providence, bequeathed to his wife a "silver possnet & the cover belonging to it." By these records we see that posnets were of various metals, and sometimes had covers. I have found no advertisements of them in early American newspapers, even with all their varied array of utensils and vessels. I fancy the name fell quickly into disuse in this country. In Steele's time, in the *Tatler*, he speaks of "a silver Posnet to butter eggs." I have heard the tiny little shallow pewter porringers, about two or three inches in diameter, with pierced handles, which are still found in New England, called posnets. They were in olden times used to heat medicine and to serve pap to infants. I have also been told that these little porringers were not posnets, but simply the samples of work made by apprentices in the pewterer's trade to show their skill and proficiency.

Tin vessels were exceedingly rare in the seventeenth century, either for table furnishings or for cooking utensils, and far from common in the succeeding one. John Wynter, of Richmond's Island, Maine, had a "tinninge basson & a tinninge platter" in 1638. In 1662 Isaac Willey, of New London, had "Tynen Pans & 1 Tynen Quart Pott;" and Zerubbabel Endicott, of Salem, had a "great tyn candlestick." By 1729, when Governor Burnet's effects were sold, we read of kitchen utensils of tin.

I do not think iron was in high favor among the colonists as a material for household utensils. It was not an iron age. They had iron pans, candlesticks, dishes, fire-dogs, and pots: the latter vessels were traded for vast and valuable tracts of land with the simple red men; but iron was not vastly in use. At an early date iron-foundries were established throughout New England, with, however, varying success.

Latten ware, which was largely composed of brass, appeared in various useful forms for table and culinary appointments. Hard-metal was a superior sort of pewter. Prince's metal (so called from Prince Rupert), a fine brass alloyed with copper and arsenicum, is occasionally named.

Leather, strangely enough, was also used on the

table in the form of bottles and drinking cups and
jacks, which were pitchers or jugs of waxed leather,
much used in ale-houses in the fourteenth and fif-
teenth century, and whose employment gave rise to
the belief of the French that Englishmen drank their
ale out of their boots.   Endicott received of Winthrop
one leathern jack worth one shilling and sixpence.
I find leathern jacks, bottles, and cups named among
the property of Connecticut colonists.

Nearly all the glass ware of the eighteenth century
was of inferior quality, full of bubbles and defects.
It was frequently fluted.   Many pieces have been
preserved that have been painted in vitrifiable colors.
the designs are crude, the colors red, yellow, blue, and
occasionally black or green.   The transparent glass
thus painted is said to be of Dutch manufacture.
The opalized glass similarly decorated is Spanish.
Drinking-glasses or flip-mugs seem to have been
most common, or, at any rate, most largely preserved.   The tradition attached to all the pieces
of Spanish glass which I have found in New England homes is that they came from the Barbadoes.
Bristol glass also was painted in colors, and came
to this country, being advertised in the *Boston News-
Letter*.

Glass bottles were frequently left by will in early
days, being rare and valuable ; but by newspaper days
glass was imported in various shapes, and soon was
plentiful enough.   In 1773 we find this advertisement :

"Very rich Cut Glass Candlesticks, cut Glass sugar Boxes & Cream Potts, Wine, Wine & Water, and Beer Glasses with cut shanks, Jelly & Syllabub Glasses, Glass Salvers, also Cyder Glasses, Free Mason Glasses, Orange & Top Glasses, Glass Cans, Glass Cream Buckets and Crewits, Royal Arch Mason Glasses, Glass Pyramids with Jelly Glasses, Globe & Barrel Lamps, Double Flynt Wyn Glasses," &c.

The most curious glass relics that are preserved are the flip-glasses or bumper-glasses; they are tumbler-shaped, and are frequently engraved or fluted. Some hold over a gallon.

The names of table furnishings varied somewhat in the eighteenth century. There were milk-pots, milk-ewers, milk-jugs, ere there were milk-pitchers; sugar-boxes, sugar-pots, sugar-basins, ere there were sugar-bowls; spoon-boats and spoon-basins ere there were spoon-holders. Terrines were imported about 1750. There were pickle-dishes and pickle-boats, twifflers, mint-stands and vegetable-basins.

One other appurtenance of a dining-room is found in all early inventories—a voider. Pewter voiders abounded and were advertised in newspapers, as were wicker and china voiders in 1740. The functions of a voider were somewhat those of a crumb-tray. They are thus given in Hugh Rhodes's "Boke of Nurture" in 1577:

> "Wyth bones & voyd morsels fyll not
> thy trenchour, my friend, full
> Avoyd them into a Voyder,
> no man will it anull.

When meate is taken quyte awaye
   and Voyders in presence
Put you your trenchour in the same
   and all your resydence.
Take you with your napkin & knyfe
   the croms that are fore thee
In the Voyder your Napkin leave
   for it is curtesye."

VI

SUPPLIES OF THE LARDER

THERE is a tradition of short commons, usually extending even to stories of starvation, in the accounts of all early settlements in new lands, and the records of the Pilgrims show no exception to the rule. These early planters went through a fiery furnace of affliction. The beef and pork brought with them became tainted, "their butter and cheese corrupted, their fish rotten." A scarcity of food lasted for three years, and there was little variety of fare, yet they were cheerful. Brewster, when he had naught to eat but clams, gave thanks that he was "permitted to suck of the abundance of the seas and the treasures hid in the sands." Cotton Mather says that Governor Winthrop, of the Bay settlement, was giving to a poor neighbor the last meal from his chest, when it was announced that the food-bearing Lion had arrived. The General Court thereat changed an appointed Fast Day to a Thanksgiving Day. By tradition—still commemorated at Forefathers' Dinner—the ration of Indian corn supplied to each person was at one time but five kernels.

Still there was always plenty of fish—the favorite

food of the English—and Squanto taught the colonists various Indian methods of catching the "treasures of the sea." With oysters and lobsters they were far from starvation. Higginson said of the latter shellfish, in 1630, "the least boy in the Plantation may both catch and eat what he will of them." He says that lobsters were caught weighing twenty-five pounds each, and that the abundance of other fish was beyond believing. Josselyn, in his "New England Rarities," enumerated two hundred and three varieties of fish; yet Tuckerman calls his list "a poor makeshift." The planters had plenty of implements with which to catch fish—"vtensils of the sea"—"quoils of rope and cable, rondes of twine, herring nets, seans, cod-lines and cod hookes, mackrill-lines, drails, spiller hooks, mussel-hooks, mackrill hooks, barbels, splitting knives, sharks hookes, basse-nettes, pues and gaffs, squid lines, yeele pots," &c. Josselyn also tells some very pretty ways of cooking fish, especially eels with herbs, showing that, like Poins, the colonists loved conger and fennel. Eels were roasted, fried, and boiled. Boiled "eals" were thus prepared :

"Boil them in half water half wine with the bottom of a manchet, a fagot of Parsly and a little Winter Savory, when they are boiled they take them out and break the bread in the broth and put in two or three spoonfuls of yest and a piece of sweet butter, pour to the eals laid upon sippets." Another way beloved by him was to stuff the eels with nutmeg and cloves, stick them with cloves, cook in wine, place on a chafing-dish, and garnish with lemons. This rich dish is

somewhat overclouded by his suggestion that the eels
be arranged in a wreath.

The frequent references to eels in early accounts
prove that they were regarded, as Izaak Walton said,
"a very dainty fish, the queen of palate-pleasure."

Next to fish, the early colonists found in Indian
corn, or "Guinny wheat"—"Turkie wheat" one traveller called it—their most unfailing food-supply.
Our first native poet wrote, in 1675, of what he called
early days:

> "The dainty Indian maize,
> Was eat with clamp-shells out of wooden trays."

Its abundance and adaptability did much to change
the nature of their diet as well as to save them from
starvation. The colonists learned from the Indians
how to plant, nourish, harvest, grind, and cook it in
many Indian ways, and in each way it formed a palatable food. The Indian pudding which they ate so
constantly was made in Indian fashion and boiled in
a bag. To the mush of Indian meal they gave the
English name of hasty-pudding. Many of the foods
made from maize retained the names given in the
aboriginal tongues, such as hominy, suppawn, pone,
samp, succotash; and doubtless the manner of cooking is wholly Indian. Hoe-cakes and ash-cakes were
made by the squaws long before the landing of the
Pilgrims. Roasting ears of green corn were made
the foundation of a solemn Indian feast and also of
a planters' frolic. It is curious to read Winthrop's
careful explanation, that when corn is parched it

turns entirely inside out, and is "white and floury within;" and to think that there ever was a time when pop-corn was a novelty to white children in New England.

Wood said that *sukquttahhash* was "seethed like beanes." Roger Williams said that "*nassaump*, which the English call Samp, is Indian corne beaten & boil'd and eaten hot or cold with milke or butter and is a diet exceeding wholesome for English bodies." *Nocake*, or *nokick*, Wood, in his "New England Prospects," thus defines: "Indian corn parched in the hot ashes, the ashes being sifted from it, it is afterward beaten to powder and put into a long leatherne bag trussed at their back like a knapsacke, out of which they take thrice three spoonsfulls a day." It was held to be wonderfully sustaining food in most condensed form. It was carried in a pouch, on long journeys, and mixed before eating with snow in winter and water in summer. Jonne-cake, or journey-cake, was also made from maize. For years the colonists pounded the corn in stone mortars, as did the Indians; then in wooden mortars with pestles. Then rude hand-mills were made—"quernes"—with upright shafts fixed immovably at the upper end, and fastened at the lower end near the outside edge of a flat, circular stone, which was made to revolve in a mortar. By turning the shaft with one hand, the corn could be supplied to the grinding-stone with the other. These hand-mills are sometimes still found in use as "samp-mills." Wind-mills and water-mills followed naturally in the train of the hand-mills.

Wheat but little availed for food in early days, being frequently blighted. Oats were raised in considerable quantity, a pill-corn or peel-corn or sil-pee variety. Josselyn, writing in 1671, gives a New England dish, which he says is as good as whitpot, made of oatmeal, sugar, spice, and a " pottle of milk ; " a pottle was two quarts. At a somewhat later date the New Hampshire settlers had a popular oatmeal porridge, in which the oatmeal was sifted, left in water, and allowed to sour, then boiled to a jelly, and was called " sowens." It is still eaten in Northumberland.

By the strict laws made to govern bakers and the number of bake-shops that were licensed, and the sharp punishments for baking short weight, etc., it seems plain that New England housewives did little home baking in early days. The bread was doubtless of many kinds, as in England—simnels, cracknels, jannacks, cheat loaves, cocket-bread, wastelbread, manchet, and buns. Pure wheaten loaves were not largely used as food — bread from corn meal dried quickly; hence rye meal was mixed with the corn, and " rye 'n' Injun " bread was everywhere eaten.

To the other bountiful companion food of corn, pumpkins, the colonists never turned very readily. Pompions they called them in " the times wherein old Pompion was a saint." Johnson, in his " Wonder-Working Providence," reproved them for making a jest of pumpkins, since they were so good and unfailing a food—" a fruit which the

Lord fed his people with till corn and cattle increased."

"We have pumpkins at morning and pumpkins at noon,
   If it were not for pumpkins we should be undone."

Pompions, and what Higginson called squanter-
squashes, Josselyn squontersquoshes, Roger Williams askutasquashes, Wood isquoukersquashes—and
we clip to squashes—grew in vast plenty. The
Indians dried the pompions on strings for winter
use, as is still done in New England farm communities. Madam Knight had them frequently offered to
her on her journey—"pumpkin sause" and "pumpkin
bred." "We would have eat a morsel ourselves, but
the Pumpkin & Indian-mixt bread had such an
Aspect." Pumpkin bread is made in Connecticut to
this day. For pumpkin "sause" we have a two-
centuries-old receipt, which was given by Josselyn, in
1671, in his "New England Rarities," and called by
him even at that day "an Ancient New England
Standing-dish."

"The Housewives manner is to slice them when ripe
and cut them into Dice, and so fill a pot with them of
two or three Gallons and stew them upon a gentle fire
the whole day. And as they sink they fill again with
fresh Pompions not putting any liquor to them and when
it is stir'd enough it will look like bak'd Apples, this
Dish putting Butter to it and a little Vinegar with some
Spice as Ginger which makes it tart like an Apple, and
so serve it up to be eaten with fish or flesh."

This must be a very good "sause," and a very good receipt when once it is clear to your mind which of them—the housewives or the pompions—sink and are to fill and be filled in a pot, and stirred and stewed and put liquor to.

In an old book which I own, which was used by many generations of New England cooks, I find this "singular good" rule to make a "Pumpion Pye :"

"Take about halfe a pound of Pumpion and slice it, a handful of Tyme, a little Rosemary, Parsley and Sweet Marjoram slipped off the stalkes, and chop them smal, then take Cinamon, Nutmeg, Pepper, and six Cloves and beat them, take ten Eggs and beat them, then mix them, and beat them altogether, and put in as much Sugar as you think fit, then fry them like a froiz, after it is fryed, let it stand til it be cold, then fill your Pye, take sliced Apples thinne rounde-wayes, and lay a row of the Froiz and layer of Apples with Currans betwixt the layer while your Pye is fitted, and put in a good deal of sweet butter before you close it, when the pye is baked take six yelks of Eggs, some White-wine or Vergis, and make a Caudle of this, but not too thicke, cut up the Lid and put it in, stir them wel together whilst the Eggs and Pompions be not perceived and so serve it up."

I am sure there would be no trouble about the pompions being perceived, and I can fancy the modest half-pound of country vegetable blushing a deeper orange to find its name given to this ambitious and compound-sentenced concoction which helped to form part of the "simple diet of the good old times." I have found no modern cook bold enough to "prove" (as the book says) this pumpion pie; but hope, if any one understands it, she will attempt it.

Potatoes were on the list of seeds, fruits, and vegetables that were furnished to the Massachusetts Bay colonists in 1628, and fifteen tons (which were probably sweet potatoes) were imported from Bermuda in 1636 and sold in Boston at twopence a pound. Winthrop wrote of "potatose" in 1683. Their cultivation was rare. There is a tradition that the Irish settlers at Londonderry, N. H., began the first systematic planting of potatoes. At the Harvard Commencement dinner, in 1708, potatoes were on the list of supplies. A crop of eight bushels, which one Hadley farmer had in 1763, was large— too large, since "if a man ate them every day he could not live beyond seven years." Indeed, the "gallant root of potatoes" was regarded as a sort of forbidden fruit—a root more than suspected of being an over-active aphrodisiac, and withal so wholly abandoned as not to have been mentioned in the Bible; and when Parson Jonathan Hubbard, of Sheffield, raised twenty bushels in one year, it is said he came very near being dealt with by his church for his wicked hardihood. In more than one town the settlers fancied the balls were the edible portion, and "did not much desire them." Nor were fashionable methods of cooking them much more to be desired. In "The Accomplisht Cook," used about the year 1700, potatoes were ordered to be boiled and blanched; seasoned with nutmeg, cinnamon, and pepper ; mixed with eringo roots, dates, lemon, and whole mace ; covered with butter, sugar, and grape verjuice, made with pastry ; then iced with rosewater and sugar, and yclept a " Secret Pye." Alas, poor, ill-used, be-sugared, secreted potato, fit but for kissing-comfits ! we can well understand your unpopularity.

Other vegetables were produced in New England in abundance. Higginson speaks of green peas, turnips, parsnips, carrots, and cucumbers, and a dozen fruits and berries. Cranberries were plentiful and soon were exported to England. Josselyn gives a very full list of fruits and vegetables and pot-herbs, including beans, which were baked by the Indians in earthen pots as they are now in Boston bake-shops.

There was a goodly supply of game. Bradford wrote of the year 1621, "beside waterfoule ther was great store of wild Turkies." Wood said these turkeys sometimes weighed forty pounds apiece, and sold for four shillings each. Josselyn assigned to them the enormous weight of sixty pounds. All agreed that they were far superior to the English domestic turkeys. Morton said they came in flocks of a hundred ; yet the Winthrops had great difficulty in getting two to breed from in 1683, and by 1690 it was rare to see a wild turkey in New England. The beautiful great bronze birds had flown away from the white man's civilization and guns.

Flocks of thousands of geese took their noisy, graceful V-shaped flight over New England, and were shot in large numbers. Dudley wrote home that doves were so plentiful that they obscured the light. Josselyn said he had bought in Boston a dozen pigeons all dressed for threepence. It is said they were sometimes sold as low as a penny a dozen. Roger Clap said it would have been counted a strange thing in early days to see a piece of roast veal, beef, or mutton, though it was not long ere there was roast goat. By 1684 a French refugee said beef, mutton, and pork were but twopence a pound in Boston. Clap says he ate his samp, or hominy, without butter or milk, but Higginson wrote in 1630, and Morton in 1624, that they had a quart of milk for a penny. John Cotton said ministers and milk were the only things cheap in New England.

By Johnson's time New Englanders had "Apple, Pear and Quince Tarts instead of their former Pumpkin Pies." They had besides apple-tarts, apple mose, apple slump, mess apple-pies, buttered apple-pies, apple crowdy and puff apple-pies—all differing.

Josselyn said the "Quinces, Cherries, & Damsins set the Dames a - work. Marmalet & Preserved Damsins is to be met with in every house." Skill in preserving was ever an English-woman's pride, and New-English women did not forget the lessons learned in their "faire English homes." They made preserves and conserves, marmalets and quiddonies, hypocras and household wines, usquebarbs and cordials. They candied fruits and made syrups. They preserved everything that would bear preserving. I have seen old-time receipts for preserving quinces, "respasse," pippins, "apricocks," plums, "damsins," peaches, oranges, lemons, artichokes, green walnuts, elecampane roots, eringo roots, grapes, barberries, cherries; receipts for syrup of clove gillyflower, wormwood, mint, aniseed, clove, elder, lemons, marigolds, citron, hyssop, liquorice; receipts for conserves of roses, violets, borage flowers, rosemary, betony, sage, mint, lavender, marjoram, and "piony;" rules for candying fruit, berries, and flowers, for poppy water, cordial, cherry water, lemon water, thyme water, Angelica water, Aqua Mirabilis, Aqua Cœlestis, clary water, mint water.

No wonder a profession of preserving sprung up. By 1731 we find advertised in June in the *Boston News Letter*, "At Widow Bonyots All Sorts of Fruits in Preserves Jellys and Surrups. Egg Cakes, All sorts of Macaroons, Marchepane Crisp Almonds. All sorts Conserves, Also Meat Jellys for the sick."

We can see plainly by these statements that New England was no Nidderland. Even in Josselyn's day he wrote, "they have not forgotten the English fashion of stirring up their appetites with variety of cooking their food." The pages of Judge Sewall's diary give many hints of his daily fare. He speaks of "boil'd Pork, boil'd Pigeons, boil'd Bacon and boil'd Venison; rost Beef, rost Lamb, rost Fowls, rost Turkey, pork and beans;" "Frigusee of Fowls," "Joll of Salmon," "Oysters, Fish and Oyl, conners, Legg of Pork, hogs Cheek and souett; pasty, bread and butter; Minc'd Pye, Aplepy, tarts, gingerbread, sugar'd almonds, glaz'd almonds;" honey, curds and cream, sage cheese, green pease, barley, "Yokhegg in milk, chockolett, figgs," oranges, shattucks, apples, quinces, strawberries, cherries, and raspberries; a very fair list of viands.

"Yokhegg" is probably "yeokheag," a name for Indian corn, parched and pounded into meal, a name by which it was known for many years in Eastern Connecticut.

Sewall was a very valiant trencher-man. He records with much zest going down the Bay to an island, or riding to Roxbury for an outing and dinner, and coming home in " brave moonshine." And, like his neighbor, Cotton Mather, he drew many a spiritual lesson from the food set before him; especially, however, at a scambling meal, or at any repast which he ate alone, and hence had naught and no one to divert therefrom his ever-religious thoughts.

From a curious account of Boston, written by a traveller named Bennet, in the year 1740, we take the following statements of the cost of food there :

" Their poultry of all sorts are as fine as can be desired, and they have plenty of fine fish of various kinds, all of which are very cheap. Take the butchers' meat all together, in every season of the year, I believe it is about twopence per pound sterling ; the best beef and mutton, lamb and veal are often sold for sixpence per pound of New England money, which is some small matter more than one penny sterling.

" Poultry in their season are exceeding cheap. As good a turkey may be bought for about two shillings sterling as we can buy in London for six or seven, and as fine a

goose for tenpence as would cost three shillings and sixpence or four shillings in London. The cheapest of all the
several kinds of poultry are a sort of wild pigeon, which
are in season the latter end of June, and so continue until
September. They are large, and finer than those we have
in London, and are sold here for eighteenpence a dozen,
and sometimes for half of that.

"Fish, too, is exceeding cheap. They sell a fine fresh
cod that will weigh a dozen pounds or more, just taken
out of the sea, for about twopence sterling. They have
smelts, too, which they sell as cheap as sprats are in London. Salmon, too, they have in great plenty, and those
they sell for about a shilling apiece, which will weigh
fourteen or fifteen pounds.

"They have venison very plenty. They will sell as fine
a haunch for half a crown as would cost full thirty shillings in England. Bread is much cheaper than we have
in England, but is not near so good. Butter is very fine,
and cheaper than ever I bought any in London; the best
is sold all summer for threepence a pound. But as for
cheese, it is neither cheap nor good."

I am somewhat surprised at Bennet's dictum with
regard to cheese, and can only feel that he had special
ill fortune in choosing his cheesemonger. For certainly the Rhode Island cheese, made from the rich
milk of the great herds of choice cows that dotted the
fertile and sunny fields of old Narragansett, was sent
to England and the Barbadoes in great quantity,
and commanded special prices there. Brissot said it
was equal to the "best Cheshire of England or Roc-
fort of France." This cheese was made from a receipt

for Cheshire cheese which was brought to Narragansett by Richard Smith's wife in the seventeenth century ; and her home is still standing, though built around, at Cocumcussett, where her husband and Roger Williams founded a colony.

We have a very distinct rendering of the items of family expense, chiefly of food, at about that time, given us by a contemporary authority, and bequeathed to us in a letter to the *Boston News Letter* of November 28, 1728. The writer refers to other " scheams of expence " for a household which have been made public, one apparently being at the rate of £250 a year for the entire outlay. This sum he thinks inadequate and " disproves in a moment." He gives his own careful estimate of the cost of keeping a family of eight persons. It is computed for " Families of Midling Figure who bear the Character of being Genteel," and reads thus :

" For Diet.   For one Person a Day.

1 Breakfast 1*d*. a Pint of Milk 2*d*.............	.03
2 Dinner. Pudding Bread Meat Roots Pickles Vinegar Salt & Cheese..........	.09

N. B.   In this article of the Dinner I would include all the Raisins Currants Suet Flour Eggs Cranberries Apples & where there are children all their Intermeal Eatings throughout the whole Year. And I think a Gentleman cannot well Dine his family at a lower Rate than this.

3 Supper As the Breakfast.......	.03
4 Small Beer for the Whole Day Winter & Summer.	1½

N. B.   In this article of the Beer I would likewise include all the Molasses used in the Family not only in Brewing but on other Occasions.

For one Person a Day in all		1s.	4½d.
For Whole Family		11s.	
For the Whole Family 365 days.................	£200	15s.	
For Butter, 2 Firkins at 68 lb. apiece, 16d. a lb..	£ 9	1s.	
For Sugar. Cannot be less than 10s. a Month or 4 weeks especially when there are children.	£ 6	10s.	
For Candles but 3 a Night Summer & Winter for Ordinary & Extraordinary occasions at 15d. for 9 in the lb.........................	£ 7	12s.	.01
For Sand 20s. Soap 40s. Washing Once in 4 weeks at 3s. a time with 3 Meals a Day at 2s. more	£ 6	5s.	
For One Maids Wages.........................	£ 10		
For Shoes after the Rate of each 3 Pair in a year at 9s. a Pair for 7 Persons, the Maid finding her own	£ 9	09s.	
In all	£249	12s.	5d.

No House Rents Mentioned Nor Buying Carting Pyling or Sawing
    Firewood

No Coffee Tea nor Chocolate

No Wine nor Cyder nor any other Spirituous Liquor

No Pipes Tobacco Spice nor Sweetmeats

No Hospitality or Occasional Entertaining either Gentlemen Strang-
    ers Relatives or Friends

No Acts of Charity nor Contributions for Pious Uses

No Pocket Expenses either for Horse Hire Travelling or Convenient
    Recreations

No Postage for Letters or Numberless other Occasions

No Charges of Nursing

No Schooling for Children

No Buying of Books of any Sort or Pens Ink & Paper

No Lyings In

No Sickness, Nothing to Apothecary or Doctor

No Buying Mending or Repairing Household Stuff or Utensils

Nothing to the Simstress nor to the Taylor nor to the Barber, nor
    to the Hatter nor to the Shopkeeper & Therefore no Cloaths."

Certainly we gain from this " scheam " a very clear notion of the style of living of this genteel Boston family.

There is, of course, no possibility of exactly picturing the serving of a meal in early days; but one peculiarity is known of the dinner—the pudding came first.   Hence the old saying, " I came in season —in pudding-time."   In an account of a Sunday dinner given at the house of John Adams, as late as 1817, the first course was a pudding of Indian corn, molasses, and butter; the second, veal, bacon, neck of mutton, and vegetables.

For many years the colonists " dined exact at noon," and on farms even half an hour earlier.   On Saturday all ate fish for dinner.   Judge Sewall frequently speaks of his Saturday dinner of fish.   Fish days had been prescribed by the King in England, in order that the fisheries might not fail of support, as was feared on account of the increased consumption of meat induced by the reformation in religion.   New Englanders loyally followed the mandate, but ate cod-fish on Saturdays, since the Papists ate fish on Fridays.

One very pleasant and friendly custom that existed among these kindly New England neighbors must be spoken of in passing.   It is thus indicated by Judge Sewall when he writes, in 1723, of Mr. and Mrs. Belcher, " my wife sent them a taste of her Diner." It appeared to be a recompensing fashion, if invited guests were unable to partake of the dinner festivities, or if neighbors were ill, for the hostess to send a " taste " of all her viands to console them for their deprivation. This truly homely and neighborly custom lingered long in old New England families under the very descriptive title of " cold party ; " indeed it lingers still in old-fashioned towns and in old-fashioned families.

In earlier days when a noble dinner seemed to be the form of domestic pleasure next in enjoyment to a funeral, a " taste of the dinner " was truly a most honorable attention, and a most pleasing one.

VII

OLD COLONIAL DRINKS AND DRINKERS

THE English settlers who peopled our colonies
were a beer-drinking and ale-drinking race — as
Shakespeare said, they were "potent in potting."
None of the hardships they had to endure in the first
bitter years of their new life caused them more annoyance than their deprivation of their beloved malt
liquors. This deprivation began even at the very
landing. They were forced to depend on the charity of
the ship-masters for a draught of beer on board ship,
drinking nothing but water ashore. Bradford, the
Pilgrim Governor, complained loudly and frequently
of his distress, while Higginson, the Salem minister,
accommodated himself more readily and cheerfully
to his changed circumstances, and boasted quaintly
in 1629, "Whereas my stomach could only digest
and did require such drink as was both strong and
stale, I can and ofttimes do drink New England
water very well." As Higginson died in a short
time, his boast of his improved health and praise
of the unwonted beverage does not carry the force
intended. Another early chronicler, Roger Clap,
writes that it was "not accounted a strange thing

in those days to drink water," and it was stated that Winthrop drank it ordinarily. Wood, in his "New England Prospects," says of New England water, "I dare not preferre it before good Beere as some have done, but any man would choose it before Bad Beere, Wheay or Buttermilk." It was also praised as being "farr different from the water of England, being not so sharp, but of a fatter substance, and of a more jettie colour ; it is thought there can be no better water in the world."

But their beerless state did not long continue, for the first luxury to be brought to the new country was beer, and the colonists soon imported malt and learned to make beer from the despised Indian corn, and established breweries and made laws governing and controlling the manufacture of ale and beer ; for the pious Puritans quickly learned to cheat in their brewing, using molasses and coarse sugar. Molasses beer is frequently mentioned by Josselyn.

By 1634, when sixpence was the legal charge for a meal, an ale-quart of beer could be bought for a penny, and a landlord was liable to ten shillings fine if he made a greater charge, or his liquor fell below a certain standard of quality. Perhaps this low price was established by the crafty Puritan magistrates in order to prevent the possibility of profit by beer-selling, and thereby reduce the number of sellers. It was also ordered that not more than an ale-quart of beer should be drunk out of meal-times. This was to prevent "bye-drinking." Josselyn complained of the petty interference of the law in drinking, saying:

" At the houses of entertainment called ordinaries into which a stranger went, he was presently followed by one appointed to that office who would thrust himself into his company uninvited, and if he called for more drink than the officer thought, in his judgment, he could soberly bear away, he would presently countermand it, and appoint the proportion beyond which he could not get one drop."

The ministers, also, who chanced to live within sight of the tavern, had a very virtuous custom of watching the tavern door and all who entered therein, and going over and " chiding them " if they remained too long within the cheerful portals. With constables, deacons, the parson, and that lab-o'-the-tongue—the tithing-man—each on the alert to keep every one from drinking but himself, the Puritan had little chance to be a toper an he would.

The colonists were fiercely intolerant of intemperance among the Indians. Laws were made as early as 1633 prohibiting the sale of strong waters to the " inflamed devilish bloudy salvages," and persons selling liquor to them were sharply prosecuted and punished. New Yorkers thought these laws oversevere, saying, deprecatingly, " to prohibit all strong liquor to them seems very hard and very turkish, rumm doth as little hurt as the ffrenchmans Brandie, and in the whole is much more wholesome." But the Puritans knew of the horrors to be dreaded from drunken Indians.

So plentiful had the sale of ale and beer become

in 1675 that Cotton Mather said every other house in Boston was an ale-house, and a century later Governor Pownall made the same assertion. The Puritan magistrates in New England made at a very early date a decided stand not only against excessive drinking by strangers, but against the habit of drunkenness in their citizens. Drunkards were in 1636, in Massachusetts, subject to fine and imprisonment in the stocks, and sellers were forbidden to furnish the tippler with any liquor thereafter. An habitual drunkard was punished by having a great D made of "Redd Cloth" hung around his neck, or sewed on his clothing, and he was disfranchised. In 1630 Governor Winthrop abolished the "Vain Custom" of drinking healths at his table, and in 1639 the Court publicly ordered the cessation of the practice because " it was a thing of no use, it induced drunkenness and quarrelling, it wasted wine and beer and it was troublesome to many, forcing them to drink more than they wished." A fine of twelve shillings was imposed on each health-drinker. Cotton Mather, however, thought health-drinking a usage of common politeness. In Connecticut no man could drink over half a pint of wine at a time, or tipple over half an hour, or drink at all at an ordinary after nine o'clock at night.

All these rigid laws had their effect, and New Englanders throughout the seventeenth century were sober and law-abiding save in a few communities, such as that at Merrymount, where "good chear went forward and strong liquors walked." Boston was an especially orderly town. Several visiting and resident clergymen testified that they had not seen a drunken man in the Massachusetts Colony in many years. The following quotation will show how rare was drunkenness and how abhorred. Judge Sewall wrote in 1686:

" Mr. Shrimpton and others came in a coach from Roxbury about nine o'clock or past, singing as they came, being inflamed with drink. At Justice Morgans they stop and drink healths and curse and swear to the great disturbance of the town and grief of good people Such high-handed wickedness has hardly before been heard of in Boston."

It is well to compare the orderly, decorous, well-protected existence in Boston, with the conditions of town life in Old England at that same date, where drunken young men of fashion under the name of Mohocks, Scourers, Hectors, Muns, or Tityriti, prowled the streets abusing and beating every man and woman they met—" sons of Belial flown with insolence and wine ; " where turbulent apprentices set upon those the Mohocks chanced to spare ; where duels and intrigues and gaming were the order of the day ; where foot-pads, highwaymen, and street ruffians robbed unceasingly and with impunity. Life in New England may have been dull and monotonous, but women could go through the streets in safety, and Judge Sewall could stumble home alone in the dark from his love-making without fear of molestation; and when he found a party of young men singing and

making too much noise in a tavern, he could go among
them uninsulted, and could get them to meekly write
down their own names with his "Pensil" for him to
bring them up and fine them the next day.

Still, the Judge, though he hated noisy revellers,
was no total abstainer. He speaks of "grace cups"
and "treating the Deputies," and sent gifts of wine
to his friends. I find in his diary references to these
drinks: Ale, beer, mead, metheglin, tea, chocolate,
sage tea, cider, wine, sillabub, claret, sack, canary,
punch, sack-posset, and black cherry brandy.

Sack, the drink of Shakespeare's day, beloved and
praised of Falstaff, was passing out of date in Sewall's
time. Winthrop tells of four ships coming into port
in 1646 with eight hundred butts of sack on board.
In 1634 ordinaries were forbidden to sell it, hence
the sack found but a poor market. Sack-posset was
made of ale and sack, thickened with eggs and cream,
seasoned with nutmeg, mace, and sugar, then boiled
on the fire for hours, and made a "very pretty drink"
for weddings and feasts.

Canary wine was imported at that time in large
quantities. In the first year's issue of the *News Letter* were advertised "Fyall wine sold by the Pipe;
Passados & Right Canary." The Winthrops in their
letters make frequent mention of Canary, as also of
"Vendredi" and "Palme Wine." Wait Winthrop
said the latter was better than Canary. Tent wine
also was sent to the colonists.

It is interesting to find that the sanguine settlers
aspired, even in bleak New England, to the home pro-

duction of wine. "Vine planters" were asked for
the colony in 1629. The use of Governor's Island
in Massachusetts Bay was granted to Governor Winthrop in 1634 for a vineyard, for an annual rental of a
hogshead of wine, which at a later date was changed to
a yearly payment of two barrels of apples. The French
settlers also planted vineyards in Rhode Island.

Claret was not much loved by the planters, who
had a taste for the sweet sack. Morton tells that for
his revellers he " broched a hogshead, caused them
to fill the Can with Lusty liquor—Claret sparklinge
neat—which was not suffered to grow pale & flat but
tipled off with quick dexterity." Mumm, a fat ale
made of oat-malt and wheat-malt, appears frequently
in early importations and accounts. The sillabub of
which Sewall speaks was made with cider and was
not boiled :

"Fill your Sillabub Pot with Syder (for that is best for
a Sillabub) and good store of Sugar and a little Nutmeg,
stir it wel together, put in as much thick Cream by two
or three spoonfuls at a time, as hard as you can as though
you milke it in, then stir it together exceeding softly
once about and let it stand two hours at least."

Other mild fermented drinks than beer were made
and drunk in colonial days in large quantities. Mead
and metheglin, wherewith the Druids and old English
bards were wont to carouse, were made from water,
honey, and yeast. Here is an old receipt for the latter drink, which some colonists pronounced as good
as Malaga sack.

"Take all sorts of Hearbs that are good and wholesome as Balme, Mint, Fennel, Rosemary, Angelica, wilde Tyme, Isop, Burnet, Egrimony, and such other as you think fit; some Field Hearbs, but you must not put in too many, but especially Rosemary or any Strong Hearb, lesse than halfe a handfull will serve of every sorte, you must boyl your Hearbs & strain them, and let the liquor stand till to Morrow and settle them, take off the clearest Liquor, two Gallons & a halfe to one Gallon of Honey, and that proportion as much as you will make, and let it boyle an houre, and in the boyling skim it very clear, then set it a cooling as you doe Beere, when it is cold take some very good Ale Barme and put into the bottome of the Tubb a little and a little as they do Beere, keeping back the thicke Setling that lyeth in the bottome of the Vessel that it is cooled in, and when it is all put together cover it with a Cloth and let it worke very neere three dayes, and when you mean to put it up, skim off all the Barme clean, put it up into the Vessel, but you must not stop your Vessel very close in three or four dayes but let it have all the vent, for it will worke and when it is close stopped you must looke very often to it and have a peg in the top to give it vent, when you heare it make a noise as it will do, or else it will breake the Vessell; sometime I make a bag and put in good store of Ginger sliced, some Cloves and Cinnamon and boyl it in, and other time I put it into the Barrel and never boyl it, it is both good, but Nutmeg & Mace do not well to my Tast."

In the list of values fixed by the Piscataqua planters in 1633, "6 Gallons Mathaglin were equal to 2 lb. Beauer." In the middle of the century metheglin was worth ten shillings a barrel in the Connecticut Valley.

Though mild, these drinks were intoxicating. One could "get fox'd e'en with foolish matheglin." Old James Howel says, "metheglin does stupefy more than any other liquor if taken immoderately and keeps a humming in the brain which made one say he loved not metheglin because he was wont to speak too much of the house he came from, meaning the hive."

Bradford tells of backsliders from Merrymount who "abased themselves disorderly with drinking too much stronge drinke aboard the Freindshipp." This strong drink was metheglin, of which two hogsheads were to be delivered at Plymouth. But after it was transferred to wooden "flackets" in Boston, these Friendship merrymakers contrived to "drinke it up under the name leackage" till but six gallons of the metheglin arrived at Plymouth.

"Cyder famed" was made at an early date from the fruitful apple-trees so faithfully planted by Endicott, Blackstone, and other settlers. Cider was cheap enough; Josselyn wrote, "I have had at the tap houses of Boston an ale-quart of cyder spiced and sweetened with sugar, for a groat."

This was not the New England nectar or Passada which he praised so highly and which was thus made—

"Take of Malligo Raisins, stamp them and put milk to them and put them to a Hippocras Bag and let it drain out of itself and put a quantity of this with a spoonful or two of Syrup of Clove Gilly-flowers into every bottle when you bottle your Syder, and your Planter will have a liquor that exceeds Passada, the Nectar of the Country."

Cider was made at first by pounding the apples by hand in wooden mortars ; sometimes the pomace was pressed in baskets.   Rude mills were then formed with a hollowed log, and a heavy weight or maul on a spring-board.   Cider soon became the common drink of the people, and it was made in vast quantities.   In 1671 five hundred hogsheads were made of one orchard's produce.   One village of forty families made three thousand barrels in 1721.   Bennet wrote in 1740, "Cider being cheap and the people used to it they do not encourage malt liquors. They pay about three shillings a barrel for cider." It was freely used even by the children at breakfast, as well as at dinner, up to the end of the first quarter of the present century, when many zealous followers so eagerly embraced the new temperance reform that they cut down whole orchards of thriving apple-trees, conceiving no possibility of the general use of the fruit for food instead of drink.

Charles Francis Adams says that "to the end of John Adams's life a large tankard of hard cider was his morning draught before breakfast."

Cider was supplied in large amounts to students at college at dinner and "bever," being passed in two two-quart tankards from hand to hand down the commons table.   It was given liberally to all travellers and wanderers who chanced to stop at the farmer's door; to all workmen and farm laborers; and an "Indian barrel," whose contents were for free gift to every tramp Indian or squaw, was found in many a farmer's cellar.

A traveller in Maine just after the Revolution said that their cider was purified by the frost, colored with corn, and looked and tasted like Madeira.

Beverige also was drunk by the colonists. This name was applied to various mild and watery drinks. In the West Indies the juice of the sugar-cane mixed with water was so called. In Devonshire, water which had been pressed through the lees of a cider-mill was called beverige. In other parts of England water, cider, and spices formed beverige. In New England the concoction varied, but was uniformly innocuous and weak—the colonial prototype of our modern "temperance drinks." In many country houses a summer drink of water flavored with molasses and ginger was called beverige. The advertisement in the *Boston News Letter*, August 16th, 1711, of the sale of the captured Neptune with her lading, at the warehouse of Andrew Fanueil, had "Wine, Vinegar and Beveridge" on the list. This must have been stronger stuff than molasses and water, to have been worth barrelling and sending across the water.

Switchel was a drink similar to beverige, but when served out to sailors was strengthened by a little vinegar and rum. The name was commonly used in New Hampshire and central Massachusetts. Ebulum was made of the juices of the elder and juniper berries mixed with ale and spices.

Perry was made to some extent from pears, and was advertised for sale in the *Boston News Letter*, and one traveller told of "peachy" made from peaches. Spruce and birch beer were brewed by mixing a decoction of sassafras, birch, or spruce bark with molasses and water, or by boiling the twigs in maple sap, or by boiling together pumpkin and apple-parings, water, malt, and roots. Many curious makeshifts were resorted to in the early days. One old song boasted

> "Oh we can make liquor to sweeten our lips
> Of pumpkins, of parsnips, of walnut-tree chips."

Fiercer liquors were not lacking. Aqua-vitæ, a general name for strong waters, was brought over in large quantities during the seventeenth century, and sold for about three shillings a gallon. Cider was distilled into cider brandy, or apple-jack ; and when, by 1670, molasses had come into port in considerable quantity through the West India trade, the forests of New England supplied plentiful and cheap fuel to convert it into " rhum, a strong water drawn from the sugar cane." In a manuscript description of Barbadoes, written in 1651, we read : "The chief fudling they make in this island is Rumbullion alias Kill Divil—a hot hellish and terrible liquor." It was called in some localities Barbadoes liquor, and by the Indians " ahcoobee " or " ockuby," a word of the Norridgewock tongue. John Eliot spelled it " rumb," and Josselyn called it plainly " that cussed liquor, Rhum, rumbullion, or kill-devil." It went by the latter name and rumbooze everywhere, and was soon cheap enough. Increase Mather said, in 1686, "It is an unhappy thing that in later years a Kind of Drink called Rum has been common among us. They that are poor, and wicked too, can for a penny or two-pence make themselves drunk." Burke said, at a later date, "The quantity of spirits which they distil in Boston from the molasses they import is as surprising as the cheapness at which they sell it, which is under two shillings a gallon; but they are more famous for the quantity and cheapness than for the excellency of their rum." In 1719, and fifty years later, New England rum was worth but three shillings a gallon, while West India rum was worth but two-pence more. New England distilleries quickly found a more lucrative way of disposing of their "kill-devil" than by selling it at such cheap rates. Ships laden with barrels of rum were sent to the African coast, and from thence they returned with a most valuable lading—negro slaves. Along the coast of Africa New England rum quite drove out French brandy.

The Irish and Scotch settlers knew how to make whiskey from rye and wheat, and they soon learned to manufacture it from barley and potatoes, and even from the despised Indian corn.

Not content with their own manufactured liquors, the thirsty colonists imported strong waters, gin and aniseseed cordial from Holland, and wine from Spain, Portugal, and the Canaries. Of these, fiery Madeiras were the favorite of all fashionable folk, and often each glass of wine was strengthened by a liberal dash of brandy.   Bennet wrote, in 1740, of Boston society, "Madeira wine and rum punch are the liquors they drink in common."   Though "spiced punch in bowls the Indians quaffed" in 1665, I do not know of the Oriental mixed drink in New England till 1682, when John Winthrop writes of the sale of a punch-bowl.   In 1686 John Dunton had more than one "noble bowl of punch," during his visit to New England.   The word punch was from the East Indian word *pauch*, meaning five.   S. M. (who was probably Samuel Mather) sent these lines to Sir Harry Frankland in 1757, with the gift of a box of lemons:

> "You know from Eastern India came
>   The skill of making punch as did the name.
>   And as the name consists of letters five,
>   By five ingredients is it kept alive.
>   To purest water sugar must be joined,
>   With these the grateful acid is combined.
>   Some any sours they get contented use,
>   But men of taste do that from Tagus choose.
>   When now these three are mixed with care
>   Then added be of spirit a small share.
>   And that you may the drink quite perfect see
>   Atop the musky nut must grated be."

Every buffet of people of fashion contained a punch bowl, every dinner was prefaced by a bowl of punch, which was passed from hand to hand and drunk from without intervening glasses.   J. Crosby, at the Box of Lemons, in Boston, sold for thirty years

lime juice and shrub and lemons, and sour oranges
and orange juice (which some punch tasters preferred
to lemon juice), to flavor Boston punches.

Double and " thribble " bowls of punch were commonly served, holding respectively two and three
quarts each, and many existing bills show what large
amounts were drunk. Governor Hancock gave a dinner to the Fusileers at the Merchants' Club, in Boston, in 1792. As eighty dinners were paid for I
infer there were eighty diners. They drank one hundred and thirty-six bowls of punch, besides twenty-
one bottles of sherry and a large quantity of cider
and brandy. An abstract of an election dinner to the
General Court of Massachusetts in 1769, showed two
hundred diners, and seventy-two bottles of Madeira,
twenty-eight bottles of Lisbon wine, ten of claret,
seventeen of port, eighteen of porter, fifteen double
bowls of punch and a quantity of cider. The clergy
were not behind the military and the magistrates. In
the record of the ordination of Rev. Joseph McKean,
in Beverly, Mass., in 1785, these items are found in
the tavern-keeper's bill :

30 Bowles of Punch before the People went to meeting.	3	
80 people eating in the morning at 16*d*................	6	
10 bottles of wine before they went to meeting........	1	10
68 dinners at 3*s*...........................	10	4
44 bowles of punch while at dinner.................	4	8
18 bottles of wine..............................	2	14
8 bowles of Brandy.............................	1	2
Cherry Rum.................................	1	10
6 people drank tea........		**9*d***

The six mild tea-drinkers and their economical beverage seem to put a finishing and fairly comic touch to this ordination bill. When we read such renderings of accounts we think it natural that Baron Reidesel wrote of New England inhabitants, "most of the males have a strong passion for strong drink, especially rum and other alcoholic beverages." John Adams said, "if the ancients drank wine as our people drink rum and cider it is no wonder we hear of so many possessed with devils."

The cost of these various drinks was thus given about Revolutionary times in Bristol, R. I.:

"Nip of Grog.. 6*d*
   Dubel bole of Tod 2*s*   9*d*
   Dubel bole of punch.................................. 8*s*
   Nip of punch... 1*s*
   Brandi Sling... 8*d*

Flip was a vastly popular drink, and continued to be so for a century and a half. I find it spoken of as early as 1690. It was made of home-brewed beer, sweetened with sugar, molasses, or dried pumpkin, and flavored with a liberal dash of rum, then stirred in a great mug or pitcher with a red-hot loggerhead or hottle or flip-dog, which made the liquor foam and gave it a burnt bitter flavor.

Landlord May, of Canton, Mass., made a famous brew thus: he mixed four pounds of sugar, four eggs, and one pint of cream and let it stand for two days. When a mug of flip was called for, he filled a quart mug two-thirds full of beer, placed in it four great

spoonfuls of the compound, then thrust in the seeth
ing loggerhead, and added a gill of rum to the creamy
mixture.   If a fresh egg were beaten into the flip the
drink was called " bellows-top," and the froth rose over
the top of the mug.   " Stone-wall " was a most intoxicating mixture of cider and rum.   " Calibogus," or
" bogus," was cold rum and beer unsweetened.
" Black-strap " was a mixture of rum and molasses.
Casks of it stood in every country store, a salted
and dried codfish slyly hung alongside—a free lunch
to be stripped off and eaten, and thus tempt, through
thirst, the purchase of another draught of black-strap.

A terrible drink is said to have been popular in
Salem—a drink with a terrible name—whistle-belly-
vengeance.   It consisted of sour household beer sim-
mered in a kettle, sweetened with molasses, filled
with brown-bread crumbs and drunk piping hot.

Of course many protests, though chiefly on the
ground of wasteful expense, were made, even in ante-
temperance days, against the drinking which grew so
prevalent with the opening of the eighteenth century.   Rev. Andrew Eliot wrote in 1735, " 'Tis surprising what prodigious sums are expended for
spirituous liquors in this one poor Province—more
than a million of our old currency in a year."   Dr.
Tenney lamented that the taverns of Exeter, N. H.,
were thronged with people who seldom retired sober.
Strenuous but ineffectual efforts were made to " prevent tippling in the forenoon," and between meals ;
but with little avail.   The temperance-reform of our
own century came none too soon.

Tea was too high priced in the first half-century of its Occidental use to have been frequently seen in New England. Judge Sewall mentioned it but once in his diary. He drank it at Madam Winthrop's house in 1709 at a Thursday lecture, but he does not note it as a rarity. In 1690, however, when not over-plentiful in old England, Benjamin Harris and Daniel Vernon were licensed to sell it " in publique " in Boston. In 1712 " green and ordinary teas " were advertised in the apothecary's list of Zabdiel Boylston. Bohea tea came in 1713, and in 1715 tea was sold in the coffee-houses. Some queer mistakes were made through the employment of the herb as food. In Salem it was boiled for a long time till bitter, and drunk without milk or sugar ; and the tea-leaves were buttered, salted, and eaten. In more than one town the liquid tea was thrown away and the carefully cooked leaves were eaten.

The new China drink did not have a wholly savory reputation. It was called a " damned weed," a " detestable weed," a " base exotick," a " rank poison far-fetched and dear bought," a " base and unworthy Indian drink," and various ill effects were attributed to it—the decay of the teeth, and even the loss of the mental faculties. But the Abbé Robin thought the ability of the Revolutionary soldiers to endure military flogging came from the use of tea. And others thought it cured the spleen and indigestion.

As the day drew near when tea-drinking was to become the great turning-point of our national liberty, the spirit of noble revolt led many dames to

join in bands to abandon the use of the unjustly
taxed herb, and societies were formed of members
pledged to drink no tea. Five hundred women so
banded together in Boston. Various substitutes were
employed in the place of the much-loved but rigidly
abjured herb, Liberty Tea being the most esteemed.
It was thus made : the four-leaved loose-strife was
pulled up like flax, its stalks were stripped of the
leaves and boiled ; the leaves were put in an iron
kettle and basted with the liquor from the stalks.
Then the leaves were put in an oven and dried. Liberty Tea sold for sixpence a pound. It was drunk at
every spinning-bee, quilting, or other gathering of
women. Ribwort was also used to make a so-called
tea—strawberry and currant leaves, sage, and even
strong medicinal herbs likewise. Hyperion tea was
made from raspberry leaves. An advertisement of
the day thus reads :

" The use of Hyperion or Labrador tea is every day
coming into vogue among people of all ranks. The virtues of the plant or shrub from which this delicate Tea is
gathered were first discovered by the Aborigines, and
from them the Canadians learned them. Before the ces-
sion of Canada to Great Britain we knew little or nothing
of this most excellent herb, but since that we have been
taught to find it growing all over hill and dale between
the Lat. 40 and 60. It is found all over New England in
great plenty and that of best quality particularly on the
banks of the Penobscot, Kennebec, Nichewannock, and
Merrimac."

The proportion of tea used in America is now less than in England, and the proportion of coffee much larger. This is wholly the result of national habits formed through patriotic abstinence from tea-drinking in those glorious "Liberty Days."

The first mention of coffee, as given by Dr. Lyon, is in the record of the license of Dorothy Jones, of Boston, in 1670, to sell "Coffe and chuchaletto." At intervals of a few years other innkeepers were licensed to sell it, and by the beginning of the eighteenth century coffee-houses were established. Coffee dishes, coffee-pots, and coffee-mugs appear in inventories, and show how quickly and eagerly the fragrant berry was sought for in private families. As with tea, its method of preparation as a beverage seemed somewhat uncertain in some minds; and it is said that the whole beans were frequently boiled for some hours with not wholly pleasing results in forming either food or drink. After a few years " coffee-powder " was offered for sale.

Chocolate became equally popular. Sewall often drank it, once certainly as early as 1697, at the Lieutenant-Governor's, with a breakfast of venison. Winthrop says it was scarce in 1698. Madam Knight took it with her on her journey in 1704. "I told her I had some chocolate if she would prepare it, which, with the help of some milk and a little clean brass kettle, she soon effected to my satisfaction." Mills to grind cocoa were quickly established in Boston, and were advertised in the *News Letter*.

Even in the early days of our Republic there were

reformers who wished to establish the use of temperance drinks, which were not, however, exactly the same liquids now so called. A writer in the *Boston Evening Post* wrote forcibly on the subject, and a Philadelphia paper published this statement on July 23d, 1788:

"A correspondent wishes that a monument could be erected in Union Green with the following inscription.

In Honour of
American Beer and Cyder.

It is hereby recorded for the information of strangers and posterity that 17,000 Assembled in this Green on the 4th of July 1788 to celebrate the establishment of the Constitution of the United States, and that they departed at an early hour without intoxication or a single quarrel. They drank nothing but Beer and Cyder. Learn Reader to prize these invaluable liquors and to consider them as the companions of those virtues which can alone render our country free and reputable.

Learn likewise to Despise
Spirituous Liquors as Anti Federal

and to consider them as the companions of all those vices which are calculated to dishonor and enslave our country."

VIII

TRAVEL, TAVERN, AND TURNPIKE

WHEN New England was colonized, the European emigrants were forced to content themselves with the rude means of transportation which were employed by the aborigines. The favorite way back and forth from Plymouth to Boston and Cape Ann was by water, by skirting the shore in birchen pinnaces or dugouts —hollowed pine logs about twenty feet long and two and a half feet wide—in which Johnson said the savages ventured two leagues out at sea. There were few horses, and the few were too valuable for domestic work to be spared for travel, hence the journeyer must go by water, or on foot. When Bradstreet was sent to Dover as Royal Commissioner, he walked the entire distance there, and back to Boston, by narrow Indian paths.

The many estuaries and river-mouths that intersected the coast also made travel on horseback difficult. Foot-passengers, however, could cross the narrow streams by natural ford-ways, or on fallen trees, which were ordered to be put in proper place by the colonial government; and the broader rivers by canoe ferries. We see, through the record of one journey, the dignified Governor of Massachusetts carried across the ford-ways pick-a-pack on the shoulders of his stalwart Indian guide.

But soon the settlers, true to their English instincts and habits, turned their attention to the breeding of horses. They imported many fine animals, and the magistrates framed laws intended to improve the imported stock. The history of horse-raising in New England is akin to that of any other country, save in one respect. In Rhode Island the breeding of horses resulted in that famous and first distinctively American breed—the Narragansett Pacers.

The first suggestion of horse-raising in Narragansett was, without doubt, given by Sewall's father-in-law, Captain John Hull, of Pine Tree Shilling fame, who was one of the original purchasers of the Petaquamscut Tract, or Narragansett, from the Indians. He wrote, in April, 1677 :

"I have often thought if we, the partners of Point Judith Neck did fence with a good stone wall at the north end thereof, that no kind of horses or cattle might get thereon, and also what other parts thereof westerly were needful, and procure a very good breed of large and fair mares and horses, and that no mongrel breed might come among them, we might have a very choice breed for coach horses, some for the saddle and some for draught ; and in a few years might draw off considerable numbers and ship them for Barbadoes Nevis or such parts of the Indies where they would vend."

This scheme was doubtless carried into effect, for in 1686 Dudley and his associates ordered thirty horses to be seized in Narragansett and sold to pay for building a jail.

In a later letter Hull accuses William Heiffernan of horse-stealing, and shows that a different and more gentle method than Western lynch-law was pursued by the Eastern settlers. He writes:

"I am informed that you were so shameless that you offered to sell some of my horses. I would have you know that they are by Gods good Providence, mine. Do you bring me some good security for my money that is justly owing and I shall be willing to give you some horses that you shall not need to offer to steal any."

Whatever the means may have been that tended to the establishment of a distinct breed of horses, the result was soon evident; by the early years of the eighteenth century the Narragansett Pacers were known throughout the colonies as a desirable breed of saddle-horses.

The local conditions for raising this breed were favorable. The soil of Narragansett was rich, the crops large, the natural formation of the land made it possible to fence it easily and with little expense— a thing of much importance in a new land. The bay, the ocean, and the chain of half salt lakes surrounding the three sides, left but a short northern length for stone wall, as Hull suggested.

It is said that the progenitor or most important

sire of this race was imported from Andalusia by
Governor Robinson. Another tradition is that this
horse, while swimming off the coast of Spain, was
picked up by a Narragansett sloop and brought to
America. Thomas Hazard contributed to the quality
of endurance in the breed by introducing into it the
blood of "Old Snip." So celebrated did the qualities
of this horse become that the "Snip breed" was not
only spoken of with regard to the horses, but of the
owners as well, and Hazards who did not possess the
distinguishing race-characteristic of self-will were said
not to be "true Snips." Old Snip was said to have
been imported from Tripoli; others assert (and it
is generally believed) that he was a wild horse running at large in the tract near Point Judith.

In the year 1711 Rip Van Dam, a prominent citizen
of New York, and at a later date Governor of the
State, wrote to Jonathan Dickinson, an early mayor
of Philadelphia, a very amusing account of his ownership of a Narragansett Pacer. The horse was
shipped from Rhode Island in a sloop, from which
he managed to jump overboard, swim ashore, and return home. He was, however, again placed on board
ship, and arrived in New York after a fourteen-days'
passage, naturally much reduced in flesh and spirits.
From New York he was sent to Philadelphia by post
—that is, ridden by the post-rider. The horse cost
£32, and his freight cost fifty shillings. He was said
to be "no beauty though so high priced, save in
his legs." "He always plays and acts and never will
stand still, he will take a glass of wine, beer or cyder,

and probably would drink a dram on a cold morning." The last extraordinary accomplishment doubtless showed contamination from the bad human company around him, while the swimming feat evinced his direct descent from the Andalusian swimmer.

Dr. McSparran, rector of the Narragansett church from 1721 to 1759, wrote a little book called "America Dissected," in which he speaks thus of the Narragansett Pacers :

"The produce of this country is principally butter, cheese, fat cattle, wool and fine horses that are exported to all parts of English America. They are remarkable for fleetness and swift pacing and I have seen some of them pace a mile in a little more than two minutes and a good deal less than three minutes. I have often upon the larger pacing horses rode fifty, nay sixty miles a day even in New England where the roads are rough, stony and uneven."

In the realm of fiction we find testimony to the qualities of the Narragansett Pacers. Cooper, in the "Last of the Mohicans," represents his heroines as mounted on these horses, and explains their characteristics in a footnote, and also in the dialogue of the story. He says that they were commonly sorrel-colored, and that horses of other breeds were trained to their gait. It is true that horses were trained to pace. Rev. Mr. Thatcher wrote in 1690 of teaching a mare to amble by cross-spanning, and again by trammelling. Logs of wood were placed across a road at certain intervals to induce a pacing gait. As late as the year 1770 men in Ipswich followed the profession of pace-trainer; but I doubt whether any other breed could ever acquire the peculiar gait of the Narragansetts, of which Isaac Hazard thus wrote: " My father described the motion of this horse as differing from others in that its backbone moved through the air in a straight line without inclining the rider from side to side, as does a rocker or pacer of the present day." That motion could scarcely be taught.

Many traits joined to make the Narragansett Pacers so eagerly sought for. Not only was their ease of motion an absolute necessity, but sureness of foot was also indispensable; this quality they also possessed. They were also tough and enduring, and could travel long distances. The stories told of them seem incredible. It was said that they could travel one hundred miles in a day, over rough roads, without tiring the rider or injury to themselves, provided they were properly cared for at the end of the journey.

There was not only in America a steady demand for these horses, but in the West Indies, as Hull predicted, they found a ready market. One farmer sent annually a hundred pacers to Cuba, and agents were sent to Narragansett from Cuba with orders to buy pacers, especially full-blooded mares, at any prices. Agents from Virginia also purchased pacers for Virginian horse-raisers. The newspapers of the latter part of the eighteenth century—especially of the

Connecticut press — abound in advertisements of horses of the "true Narragansett breed," yet it is said that in the year 1800 but one full-blooded Narragansett Pacer was known to be living. In the War of 1812 the British man-of-war Orpheus cruised the waters of Narragansett Bay, and her captain endeavored through agents to obtain a Narragansett Pacer as a gift for his wife, but in vain—not a horse of the true breed could be found.

It has been said that the reckless exportation to the West Indies caused this extermination, but it is difficult to believe that so shrewd a race as were the Narragansett planters ever would have committed such a killing of a goose of golden eggs. The decay of the race was the action of a simple law—cause and effect. The conditions which rendered the pacer so desirable did not exist after the Revolution. Roads were improved, carriages became common, the saddle less used, and the American trotter was evolved, who was a better carriage horse, and a more useful one, as he could be employed for both light and heavy work, while heavy draughting stiffened the joints of the pacer, and destroyed the very qualities for which he was most valued. Thus, being no longer needed, the Narragansett Pacer ceased to exist.

There died in Wickford, R. I., a few years ago, a Narragansett Pacer that was nearly full blooded. She was a villainously ugly animal of faded, sunburnt sorrel color. She was so abnormally broad-backed and broad-bodied that a male rider who sat astride her was forced to stick his legs out at a most awkward and ridiculous angle. That broad back carried, however, most comfortably a side-saddle or a pillion. Being extremely short-legged this treasured relic was unprecedentedly slow, and altogether I found the Narragansett Pacer, though an object of great pride and even veneration to her owner, not all my fancy had painted her.

From the earliest days when horses were imported, women rode on pillions behind the men. Lechford in his note-book refers to a " womans pillion " lost on the Hopewell. A pillion was a cushion strapped on behind a man's saddle, and from it sometimes hung a small platform or double stirrup on which a woman rider could rest her feet. One horse was sometimes made also to carry two men riding astride. Horseflesh was also economized by the ride-and-tie system : two persons would start on horseback, ride a mile or two, dismount, tie the animal by the roadside, leaving him for another couple (who had started afoot) to mount, ride on past the first couple, and dismount and tie in their turn.

Coaches were not a wholly popular means of conveyance in the first half of the seventeenth century, even among Englishmen on English roads, and they would have been wholly useless in New England. John Winthrop had one in 1685. Sir Edmund and Lady Andros rode in a coach in Boston in 1687, and there were then a few other carriages in town. Their purchase and use were deplored and discouraged by Puritan authorities, as were other luxurious fashions. Outside of the town wheeled vehicles were of little use as they had to be lashed clumsily in two canoes and laboriously ferried across the rivers, while the horses were similarly transferred to the opposite shore, or allowed to swim over. The early carriages were calashes and chariots. Henry Sharp of Salem had a calash in 1701. William Cutler's "collash with ye furniture" was worth £10 in 1723. Chairs—two-wheeled gigs without a top—and chaises, a vehicle with similar body and a top, were early forms of carriages. The sulky had in early days, as now, seating room but for one person. All these were hung on thorough braces instead of springs.

In an account of the funeral of Lieutenant Governor Tailor, in 1732, it is mentioned that a "great number of the gentry attended in their coaches and chaises;" but even by that date coaches were of little avail for long journeys. The anxious letters of Waitstill Winthrop to his son in 1717, at the latter's proposal of bringing a coach overland from Boston to New London, show the obstacles of travel. He warns that there are no bridges in Narragansett; he urges him to bring a mounted servant with an axe to "cut bows in the way," "to bring a good pilate that knows the cart ways," to be sure to keep the coachman sober, to have axle and hubs prepared for rough usage—and in every way discourages so rash an endeavor.

Though I have seen a New England inventory of the year 1690 in which a "sley" appears, I do not find that they were frequently used until the second or third decade of the succeeding century, though a few Bostonians had them in the year 1700. They were largely used by the Dutch in New York, and Connecticut folk occasionally followed Dutch fashions.

When sedan-chairs were so fashionable and plentiful in England, they were sure to be used to some extent in New England towns. Governor Winthrop had a very elegant Spanish sedan-chair, which was given him in 1646 by Captain Cromwell, who captured it from a Spanish galleon. This fine chair was worth £50 and was an intended gift of the Viceroy of Mexico to his sister. When Parson Oxenbridge was striken with apoplexy in the pulpit of the First Church in Boston, he was "carried home in a Cedan." On August 3, 1687, Judge Sewall wrote in his diary: " Capt. Gerrish is carried in a Sedan to the Wharf and so takes boat for Salem." Again he writes on May 31, 1715 : "The Gov'r comes first to Town, was carried from Mr. Dudleys to the Town-House in Cous. Dumers Sedan; but 'twas too tall for the Stairs, so was fain to be taken out near the top of them." The Governor had had a bad attack of gout.

On September 11, 1706, Sewall writes: "Five Indians carried Mr. Bromfield in a chair." And though I have never seen the sale of a sedan mentioned, several times I have fancied that the reference to the sale of a chair meant a sedan-chair. In the memoirs of Eliza Quincey she speaks of riding in a sedan, and of seeing Dr. Franklin in one in 1789.

At a surprisingly early date, when we consider the limited opportunities for travel, the colonial authorities licensed taverns or ordinaries, and also made strict laws governing them. The landlords could not sell sack or strong water; nor permit games to be played in their precincts; nor allow dancing or singing; nor could tobacco be used within their walls; nor could they sell cakes or buns indiscriminately. Samuel Cole, the Boston comfit-maker, received his license in 1634, though one can hardly understand, with such manifold rules of narrow limit, how he could wish it. Previously other freemen had obtained permission "to draw wine and beer" to sell at retail to their neighbors and to travellers. In New Haven the tavern-keeper had been given twenty acres of land in 1645, in which travellers' horses could be pastured. In Hartford and other river towns the establishment of taverns was compulsory. The ordinaries quickly multiplied in number and increased in pretension. In Boston, in 1651, the King's Arms and its furniture were held to be worth £600. Board was cheap enough. In 1634 the Court set the price of a single meal at sixpence, and an ale quart of beer at a penny. At the Ship Tavern a man had "fire and bed, dyet, wyne and beere betweene meals" for three shillings a day. The wine was limited to "a cupp each man at dynner & supp & no more." Following the English fashion of Shakespeare's time, the inn chambers were each named: The Exchange Chamber, Rose and Sun Chamber, Star Chamber, Court Chamber, Jerusalem Chamber, etc. The names of the inns also followed English nomenclature: The Bunch of Grapes, Dog & Pot, Turk's Head, Green Dragon, Blue Anchor, King's Head, etc. The Good Woman bore on its

painted sign the figure of a headless woman. The
Ship in Distress had these lines :

> " With sorrows I am compassed round,
> Pray lend a hand—my ship's aground."

Another Boston tavern had this rhyme :

> " This is the bird that never flew,
> This is the tree that never grew,
> This is the ship that never sails,
> This is the can that never fails."

The Sun Tavern bore these words :

> " The Best Ale and Beer under the Sun."

This tavern was removed to Moon Street, and was
kept by Mrs. Milk.   Her neighbors' names were Waters, Beer, and Legg.   The Salutation Inn, with its
sign-board bearing the picture of two men shaking
hands, was commonly known as the Two Palaverers.

I know no more attractive picture of olden-time
hospitality, nothing better "under the notion of a
tavern," than the old Palaverer tavern at Medford.
On either side of its front door grew a great tree, and
in the spreading branches of each tree was built a
platform or balcony.   The two were connected by a
hanging bridge or scaffolding, and also connected by
a similar foot-bridge with the tavern itself.   In these
leafy tree-arbors, through the sunny summer months,
from dawn till twilight, whilom travellers rested and
drank their drams, or, perchance, their cups of tea,

and watched the arrival and departure of coaches and horsemen at "mine inn."

John Adams wrote frequently of the inns of the time. He said of the Ipswich innkeeper in 1771: "Landlord and Landlady are some of the grandest people alive. Landlady is the great granddaughter of Governor Endicott, and has all the notions of greatest family. As to Landlord, he is as happy, and as big, as proud, as conceited as any nobleman in England, always calm and good-natured and lazy."

Of the Enfield landlord he wrote: "Oated and drank tea at Peases—a smart house and landlord truly; well dressed with his ruffles &c. and upon inquiry I found he was the great man of the town, their representative as well as tavern-keeper." In a paper which he wrote upon licensed houses, Adams stated that "retailers and taverners are generally, in the country, assessors, selectmen, representatives, or esquires."

Members of our best and most respected families throughout New England were innkeepers. The landlord was frequently a local magistrate, a justice of the peace, or a sheriff. Notices of town-meetings, of elections, of new laws and ordinances of administration were posted at the tavern, just as legal notices are printed in the newspapers nowadays. Bills of sales, of auctions, records of transfers were naturally posted therein; the taverns were the original business exchanges. No wonder all the men in the township flocked to the tavern—they had to to know anything of town affairs, to say nothing of local scandals. Distances were given in almanacs of the day, not from town to town, but from tavern to tavern.

Of the good quality of New England inns many travellers testify. Lafayette wrote to his wife in 1777 : " Host and hostess sit at the table with you and do the honors of a comfortable meal, and on going away you pay your fare without higgling." Dr. Dwight said the best old-fashioned New England inns were superior to any of the modern ones. Brissot said : " You meet with neatness, dignity and decency, the chambers neat, the beds good, the sheets clean, supper passable, cyder tea punch and all for fourteen pence a head." Alackaday! the good old times.

Next in importance to the landlord came the stage-driver. He was so popular and such a kindly fellow that he had to be prohibited by law from carrying any parcels or letters for persons along the route, else he were overburdened with troublesome and hinder-ing business, detrimental to the postal and carriage income of the government. He was so importuned to drink at each stopping-place that he might have lain drunk the whole year round. He was of so much consequence and so looked up to, that little Jack Men-dum, who drove the Salem mail-coach, hardly exagger-ated his position when he roared out angrily to a hun-gry passenger who urged him to drive faster : " While I drive this coach I am the whole United States of America." Stage-driving was an hereditary gift ; it went in families. Four Potters, three Ackermans, three Annables drove in Salem. Patch and Peach,

Tozzer and Blumpy, Canney and Camp, were well-known stage-driving names.

The stage-agent also, that obsolete functionary, was a man of much local consequence and of many affairs; he was established in many a tavern as a necessary and almost immovable piece of bar-room furniture.

To show the importance of tavern, tavern-keeper, stage-agent, and stage-driver in early Federal days, let me give a single instance. Haverhill was the great staging centre of New Hampshire; six or eight lines of coaches left there each day. There were lines direct to Boston, New York, and Stanstead, Canada. Of course there was a vast bustle and commotion on the arrival and departure of each coach, and a goodly number of passengers were deposited at the tavern that formed the coach office—sometimes one hundred and fifty a day. It can readily be seen what a news centre such a tavern must have been, how much knowledge of the world must have been gathered by its occupants. It must be remembered that our universal modern source of information, the news-paper, did not then exist; there were a few journals, of course, of scant circulation, but of what we now deem news they contained nothing. Information of current events came through hearing and talking, not through reading. Hence it came to be that an innkeeper was not only influential in local affairs, but was universally known as the best-informed man in the place; reporters, so to speak, rendered their accounts to him; items of foreign and local news were sent to him; he was in himself an entire Associated Press.

The earliest roads for travel throughout New England followed the Indian trails or paths, and were but two or three feet wide. The Old Plymouth or Coast Road, of much importance because connecting Boston and Plymouth, the capitals of separate colonies, was provided for by action of the General Court in 1639. It ran through old Braintree. The Old Connecticut Road or Path started from Cambridge, ran to Marlborough, thence to Grafton, Oxford, and Woodstock, and on to Springfield and Albany. It was intersected at Woodstock by the Providence Path, which ran through Narragansett and Providence plantations, and also by the Nipmuck Path which came from Norwich.

The New Connecticut Road ran as did the old road, from Boston to Albany. It was known at a later date as the Post Road. From Boston it ran to Marlborough, thence to Worcester, thence to Brookfield, and so on to Springfield and Albany.

The famous Bay Path, laid out in 1673, left the Old Connecticut Path at Happy Hollow, now Wayland, and ran through Marlborough to Worcester, Oxford, Charlton, and Brookfield, when it separated in two paths, one—the Hadley Path—running to Ware, Belchertown, and Hadley, and the other returning to the Old Connecticut Path and on to Springfield.

An inexplicable charm still attaches itself to these old Indian paths, a delight in attempting to trace their unused and overgrown roadways, as they leave the main road in devious twists and turns till they again join its beaten way. And the halo of early romance and adventure surrounds them. Holland felt the charm when he wrote thus of the Bay Path:

"It was marked by trees a portion of the distance and by slight clearings of brush and thicket for the remainder. No stream was bridged, no hill graded, and no marsh drained. The path led through woods which bore the mark of centuries, over barren hills that had been licked by the Indian hounds of fire, and along the banks of streams that the seine had never dragged. A powerful interest was attached to the Bay Path. It was the channel through which laws were communicated, through which flowed news from distant friends, and through which came long, loving letters and messages. That rough thread of soil chopped by the blades of a hundred streams was a bond that radiated at each terminus into a thousand fibres of love and interest and hope and memory. Every rod had been prayed over by friends on the journey and friends at home."

Hawthorne felt it also and said:

"The forest-track trodden by the hob-nailed shoes of these sturdy and ponderous Englishmen has now a distinctness which it never could have acquired from the light tread of a hundred times as many moccasins. It goes onward from one clearing to another, here plunging into a shadowy strip of woods, there open to the sunshine, but everywhere showing a decided line along which human interests have begun to hold their career. . . . And

the Indians coming from their distant wigwams to view
the white man's settlement marvel at the deep track which
he makes, and perhaps are saddened by a flitting pre-
sentiment that this heavy tread will find its way over all
the land, and that the wild woods, the wild wolf, and the
wild Indian will alike be trampled beneath it."

For many years these paths were travelled, gradually widening from foot - paths to bridle - ways, to
cart-tracks, to carriage-roads, until they became the
post-roads, set thick with cheerful country homes.   In
some portions of New England they still are travelled
and form the general thoroughfare, but in many lonely
townships the old paths are deserted, and traffic and
passage over the post or county road is gone forever.
Bushes flourish and meet gloomily across the grass-
grown track; forest trees droop heavily over it in
summer and fall unheeded across it in winter.   On
either side moss - grown, winter - killed apple - trees
and ancient stunted currant-bushes struggle for life
against sturdy young pine and spruce and birch.
Many a rod of heavy tumble-down stone wall—New
England Stonehenges—may be seen, not as of old
dividing cleared and fertile fields, but in the midst of
a forest of trees or underbrush :

> " Far up on these abandoned mountain farms
>   Now drifting back to forests wild again,
>   The long gray walls extend their clasping arms
>   Pathetic monuments of vanished men."

Or more pathetic monuments still of hard and wasted work. On either side of the way, at too sadly frequent intervals, ruined wells or desolate yawning cellar-holes, with tumbling chimneys standing like Druid ruins, show that fair New England homes once there were found. Flaming orange tiger-lilies, most homely and cheerful bloom of country gardens, have spread from the deserted dooryards, across the untrodden foot-paths, in weedy thickets a-down the hill, and shed their rank odor unheeded on the air.

Some of the old provincial mile-stones, however, remain, and put us closely in touch with the past. In the southern part of New London County, and at Stratford, Conn., on the old post-road—the King's Highway—between Boston and Philadelphia, there are mossgrown stones that were set under the supervision of Benjamin Franklin when he was colonial Postmaster-General. After that highway was laid out, the placing and setting of the mile-stones were entrusted to Franklin, and he transacted the business, as he did everything else, in a thoroughly original way. He drove over the road in a comfortable chaise, followed by a gang of men and heavy teams loaded with the mile-stones. He attached to his chaise a machine which registered by the revolution of the chaise-wheels the number of miles travelled, and he had the mile-stones set by that record, and marked with the distance to the nearest large town. Thus the Stratford stone says : "20 Mls to N. H."—New Haven.

By provincial enactment in Governor Hutchin-

son's time, mile-stones were set on all the post-roads
throughout Massachusetts.   Some of these stones are
still standing.   There is one in the middle of the city
of Worcester, on Lincoln Street—the " New Connecticut Path ; " it is of red sandstone, and is marked, "42
Mls to Boston, 50 Mls to Springfield, 1771."

In Sutton, on the "Old Connecticut Path," stands
still the king of all these 1771 mile-stones.   It is of
red sandstone, is five feet high, and nearly three feet
wide.   It is marked, " 48 Mls to Boston 1771 B. W."
The letters B. W. stand for Bartholomew Woodbury,
a jovial and liberal old Sutton tavern - keeper who
died in 1775.   When the mile-stones were set out
by the provincial government, the place for this
Sutton stone fell a few rods from Landlord Woodbury's house; but he obtained permission and set
up this handsome stone at his own expense, beside his great horse-block under his swinging sign at
his open, welcoming door.   He fancied, perhaps, that
it would attract the attention, and thus cause the halt-
ing of travellers.   Tavern-keeper and tavern are gone ;
no vestiges even of cobblestone chimneys or cellar
walls remain.   The old post-road is now but little
travelled, but the great mile-stone and its neighbor,
the worn stepping-block, still stand, lonely monuments of past days and past pleasures.   On warm
summer nights perhaps the silent old mile-stone
awakes and sadly tells his companion of the gay
coaches that rattled by, and the rollicking bucks and
blades, the gallant soldiers that galloped past him
in the days of his youth, a century ago.   And the

stepping-block may tell in turn of the good old days when her broad sunny face was pressed by the feet of fair colonial dames who, with faces hidden in riding-hoods and masks, stepped lightly from saddle or pillion to "board and bait" at Bartholomew Woodbury's cheerful inn.

In Roxbury, Mass., there still stands at the corner of Centre and Washington Streets the famous Roxbury Parting Stone. It is a great square stone, bearing on one face the words: "The Parting Stone 1744. P. Dudley;" on another face the words: "Dedham—Rhode Island," and on a third "Cambridge—Watertown." It has had set on it recently an iron frame or fixture for a gas-lamp. This stone, with many others in Norfolk County, was placed by Paul Dudley at his own expense in the middle of the last century. It has seen the separation or "parting" of many a brave company that had ridden out to it from Boston. Many a distinguished traveller has passed it and glanced at its carved words. Lord Percy's soldiers took counsel of it one hot April morning to find the road to Lexington.

Governor Belcher set out a row of mile-stones from Boston Town House to his home in Milton. Some of them are still standing, the seventh and eighth in Milton, one marked "8 miles to B. Town House. The Lower Way, 1734." The ninth and twelfth stand as historical landmarks in Quincy, on the old Plymouth Road, and bear the dates 1720 and 1727.

In Wenham another mile-stone near the graveyard bears the date 1710, shows the distance to Ipswich and Boston, and gives these words of timely warning: "I know that Thou wilt Bring me to Death and to the house appointed for all Living."

A marked improvement in facilities for travel came in turnpike days. These well laid out and well kept roads fairly changed the face of the country. They sometimes shortened by half the distance to be travelled between two towns. Stock companies were formed to build bridges and grade these turnpikes, and the stock formed a good investment and was also vastly used in speculation. The story of the turnpike is as interesting as that of the Indian path, but cannot be told at length here. They, too, have had their day; in some counties the turnpike is as deserted as the path and seems equally ancient.

New England roads and turnpikes have seen many a gay sight, for the custom of speeding the parting guest "agatewards" for some miles, with an accompanying escort on foot or on horseback, to some ford or natural turning-point or bourn, was a universal mark of interest and affection, and of courtesy as well. Judge Sewall records, on one occasion, with much indignation, that "not one soul rode with us to the ferry." Ere the days of turnpikes, the old Indian paths witnessed many a sad and pathetic parting in the wilderness, such as was recorded in simple language in Parson Thatcher's diary in 1680, when he left Barnstable to go to a new parish:

"A great company of horsemen 7 & 50 horse & 12 of them double, went with us to Sandwich & there got me to go to prayer with them, and I think none of them parted with me with dry eyes."

This is indeed a strong picture for the brush of a painter, the golden September light, nowhere more radiantly beautiful than on

> "the narrowing Cape
> That stretches its shrunk arm out to all the winds,
> And the relentless smiting of the waves,"

and the sad-faced band in Puritan garb, armed and mounted, gathered around their departing leader in reverent prayer.

Perhaps the turnpike saw no more characteristic scene than the winter ride to market. Though summer and fall were the New England farmer's time of increase, winter was his time of trade and his time of recreation as well. When wintry blasts grew chill, and snow and ice covered deep the desolate fields and country roads, then he prepared with zest and with delight for his gelid time of outing, his Arctic red-letter day, his greatest social pleasure of the entire year. The friendly word was circulated by a kind of estafet from farm to farm, was carried by neighbor or passing traveller, or was discussed and planned and agreed upon in the noon-house, or at the tavern chimney-side on Sunday during the nooning, that on a certain date—unless there set in the tantalizing and swamping January thaw, a thaw which might be pushing and unseasonable enough to rush in in December and quite as often hung off and dawdled into February

—that on the appointed date, at break of day, the annual ride to market would begin. Often fifty or sixty neighbors would respond to the call, would start together on the road. For farmers in western Vermont and Massachusetts the market town was Troy or other Hudson valley towns. In Maine, from Bath and Hallowell and neighboring towns, the winter procession rode to Portland. In central Massachusetts some drove to Northampton, Springfield, or Hartford; but the greatest number of farmers and the largest amount of farm produce went to the towns of the Massachusetts coast, to Salem, to Newburyport, and, above all, to Boston.

The two-horse pung or the single-horse pod, shod with steel shoes an inch thick, was closely packed with the accumulated farm wealth—whole pigs, perhaps a deer or two, firkins of butter, casks of cheese, four cheeses in each cask, bags of beans, pease or corn, skins of mink, fox, and fisher-cat that the boys had trapped, birch brooms that the boys had made, yarn that their sisters had spun, and stockings and mittens that they had knitted—in short, anything that a New England farm could produce that would sell to any profit in a New England town. So closely was the sleigh packed, in fact, that the driver could not be seated. The sturdy and hardy farmer stood on a little semicircular step in the rear of the sleigh, his body protected by the high sleigh back against the sharp icy blasts. At times he ran alongside or behind his vehicle to keep his blood in brisk circulation.

Though every inch of the sleigh was packed to
its fullest extent, there was always found room in
some corner for plenty of food to last the thrifty
traveller through his journey; often enough to liberally supply him even on his return trip—cold roasted
spare ribs of pork, doughnuts, loaves of "rye an'
Injun" bread, and invariably a bountiful mass of
frozen bean porridge. This latter was made and
frozen in a tub, and when space was hard to find
in the crowded vehicle, the solid mass was furnished
with a loop of twine by which to hang it to the side
of the pung. A small hatchet with which to chop off a
chunk of porridge formed the accompaniment of this
unalluring Arctic provender. Oats and hay to feed
his horses did the farmer also carry.

There were plenty of taverns in which he could
obtain food if he needed it, in which, indeed, he did
obtain liquid sustenance to warm his bones and stir
his tongue, and make palatable the half-thawed porridge which he ate in front of the cheerful tavern
fire. But it was the invariable custom, no matter
what the wealth of the farmer, to carry a supply of
food for the journey. This kind of itinerant picnic
was called "tuck-a-nuck"—a word of Indian origin,
or "mitchin," while the box or hamper or bucket
that held the provisions was called a "mitchin-box."
I can fancy that no thrifty or loving housewife allowed the man of her household to go to market with
too meanly filled a mitchin-box, but took an honest
pride in sending him off with a full stock of rich
doughnuts, well-baked bread, well-filled pies, and at

least well-cooked porridge, which he could devour without shame before the eyes of his neighbors.

The traveller did not carry his meals from home because the tavern fare was expensive; at the inn where he paid ten cents a night for his lodging, he was uniformly charged but twelve and a half cents for a "cold bite," and but twenty-five cents for a regular meal; but it was not the fashion to purchase meals at the tavern; the host made his profits from the liquor he sold and from the sleeping-room he gave. Sometimes the latter was simple enough. A great fire was built in the fireplace of either front room—the bar-room and parlor—and round it, in a semicircle, feet to the fire and heads on their rolled-up buffalo robes, slept the tired travellers. A few sybaritic or rheumatic tillers of the soil paid for half a bed in one of the double-bedded rooms which all taverns then contained, and got a full bed's worth, in deep hollows and high billows of live-geese feathers, warm homespun blankets, and patchwork quilts.

It was certainly a gay winter's scene as sleigh after sleigh dashed into the tavern barn or shed, and the stiffened driver, after "putting up" his steed, walked quickly to the bar-room, where sat the host behind his cage-like counter, where ranged the inspiring barrels of old Medford or Jamaica rum and hard cider, and

"Where dozed a fire of beechen logs that bred
Strange fancies in its embers golden-red,
And nursed the loggerhead, whose hissing dip,
Timed by nice instinct, creamed the bowl of flip."

Many a rough joke was laughed at, many a story told ere the tired circle slept around the fire; but four o'clock saw them all bestirring, making a fresh start on their city-ward journey.

In town the traveller was busy enough; he not only had his farm products to sell, but since he sometimes got the enormous sum of fifty dollars for his sleigh load, and it was estimated that two dollars was a liberal allowance for a week's travelling expenses, he had much to spend and many purchases to make—spices and raisins for the home table, fish-hooks and powder and shot, pewter plates, or a few pieces of English crockery, a calico gown or two, a shawl, or a scarf, or a beaver hat; and thus brought to dreary New England farms their sole taste of town life in winter.

For many years travel, especially to New York and other seaport towns, was largely by water, on sloop or pink or snow; and many stories of the discomforts of such trips have come down to us.

The first passenger steamboat which ran between New York and Providence made its trial trip in 1822. The boats made the passage from town to town in twenty-three hours, which was monstrous fast time. On one of the first trips the boat lay by near Point Judith to repair a slight damage to machinery, and all the simple country-folk who came down to the shore expecting to find a wreck, were amazed to see the boat—apparently burning up—go quickly sliding away without sails over the water until out of sight. Many whispered that the devil had a hand in it, and perhaps was on board in person. The new means of conveyance proved at once to be the favored one for all genteel persons wishing to travel between Boston and New York. The forty-mile journey between Boston and Providence was made in fine stage-coaches, which were always crowded. Often eighteen or twenty full coach-loads were carried each way each day. The editor of the *Providence Gazette* wrote at that time: "We were rattled from Providence to Boston in four hours and fifty minutes—if any one wants to go faster he may send to Kentucky and charter a streak of lightning!"

The fare on these coaches was three dollars for the trip between Providence and Boston. This exorbitant sum was a sore annoyance to all thrifty men, and indignantly did they rail and protest against it. At last a union was formed, and a line of rival coaches was established, on which the fare was to be two dollars and a half a trip. This caused great dismay to the regular coach company, who at once reduced their fare to two dollars. The rival line, not to be outdone, announced their reduction to a dollar and a half. The regulars then widely advertised that their fare would thenceforth be only one dollar. The rivals then sold seats for the trip for fifty cents apiece; and in despair, after jealously watching for weeks the crowded coaches of the new line, the conquered old line mournfully announced that they would make trips every day with their vehicle filled with the first applicants who chanced to be on time at the starting-place, and that these lucky dogs would be carried for nothing.

The new stage-coaches were now in their turn de-

serted, and the proprietors pondered for a week trying to invent some way to still further cut down the
entirely vanished rates.   They at last placarded the
taverns with announcements that they would not only
carry their patrons free of expense, but would give
each traveller on their coaches a good dinner at the
end of his journey.   The old coach-line was rich and
at once counter-advertised a free dinner and a good
bottle of wine too, to its patrons—and there, for a
time, the fierce controversy came to a standstill, both
lines having crowded trips each day.

Mr. Shaffer, who was a fashionable teacher of
dancing and deportment in Boston, and a well-known
" man about town," a jolly good fellow, got upon the
Providence coach one Monday morning in Boston,
had a gay ride to Providence and a good dinner and
bottle of wine at the end of the journey, all at the
expense of the coach company.   On Tuesday he rode
more gayly still back to Boston, had his dinner and
his wine, and was up on Wednesday morning to
mount the Providence coach for the third ride and
dinner and bottle.   He returned to Boston on Thursday in the same manner.   On Friday the fame of his
cheap fun was thoroughly noised all over Boston, and
he collected a crowd of gay young sparks who much
enjoyed their frolicking ride and the fine Providence
dinners and wine.   All returned in high spirits with
Shaffer to Boston on Saturday to meet the sad, sad
news that the rival coach lines had made a compro-
mise and had both signed a contract to carry passengers thereafter for two dollars a trip.

Upon Tremont Street, near Winter Street, in Boston, there stood at that time in a garden a fine old house which was kept as a restaurant, and was a pleasant summer lounging-place for all gay cits.   One day a very portly, aldermanic man presented himself at the entrance of the restaurant and asked the price of a dinner.   Shaffer, who was present, immediately assumed all the obsequious airs of a waiter, and calling for a tape-measure, proceeded to measure the distance around the protuberant waist of the astonished and insulted inquirer, who could hardly believe his sense of hearing when the impudent Shaffer very politely answered, "Price of dinner, sir! — about four dollars, sir! — for that size, sir!"   Such were the practical jokes of stage and tavern life in olden days.

IX

HOLIDAYS AND FESTIVALS

THE first century of colonial life saw few set times
and days for pleasures. The holy days of the English Church were as a stench to the Puritan nostrils,
and their public celebration was at once rigidly forbidden by the laws of New England. New holidays
were not quickly evolved, and the sober gatherings
for matters of Church and State for a time took their
place. The hatred of "wanton Bacchanallian Christ-
masses" spent throughout England, as Cotton said,
in "revelling, dicing, carding, masking, mumming,
consumed in compotations, in interludes, in excess of
wine, in mad mirth," was the natural reaction of intelligent and thoughtful minds against the excesses
of a festival which had ceased to be a Christian holiday, but was dominated by a lord of misrule who
did not hesitate to invade the churches in time of service, in his noisy revels and sports. English Church-
men long ago revolted also against such Christmas
observance.

Of the first Pilgrim Christmas we know but little,
save that it was spent, as was many a later one, in
work. Bradford said : "Ye 25 day begane to erect

ye first house for comone use to receive them and
their goods." On the following Christmas the governor records with grim humor a "passage rather of
mirth than of waight." Some new company excused
themselves from work on that day, saying it went
against their consciences. The governor answered
that he would spare them until they were better informed. But returning at mid-day and finding them
playing pitch-the-bar and stool-ball in the streets, he
told them that it was against *his* conscience that they
should play and others work, and so made them cease
their games.

By 1659 the Puritans had grown to hate Christmas
more and more ; it was, to use Shakespeare's words,
" the bug that feared them all." The very name
smacked to them of incense, stole, and monkish jar-
gon ; any person who observed it as a holiday by for-
bearing of labor, feasting, or any other way was to
pay five shillings fine, so desirous were they to
"beate down every sprout of Episcopacie." Judge
Sewall watched jealously the feeling of the people
with regard to Christmas, and noted with pleasure
on each succeeding year the continuance of common
traffic throughout the day. Such entries as this
show his attitude : " Dec. 25, 1685. Carts come to
town and shops open as usual. Some somehow observe the day, but are vexed I believe that the Body
of people profane it, and blessed be God no authority
yet to compel them to keep it." When the Church
of England established Christmas services in Boston
a few years later, we find the Judge waging hopeless

war against Governor Belcher over it, and hear him praising his son for not going with other boy friends to hear the novel and attractive services. He says : "I dehort mine from Christmas keeping and charge them to forbear."

Christmas could not be regarded till this century as a New England holiday, though in certain localities, such as old Narragansett—an opulent community which was settled by Episcopalians—two weeks of Christmas visiting and feasting were entered into with zest by both planters and slaves for many years previous to the Revolution.

Thanksgiving, commonly regarded as being from its earliest beginning a distinctive New England festival, and an equally characteristic Puritan holiday, was originally neither.

The first New England Thanksgiving was not observed by either Plymouth Pilgrim or Boston Puritan. "Gyving God thanks" for safe arrival and many other liberal blessings was first heard on New England shores from the lips of the Popham colonists at Monhegan, in the Thanksgiving service of the Church of England.

Days set apart for thanksgiving were known in Europe before the Reformation, and were in frequent use by Protestants afterward, especially in the Church of England, where they were a fixed custom long before they were in New England. One wonders that the Puritans, hating so fiercely the customs and set days and holy days of the Established Church, should so quickly have appointed a Thanksgiving

Day. But the first New England Thanksgiving was not a day of religious observance, it was a day of recreation. Those who fancy all Puritans, and especially all Pilgrims, to have been sour, morose, and gloomy men should read this account of the first Thanksgiving week (not day) in Plymouth. It was written on December 11, 1621, by Edward Winslow to a friend in England :

" Our harvest being gotten in ourgov ernor sent four men on fowling that so we might after a special manner rejoice together after we had gathered the fruits of our labors. They four killed as much fowl as with a little help beside served the company about a week. At which times among other recreations we exercised our arms, many of the Indians coming amongst us, and among the rest their greatest king Massasoyt with some ninety men, whom for three days we entertained and feasted, and they went out and killed five deer which they brought and bestow'd on our governor, and upon the captains and others."

As Governor Bradford specified that during that autumn "beside waterfoule ther was great store of wild turkies," we can have the satisfaction of feeling sure that at that first Pilgrim Thanksgiving our forefathers and foremothers had turkeys.

Thus fared the Pilgrims better at their Thanksgiving than did their English brothers, for turkeys were far from plentiful in England at that date.

Though there were but fifty-five English to eat the Pilgrim Thanksgiving feast, there were "partakers in plenty," and the ninety sociable Indian visitors did not come empty-handed, but joined fraternally in provision for the feast, and probably also in the games.

These recreations were, without doubt, competitions in running, leaping, jumping, and perhaps stool-ball, a popular game played by both sexes, in which a ball was driven from stool to stool or wicket to wicket.

During that chilly November week in Plymouth, Priscilla Mullins and John Alden may have " recreated " themselves with this ancient form of croquet—if any recreation were possible for the four women of the colony, who, with the help of one servant and a few young girls or maidekins, had to prepare and cook food for three days for one hundred and twenty hungry men, ninety-one of them being Indians, with an unbounded capacity for gluttonous gorging unsurpassed by any other race. Doubtless the deer, and possibly the great turkeys, were roasted in the open air. The picture of that Thanksgiving Day, the block-house with its few cannon, the Pilgrim men in buff breeches, red waistcoats, and green or sad-colored mandillions ; the great company of Indians, gay in holiday paint and feathers and furs ; the few sad, overworked, homesick women, in worn and simple gowns, with plain coifs and kerchiefs, and the pathetic handful of little children, forms a keen contrast to the prosperous, cheerful Thanksgivings of a century later.

There is no record of any special religious service during this week of feasting.

The Pilgrims had good courage, stanch faith, to thus celebrate and give thanks, for they apparently had but little cause to rejoice. They had been lost in the woods, where they had wandered surbated, and had been terrified by the roar of "Lyons," and had met wolves that "sat on thier tayles and grinned" at them; they had been half frozen in their poorly built houses; had been famished, or sickened with unwonted and unpalatable food; their common house had burned down, half their company was dead—they had borne sore sorrows, and equal trials were to come. They were in dire distress for the next two years. In the spring of 1623 a drought scorched the corn and stunted the beans, and in July a fast day of nine hours of prayer was followed by a rain that revived their "withered corn and their drooping affections." In testimony of their gratitude for the rain, which would not have been vouchsafed for private prayer, and thinking they would "show great ingratitude if they smothered up the same," the second Pilgrim Thanksgiving was ordered and observed.

In 1630, on February 22d, the first public thanksgiving was held in Boston by the Bay Colony, in gratitude for the safe arrival of food-bearing and friend-bringing ships. On November 4, 1631, Winthrop wrote again : " We kept thanksgiving day in Boston." From that time till 1684 there were at least twenty-two public thanksgiving days appointed in Massachusetts—about one in two years; but it was not a regular biennial festival. In 1675, a time of deep gloom through the many and widely separated attacks from the fierce savages, there was no public thanksgiving celebrated in either Massachusetts or Connecticut. It is difficult to state when the feast became a fixed annual observance in New England. In the year 1742 were two Thanksgiving Days.

Rhode Islanders paid little heed in early days to Thanksgiving—at any rate, to days set by the Massachusetts authorities. Governor Andros savagely prosecuted more than one Rhode Islander who calmly worked all day long on the day appointed for giving thanks. In Boston, William Veazie was set in the pillory in the market-place for ploughing on the Thanksgiving Day of June 18, 1696. He said his king had granted liberty of conscience, and that the reigning king, William, was not his ruler; that King James was his royal prince, and since he did not believe in setting apart days for thanksgiving he should not observe them.

Connecticut people, though just as pious and as prosperous as the Bay colonists, do not appear to have been as grateful, and had considerable trouble at times to " pick vppon a day " for thanksgiving ; and the festival was not regularly observed there till 1716.

Thanksgiving was not always appointed in early days for the same token of God's beneficence. Days of thanks were set in gratitude for and observance of great political and military events, for victories over the Indians or in the Palatinate, for the accession of kings, for the prospect of royal heirs to the throne, for the discovery of conspiracy, for the "healing of

breaches," the "dissipation of the Pirates," the abate-
ment of diseases, for the safe arrival of "psons of
spetiall use and quality," as well as in gratitude for
plentiful harvests—that "God had not given them
cleannes of teeth and wante of bread."

The early Thanksgivings were not always set upon
Thursday. It is said that that day was chosen on account of its reflected glory as lecture day. Judge Sewall told the governor and his council, in 1697, tha the
"desir'd the same day of the week might be for
Thanksgiving and Fasts," and that "Boston and Ipswitch Lectures led us to Thorsday." The feast of
thanks was for many years appointed with equal frequency upon "Tusday com seuen-night," or "vppon
Wensday com fort-nit." Nor was any special season
of the year chosen : in 1716 it was appointed in August; in 1713, in January; in 1718, in December; in
1719, in October. The frequent appointments in
gratitude for bountiful harvests finally made the autumn the customary time.

The God of the Puritans was a jealous God, and
many fasts were appointed to avert his wrath, as shown
in blasted wheat, moulded beans, wormy pease, and
mildewed corn ; in drought and grasshoppers; in Indian invasions ; in caterpillars and other woes of New
England; in children dying by the chincough; in the
"excessive raigns from the botles of Heaven"—all
these evils being sent for the crying sins of wig-wearing, sheltering Quakers, not paying the ministers, etc.
A fast and a feast kept close company in Puritan
calendars. A fast frequently preceded Thanksgiving

Day, and was sometimes appointed for the day succeeding the feast—a clever plan which had its good
hygienic points.   Days of private as well as of public
fast and thanksgiving were also observed by individuals.   Judge Sewall took the greatest satisfaction in
his fastings, and carefully outlined his plan of prayer
throughout the fast day, which he spent in his chamber—a plan which included and specified ministers,
rulers and magistrates, his family, and every person
whom he said " had a smell of relation " to him ; and
also every nation and people in the known world. He
does not note Thanksgiving Day as a holiday of any
importance.

Though in the mind of the Puritan, Christmas
smelled to heaven of idolatry, when his own festival, Thanksgiving, became annual, it assumed many
of the features of the old English Christmas ; it was
simply a day of family reunion in November instead
of December, on which Puritans ate turkey and Indian pudding and pumpkin-pie, instead of " superstitious meats " such as a baron of beef, boar's head, and
plum-pudding.

Many funny stories are told of the early Thanksgiving Days, such as the town of Colchester calmly
ignoring the governor's appointed day and observing
their own festival a week later in order to allow time
for the arrival, by sloop from New York, of a hogshead of molasses for pies.   Another is recounted of
a farmer losing his cask of Thanksgiving molasses
out of his cart as he reached the top of a steep hill,
and of its rolling swiftly down till split in twain

by its fall. His helpless discomfiture and his wife's acidity of temper and diet are comically told.

There is in the possession of the Massachusetts Historical Society a broadside announcing a thanksgiving for victory in King Philip's War; and during the following year, 1677, the first regular Thanksgiving proclamation was printed.

But Thanksgiving Day was not the chief New England holiday. Ward, writing in 1699, does not name it, saying of New Englanders: "Election, Commencement and Training Days are their only Holy Days."

It was natural in New England, a state planted by men of exceptional intelligence, that all should think as one minister said, "If the college die, the church cannot long live;" and in the Commencement Day of their colleges they found matter of deep interest, of pride, of recreation. Judge Sewall always notes the day at Harvard, its exercises, its dinner, its plentiful wine, and the Commencement cake, which he carried to his friends. The meagre entries in the diaries and almanacs of many an old New England minister show that Commencement Day was one of their proudest holidays. After 1730, Commencement Day was usually set for Friday, in order that there might be, as President Wadsworth said in his diary, "less remaining time in the week to be spent in frolicking."

Training Day may be called the first New England holiday, though Hawthorne thought the day of too serious importance in early warlike times to be classed under the head of festivals.   At the first Pilgrim Thanksgiving they " exercised their arms," and for some years they had six trainings a year ; no wonder they were said to be " diligent in traynings."   The all-powerful Church Militant held sway even over these gatherings of New England warriors.   The military reviews and exercises were made properly religious by an opening exercise of prayer and psalm-singing, the latter sometimes at such inordinate length as to provoke criticism and remarks from the rank and file, remonstrance which was at once pleasantly rebuked by pious Judge Sewall.   Relig-ious notices were also given before the company broke line.   A noble dinner somewhat redeemed the sobriety of the opening exercises, a dinner given in Boston to gentlemen and gentlewomen in tents on the Common ; and the frequent firing of guns and cannon further enlivened the day.

Boston mustered a very fair military force at train-ings, even in early days.   Winthrop writes that at the May training in 1639 one thousand men exercised, and in the autumn twelve hundred bore arms, and not an oath or quarrel was heard and no drunkenness seen.   The training field was Boston Common.   At these trainings prizes were frequently offered for the best marksmanship; in Connecticut, a silk handker-chief or some such trinket.   Judge Sewall offered a silver cup, and again a silver-headed pike ; since he was an uncommonly poor shot himself, his gener-osity shows out all the more plainly.   With barbaric openness of cruel intent, a figure stuffed to represent

a human form was often the target, and it was a
matter of grave decision whether a shot in the head
or bowels were the fatal one. Sometimes the day was
enlivened by a form of amusement ever beloved
of the colonists—by public punishments. For instance, at the training day at Kittery, Me., in 1690,
two men " road the woodin Horse for dangerous and
churtonous carig and mallplying of oaths."

The training days of colony times developed into
Muster Days, the crowning pinnacle of gayety, dissipation, and noise in a country boy's life in New England for over a century.

We owe much to these trainings and these trials of
marksmanship. In conjunction with the universal
skill in woodcraft and in hunting, they made our
ancestors more than a match for the Indian and the
Frenchman, and in Revolutionary times gave them
their ascendency over the English.

Election Day was naturally a time of much excitement to New Englanders in olden times, as nowadays. In fact, the entire week partook of the flavor
of a holiday. This did not please the ministers.
Urian Oakes wrote sadly that Election Day had become a time " to meet, to smoke, carouse and swag-
ger and dishonor God with the greater bravery."
Various local customs obtained. " 'Lection cake,"
a sort of rusk rich with fruit and wine, was made
in many localities; indeed, is still made in some families that I know; and sometimes " 'lection beer "
was brewed. In early May the herb gatherers (many
of them old squaws) brought to town various barks

and roots for this beer, and they also vended it on the streets during Election week. An Election sermon was also preached.

Boston had two Election Days. "Nigger 'Lection" was so called in distinction from Artillery Election. On the former anniversary day the election of the governor was formally announced, and the black population was allowed to throng the Common, to buy gingerbread and drink beer like their white betters. On the second holiday the Ancient and Honorable Artillery had a formal parade, and chose its new officers, who received with much ceremony, out-of-doors, their new commissions from the new governor. Woe, then, to the black face that dared be seen on that grave and martial occasion! In 1817 a negro boy named William Read, enraged at being refused the high privileges and pleasures of Artillery Day, blew up in Boston Harbor a ship called the Canton Packet. For years it was a standing taunt of white boys in Boston to negroes:

> "Who blew up the ship?
> Nigger, why for?
> 'Cause he couldn't go to 'lection
> An' shake paw-paw."

Paw-paw was a gambling game which was played on the Common with four sea-shells of the *Cyprœa Moneta.*

The 14th of July was observed by Boston negroes for many years to commemorate the introduction of measures to abolish the slave trade. It was deri-

sively called Bobalition Day, and the orderly conven-
tion of black men was greeted with a fusillade of rotten
fruit and eggs and much jesting abuse. It was at
one of these Bobalition-Day celebrations that this
complimentary toast was seriously given and recorded
in honor of the newly elected governor : " Governor
Brooks—May the mantelpiece of Caleb Strong fall on
the hed of his distinguished Predecessor."

In other localities, notably on the Massachusetts
coast, in Connecticut, and in Narragansett, the term
" Nigger 'Lection " was applied to the election of a
black governor, who held his sway over the black
population. Wherever there was a large number of
negroes the black governor was a man of much dignity and importance, and his election was a scene of
much gayety and considerable feasting, which the
governor's master had to pay for. As he had much
control over his black constituents, it is plain that
the black governor might be made useful in many
petty ways to his white neighbors. Occasionally the
" Nigger 'Lection " had a deep political signification
and influence. " Scaeva," in his " Hartford in the
Olden Times," and Hinman, in the " American Revolution," give detailed and interesting accounts of
" Nigger 'Lection."

A few rather sickly and benumbed attempts were
made in bleak New England to celebrate in old English fashion the first of May. A May-pole was erected
in Charlestown in 1687, and was promptly cut down.
The most unbounded observance of the day was held
at Merry Mount (now the town of Quincy) in 1628 by

roystering Morton and his gay crew.   Bradford says: "They set up a May-pole, drinking and dancing aboute it many days togeather, inviting the Indian women for their consorts, dancing and frisking togeather like so many fairies or furies rather."   This May-pole was a stately pine-tree eighty feet high, with a pair of buck's horns nailed at the top, and with "sundry rimes and verses affixed."   Stern Endicott rode down ere long to investigate matters, and at once cut the "idoll Maypole" down, and told the junketers that he hoped to hear of their "better walking, else they would find their merry mount but a woful mount."

To eat pancakes on Shrove Tuesday was held by the Puritans to be a heathenish vanity ; and yet, apparently with the purpose of annoying good Boston folk, some attempts were made to observe the day. One year a young man went through the town "carrying a cock on his back with a bell in 's hand."   Several of his fellows followed him blindfolded, and, under pretence of striking him with heavy cart-whips, managed to do considerable havoc in the surrounding crowd.   We can well imagine how odious this horse-play was to the Puritans, aggravated by the fact that it was done to note a holy day.   On Shrove Tuesday, in 1685, there was "great disorder in town by reason of Cock-skailing."   This was the barbarous game of cock-steling, or cock-throwing, or cock-squoiling—a game as old as Chaucer's time, a universal pastime on Shrove Tuesday in England, where scholars also had cock-fights in the school-rooms.

The observance, or even notice, of the first day of

the year as a " gaudy-day "—of New-Year's tides in any way—was thought by Urian Oakes to savor strongly of superstitious reverence for the heathen god Janus; the Pilgrims made no note of their first New-Year's Day in the New World, save by this very prosaic record, " We went to work betimes." Yet Judge Sewall, as rigid and stern a Puritan as any of the earliest days, records with some pride his being greeted with a levet, or blast of trumpets, under his window, early on the morning of January 1, 1697 ; while he himself celebrated the opening of the new century with a very poor poem of his own making, which he caused to be cried or recited throughout the. town of Boston by the town bellman.

Guy Fawkes' Day, or " Pope's Day," was observed with much noise throughout New England for many years by burning of bonfires, preceded by parades of young men and boys dressed in fantastic costumes and carrying " guys " or " popes " of straw. Fires are still lighted on the 5th of November in New England towns by boys, who know not what they commemorate. In Newburyport, Mass., and Portsmouth, N. H., Guy Fawkes' Day is still celebrated. In Newcastle, N. H., it is called " Pork Night." In New York and Brooklyn, the bonfires on the night of election, and the importunate begging on Thanksgiving Day of ragged fantastics, usually children of Roman Catholic parents, are both direct survivals of the ancient celebration of " Pope's Day."

In Governor Belcher's time, in Massachusetts, the stopping of pedestrians on the street, by "loose and dissolute people," who were wont to levy contributions for paying for their bonfires, became so universally annoying that the governor made proclamation against them in the newspapers. Tudor, in his "Life of Otis," gives an account of the observance of the day and its disagreeable features. He says the intruders paraded the streets with grotesque images, forcibly entered houses, ringing bells, demanding money, and singing rhymes similar to those sung all over England:

> "Don't you remember
> The Fifth of November,
> The Gunpowder Treason and plot,
> I see no reason
> Why Gunpowder Treason
> Should ever be forgot.

> From Rome to Rome
> The Pope is come,
> Amid ten thousand fears,
> With fiery serpents to be seen
> At eyes, nose, mouth, and ears.
> Don't you hear my little bell
> Go chink, chink, chink,
> Please give me a little money
> To 'buy my Pope some drink."

The figure of the Pretender was added to that of the pope and devil in 1702; and on Pope's Day, in 1763, American politics took a share. I read in a diary of that date, " Pope, Devil, and Stampman were hung together." After the Revolution the effigy of Benedict Arnold was burnt alongside that of Guy Fawkes.

Though we retained Pope's Day until Federal times, the Declaration of Independence struck one holiday off our calendar. The king's birthday was, until then, celebrated with a training, a salute of cannon, a dinner, and an illumination.

Other holidays were evolved by circumstances. Anniversary Day was a special festival for the ministers, who gathered together in the larger towns for spiritual intercourse and the material refreshment of a good dinner. It was originally held in Massachusetts at the May meeting of the General Court. Forefathers' Day, the anniversary of the landing at Plymouth, was celebrated by dinners, prayer, and praise.

Many other annual scenes of gayety were developed by the various food harvests. Thus the time when the salmon and shad came up the rivers had been a great merry-making and season of feasting for the Indian, and became equally so for the white man. As years passed on it became also a time of much drunkenness and revelry. Men rode a hundred miles for these gay holidays, and went home with horses laden down with fish. Shad were so plentiful that they were thrown away, would sell for but a penny apiece, and no persons of social importance or of good taste would eat them except in secret. Salmon, too, were so plentiful and so cheap that farm-servants on the banks of the Connecticut stipulated that they should have salmon for dinner but thrice a week, as the rich fish soon proved cloying.

In many localities, in Narragansett in particular,

the autumnal corn-huskings almost reached the dignity of holidays, being conducted in a liberal fashion and with unbounded hospitality, which included and entertained whole retinues of black servants from neighboring farms, as well as the planters and their families. Apple-parings, maple-sugar makings, and timber-rollings were merry gatherings.

In Vermont and down the Connecticut valley the annual sheep-shearing was a lively scene. On Nantucket there took place annually a like sheep-shearing, which, though a characteristic New England festival, was like the scene in the "Winter's Tale." The broad plains outside the town were used as a common sheep-pasture throughout the year; sometimes fifteen or sixteen thousand sheep were kept thereon. About two miles from the town was a sheep-fold, near the margin of a pond, where the sheep could be washed. It was built of four or five concentric fences, which thus formed a sort of labyrinth, into which and through which the sheep and lambs were driven at shearing-time, and in it they were sorted out and placed in cotes or pens erected for each sheep-owner. The existence of carefully registered ear-marks, with which each lamb was branded, formed a means of identifying each owner's sheep and lambs. Of course, this gathering brought together all the sheep drivers and herders, the sheep washers and shearers. Vast preparations of food and drink were made for their entertainment, and tents were reared for their occupancy, and, of course, fiddlers and peddlers, like Autolycus, flocked there also, and much amusement and frolicking accompanied the shearing. Even the sheep, panting with their heavy wool when within the folds, and the shorn and shivering creatures running around outside and bleating for their old long-wooled companions, added to the excitement of the scene. Perhaps the maritime occupation of the Islanders made them enjoy with the zest of unwontedness this rural " shore-holiday." But it exists no longer; the island is not now one vast sheep-pasture, and there are no longer any sheep-shearings.

X

SPORTS AND DIVERSIONS

THE Puritans of the first century of colonial life—
the "true New England men," not only of Winthrop
and Bradford's time, but of the slowly degenerating
days of Cotton Mather and Judge Sewall—thought
little and cared little for any form of amusement;

> "Not knowing this, that Heaven decrees
> Some mirth t'adulce man's miseries."

Of them it may be said, as Froissart said of their
ancestors, "They took their pleasures sadly—after
their fashion." " 'Twas no time for New England to
dance," said Judge Sewall, sternly; and indeed it was
not. The struggle of planting colonies in the new,
bleak land left little time for dancing.

The sole mid-week gathering, the only regular diversion of early colonial life, took naturally a religious
and sombre cast, and was found in the "great and
Thursday lecture." "Truly the times were dull when
these things happened," for so eager were the colonists for this sober diversion that it soon became a
pious dissipation. Cotton said, in his "Way of the

Churches," in 1639, that so many lectures did damage to the people ; and the largeness of the assemblies alarmed the magistrates, who saw persons who could ill afford the time from their work, gadding to mid-day lectures in three or four different towns the same week. Young people, not having acquired that safety-valve, the New England singing-school, gladly seized these religious meetings as a pretext and a means for enjoyable communion, and attended in such numbers that the hospitality shown in providing food for the visiting lecture-lovers seemed to be in danger of be-coming a burdensome expense. In 1633 the magis-trates set the lecture hour at one o'clock, that lecture-goers might eat their dinner at noon at home; and they attempted to have each minister give but one lecture in two weeks, and planned that contiguous towns should offer but two temptations a week. But the law-makers overstepped the mark, and the lect-ure and the ministers resumed weekly sway, which they held for a century.

Hawthorne thus described the opening hours of the colonial Lecture-day:

"The breakfast hour being passed, the inhabitants do not as usual go to their fields or work-shops, but remain within doors or perhaps walk the street with a grave sobriety yet a disengaged and unburdened aspect that belongs neither to a holiday nor the Sabbath. And in-deed the passing day is neither, nor is it a common week day, although partaking of all three. It is the Thursday Lecture; an institution which New England has long ago relinquished, and almost forgotten, yet which it would have been better to retain, as bearing relations both to the spiritual and ordinary life. The tokens of its observance, however, which here meet our eyes are of a rather questionable cast. It is in one sense a day of public shame; the day on which transgressors who have made themselves liable to the minor severities of the Puritan law receive their reward of ignominy. At this very moment the constable has bound an idle fellow to the whipping - post and is giving him his deserts with a cat-o-nine-tails. Ever since sunrise Daniel Fairfield has been standing on the steps of the meeting-house, with a halter about his neck, which he is condemned to wear visibly throughout his lifetime; Dorothy Talby is chained to a post at the corner of Prison Lane with the hot sun blazing on her matronly face, and all for no other offence than lifting her hand against her husband; while through the bars of that great wooden cage, in the centre of the scene, we discern either a human being or a wild beast, or both in one. Such are the profitable sights that serve the good people to while away the earlier part of the day."

Not only were criminals punished at this weekly gathering, but seditious books were burned just after the lecture, intentions of marriage were published, notices were posted, and at one time elections were held on Lecture-day. The religious exercises of the day resembled those of the Sabbath and were sometimes five hours in length.

In primitive amusements, the sports of the woods and waters, even a Puritan could find occasional and proper diversion without entering into frivolous and sinful amusement. The wolf, most hated and most destructive of all the beasts of the woods, a "ravening runnagadore," was a proper prey. Wolves were caught in pits, in log pens, in traps; they were also hooked on mackerel hooks bound in an ugly bunch and dipped in tallow, to which they were toled by dead carcasses. The swamps were "beat up" in a wolf-drive or wolf-rout, similar to the English "drift of the forest." A ring of men surrounded a wooded tract and drew inward toward the centre, driving the wolves before them. The excitement of such a wolf-rout, constantly increasing to the end, can well be imagined. The wolves were not always killed outright. Josselyn tells that the inhuman sport of wolf-baiting was popular in New England, and he describes it thus: "A great mastiff held the Wolf. . . . Tying him to a stake we bated him with smaller doggs and had excellent sport, but his hinder legg being broken we soon knocked his brains out." Wolves also were dragged alive at a horse's tail, a sport equally cruel to both animals. These fierce and barbarous traits had been nourished in England by the many bear and bull baitings, and even horse-baitings, and the colonists but carried out here their English training. Wood wrote in his "New England's Prospects:" "No ducking ponds can afford more sport than a lame cormorant and two or three lusty doggs." Though we do not hear of cock-fights, I doubt not the wealthy and sportsmanlike Narragansett planters, who resembled in habits and occupations the Virginian planters, had many a cock-fight, as they had horse-races.

Bears were "hunted with doggs; they take to a tree where they shoot them." Nothing was "more sportfull than bearbayting." Killing foxes was also the "best sport in depth of winter." On a moonlight night the hunters placed a sledge-load of codfish heads on the bright side of a fence or wall, and hiding in the shadow "as long as the moon shineth" could sometimes kill ten of the wary creatures in a night. Squirrel hunts were also prime sport.

Shooting at a mark or at prizes became a popular form of amusement. We read in the *Boston Evening Post* of January 11, 1773: "This is to give Notice That there will be a Bear and a Number of Turkeys set up as a Mark next Thursday Beforenoon at the Punch Bowl Tavern in Brookline."

The "Sports of the Inn yards" found few participants in New England. In 1692 the Andover innkeeper was ordered not to allow the playing of "Dice, Cards, Tables, Quoits, Loggits, Bowles, Ninepins or any other Unlawful Game in his house yard Garden or Backside after Saturday P.M." Henry Cabot Lodge says the shovelboard of Shakespeare's time was almost the only game not expressly prohibited. A Puritan minister, Rev. Peter Thatcher, of Milton, bought in 1679 a "pack of ninepins and bowle," for which he paid five shillings and sixpence, and enjoyed playing with them too; but I fancy few ministers played either that or like games. On the second Christmas, at Plymouth, we find some of the Pilgrims playing pitch-the-bar and stool-ball. Pitch-the-bar was a trial of strength rather than of skill, and was popular with sturdy Nantucket whalers till into this century, though deemed hopelessly plebeian in old England.

We hear of foot-ball being played by Boston boys in Boston streets and lanes; of the Rowley Indians playing it in 1686 on the broad sandy shore, where it was "more easie," since they played barefooted. Dunton adds of their sport: "Neither were they so apt to trip up one anothers feet and quarrel as I have often seen 'em in England"—and I may add, as I have often seen 'em in New England.

Playing-cards — the devil's picture-books — were hated by the Puritans like the very devil; and, as ever with forbidden pleasures, were a constant temptation to Puritan youth. Their importation, use, and sale were forbidden. As late as 1784 a fine of $7 was ordered to be paid for every pack of cards sold; and yet in 1740 we find Peter Fanueil ordering six gross of best King Henry's cards from England. Jolley Allen had cards constantly for sale— "Best Merry Andrew, King Harry and Highland Cards a Dollar per Doz." and also "Blanchards Great Mogul Playing Cards." The fine for selling these cards must have been a dead letter, for we find in the newspapers proof of the prevalence of card-playing.

One use for playing-cards other than their intended one was found in their employment to inscribe invitations upon. Ball invitations were frequently written upon the backs of playing-cards, and dinner invitations also.

In the *Salem Gazette*, in 1784, appeared "New In Laid Cribbage Boxes, Leather Gammon Tables, and Quadrille Pools." In the *Evening Post*, in 1772, may be seen "Quadrille Boxes and Pearl Fishes;" and I do not doubt that many a gay Boston belle or beau (as well as Mrs. Knox) gambled all night at quadrille and ombre, as did their cousins in London. Captain Goelet had many a game of cards in his travels through New England, in 1750.

On April 30, 1722, the *New England Courant* advertised that any gentleman that "had a Mind to Recreate themselves with a Game of Billiards" could do so at a public house in Charlestown.

It is curious to find how eagerly the staid colonists turned to dancing. Mr. Eggleston says:

"The savages themselves were not more fond of dancing than were the colonists who came after them. Dancing schools were forbidden in New England by the authorities but dancing could not be repressed in an age in which the range of conversation was necessarily narrow and the appetite for physical activity and excitement almost insatiable."

Dancing was forbidden in Massachusetts taverns and at weddings, but it was encouraged at Connecticut ordinations. In a letter written by John Cotton, that good man specifies that his condemnation is not of dancing "even mixt" as a whole, but of "lascivious dancing to wanton ditties with amorous gestures and wanton dalliances;" an objection in which I hope he is not singular, an we be not Puritan ministers ; and an objection which makes us suspect, an he were a Puritan minister, that he had been in some very singular company.

In 1713 a ball was given by the governor in Boston, at which light-heeled and light-minded Bostonians of the governor's set danced till three in the morning. As balls and routs began at six in the afternoon, this gave long dancing-hours. On the other hand, we find sober folk reading " An Arrow against Profane and Promiscuous Dancing Drawn out of the Quiver of the Scriptures By the Ministers of Christ at Boston." And though one dancing-master was forbidden room to set up his school, we find that " Abigaill Hutchinson was entered to lern to dance " somewhere in Boston in 1717, probably at the school of Mr. George Brownell. By Revolutionary times old and young danced with zest at balls, at " turtle-frolicks," at weddings. President Washington and Mrs. General Greene "danced upwards of three hours without once sitting down," and General Greene called this diversion of the august Father of his Country " a pretty little frisk." By 1791 we find Rev. John Bennett, in his "Letters to a Young Lady," recommending dancing as a proper and healthful exercise. Queer names did early contra-dances bear: Old Father George, Cape Breton, High Betty Martin, Rolling Hornpipe, Constancy, Orange Tree, Springfield, Assembly, The President, Miss Foster's Delight, Pettycoatee, Priest's House, The Lady's Choice, and Leather the Strap. By Federal times came Federal dances.

Such care was paid by New Englanders to the raising and improving of horses that I presume horse-races did not seem so wicked as card-playing or dancing, for I find hint of a horse-race in the *Boston News Letter* of August 29, 1715, for Jonathan Turner therein challenged the whole country to match his black gelding in a race for a hundred pounds, to take place on Metonomy Common or Chelsea Beach. Many pace-races took place in Narragansett on Little Neck Beach, at which the prizes were silver tankards. And if we can believe Dr. MacSparran, or, rather, since we would not appear to doubt the word of a clergyman, especially upon the speed of a horse, if he took the time of " a little over two minutes " with any care and had a good watch, there must have been some very good sport on Little Neck Beach.

Though the Puritan magistrates denounced shows as a great "mispense of time," yet after a century's existence in the New World, the people was so amusement hungry that all turned avidly to any kind of exhibition, and but little was necessary to make an exhibition. A " Lyon of Barbary " was in Boston in 1716 ; and I believe the " lyons hair," which was "cut by the keeper" and sent by Wait Winthrop to be placed as a strengthening tonic under the armpits of his sickly little grandchild, was abstracted from this very lion. In 1728 another lonely king of the beasts made the round of all the provinces on a cart drawn by four oxen, with as much eclat as if he had been a whole menagerie. He lodged in New London in

Madam Winthrop's barn, and " put up " elsewhere at the very best taverns, as became a royal visitor, yet seems a semi-pathetic figure—a tropical king in slavery and alone in a strange, cold land.

In December, 1733, and in 1734, rivals appeared at a Boston tavern, and were advertised in the *Weekly Rehearsal*.

" A Fine Large White Bear brought from Greenland, the like never been seen before in these Parts of the World. A Sight far preferable to the Lion in the Judgment of all Persons who have seen them both. N.B. He is certainly going to London in about 3 Weeks & his Farewel Speech will be publish'd in a day or two."

" To be seen at the Shop of Mr. Benjamin Runker Tinman near the Market House on Dock Square a very Strange & Wonderful Creature called a Sea Lion lately taken at Monument Pond near Plimouth The like of which never seen in these Paris before. He is Nine Feet long from His Rump to his Head & near 4 feet wide over his back with Four Large Feet & Five Strong Claws on Each. Also Two Large Strong Teeth as white as Ivory sticking out of his mouth five or six Inches long with many other Curiosities too Tedious to mention here. Price Sixpence for a Man or Woman & 2 Pence for a child."

The *Boston Gazette* of April 20, 1741, thus advertised :

" To be seen at the Greyhound Tavern in Roxbury a wild creature which was caught in the woods about 80 miles to the Westward of this place called a Cattamount. It has a tail like a Lyon, its legs are like Bears, its Claws like an Eagle, its Eyes like a Tyger. He is exceedingly ravenous and devours all sorts of Creatures that he can come near. Its agility is surprising.. It will leap 30 feet at one jump notwithstanding it is but 3 months old. Whoever wishes to see this creature may come to the place aforesaid paying one shilling each shall be welcome for their money."

Salem had the pleasure of viewing a "Sapient Dog" who could light lamps, spell, read print or writing, tell the time of day, or day of the month. He could distinguish colors, was a good arithmetician, could discharge a loaded cannon, tell a hidden card in a pack, and jump through a hoop, all for twenty-five cents. About the same time Mr. Pinchbeck exhibited in the same town a "Pig of Knowledge" who had precisely the same accomplishments.

In 1789 a pair of camels went the rounds—"19 hands high, with 4 joints in their hind legs." A mermaid also was exhibited—defunct, I presume—and a living cassowary five feet high, that swallowed stones as large as an egg. A white sea bear appeared in the port of Pollard's Tavern and could be seen for half a pistareen. A forlorn moose was held in bondage at Major King's tavern and shown for nine pence, while to view the "leapord strongly chayned" cost a quarter. The big hog, being a home production, could be seen cheaply—for four pence. It is indeed curious to find a rabbit among "curious wild beasts." The Winthrops had tried to breed rabbits in 1633 and again in 1683, and if they had not succeeded were the only souls known to fail in that facile endeavor. To their shame be it told, Salem folk announced in 1809 a bull-fight at the Half-Way House on the new turnpike, and after the bull-fight a fox-chase. In 1735 John Burlesson had some strange animals to show, and was not always allowed to exhibit them either: " the Lyon, the Black and Whight bare and the Lanechtskipt were shown by me that had their limbs as long as they pleased."

There were also exhibitions of legerdemain—a "Posture Master Boy who performed most surprizing Postures, Transforming Himself into Various Shapes;" performers on the "tort rope;" solar microscopes; "Italian Matcheans or Moving Pictures wherein are to be seen Windmills and Water-mills moving around Ships sayling in the Seas, and various curious figures;" electrical machines; "prospects of London" or of "Royall Pallaces;" but, to their credit and good taste be it recorded, I find no notices of monstrosities either in shape of man or beast. Exhibitions of wax figures were given and museums were formed. Gentlemen sailing for foreign ports were begged to collect for museums and collections of curiosities, and did so in a thoroughly public-spirited manner.

Shortly after the invention of balloons came their advent as popular shows into New England towns. In Hartford they appeared under the pompous title of "Archimedial Phaetons, Vertical Aerial Coaches, or Patent Fœderal Balloons," and the public was notified that "persons of timid nature might enter with full assurance of safety." These fœderal balloons not only served to amuse New Englanders, but were strongly recommended to " Invaletudinarians" as hygienic and medicinal factors, in that through their employment as carriers they caused "sudden revulsion of the blood and humours" to the benefit of the aeronautic travellers.

The first stepping-in of theatrical performances was to the lively tunes of jigs and corams on a stage. In 1713 permission was asked to act a play in the Council House in Boston. Judge Sewall's grief and amazement at this suggestion of " Dances and Scenical Divertessiments " within those solemn walls can well be imagined. Ere long little plays called drolls were exhibited ; puppet shows such as " Pickle Herring," or the "Taylor ryding to Brentford," or " Harlequinn and Scaramouch." About 1750 two young English strollers produced Otway's " Orphans " in a Boston coffee-house. Prompt and strict measures by Boston magistrates nipped in the bud this feeble dramatic plant, and Boston had no more plays for many years.

Many ingenious ruses were invented to avoid the legal obstructions placed in the way of play-acting. " Histrionic academies " tried to sneak in on the stage ; and in 1762 a clever manager gave an entertainment whose playbill I present as the most amusing example of specious and sanctimonious truckling extant.

KINGS ARMS TAVERN—NEWPORT RHODE ISLAND.

On Monday, June 10th, at the Public Room of the above Inn will be delivered a series of

MORAL DIALOGUES

in Five Parts

Depicting the evil effects of jealousy and other bad passions and Proving that happiness can only spring from the pursuit of Virtue.

Mr Douglass—Will represent a noble and magnanimous Moor called Othello, who loves a young lady named Desdemona, and after he marries her, harbours (as in too many cases) the dreadful passion of jealousy.

> *Of jealousy, our beings bane,*
> *Mark the small cause, and the most dreadful pain.*

Mr Allyn—Will depict the character of a specious villain, in the regiment of Othello, who is so base as to hate his commander on mere suspicion, and to impose on his best friend. Of such characters, it is to be feared, there are thousands in the world, and the one in question may present to us a salutary warning.

> *The man that wrongs his master and his friend,*
> *What can he come to but a shameful end?*

Mr Hallam—Will delineate a young and thoughtless officer who is traduced by Mr. Allyn, and, getting drunk, loses his situation and his generals esteem. All young men whatsoever, take example from Cassio.

> *The ill effects of drinking would you see*
> *Be warned and fly from evil company.*

Mr Morris—Will represent an old gentleman, the father of Desdemona, who is not cruel or covetous, but is foolish enough to dislike the noble Moor, his son-in-law, because his face is not white, forgetting that we all spring from one root. Such prejudices are very numerous and very wrong.

> *Fathers, beware what sense and love ye lack,*
> *'Tis crime, not colour, makes the being black.*

Mr Quelch—Will depict a fool who wishes to become a knave, and trusting to one, gets killed by one. Such is the friendship of rogues. Take heed !

> *Where fools would knaves become, how often you'll*
> *Perceive the knave not wiser than the fool.*

Mrs Morris—Will represent a young and virtuous wife, who, being wrongfully suspected, gets smothered (in an Adjoining room) by her husband.

> *Reader, attend, and ere thou goest hence,*
> *Let fall a tear to hapless innocence.*

Mrs Douglass—Will be her faithful attendant, who will hold out a good example to all servants, male and female, and to all people in subjection.

> *Obedience and gratitude,*
> *Are things as rare as they are good.*

Various other Dialogues, too numerous to mention here, will be delivered at night, all adapted to the improvement of the mind and manners. The whole will be repeated on Wednesday and on Saturday. Tickets, six shillings each ; to be had within. Commencement at 7. Conclusion at half past 10 ; in order that every spectator may go home at a sober hour, and reflect upon what he has seen, before he retires to rest.

> God save the King,
> And long may he sway,
> East, north and south
> And fair America.

The Continental Congress of 1774 sought to pledge the colonists to discountenance "all exhibitions of shews, plays, and other expensive diversions and entertainments," and such exhibitions languished naturally in war times ; but with peace came new life to shows and theatres.

We catch a glimpse at Hartford of the "New

Theatre" in 1795. The play began at half after six. Following the English fashion, servants were sent in advance to keep seats for their masters and mistresses. They were instructed to be there "by Five at the Farthest." If ladies "chused to sit in the Pit" a place was partitioned off for them. The admission price was a dollar. There was variety in the entertainment furnished. One actor gave a character recitation entitled "The New Bow Wow." In this he played the "Sly Dog, the Sulky Dog, the Hearty Dog, and many other dogs in his character of Odd Dog."

In 1788 the "Junior Sophister Class" of Yale College gave a theatrical performance, during Election week, of "Tancred and Sigismunda," and followed it with a farce of the students' own composing, relating to events in the Revolutionary War. A letter of Rev. Andrew Eliot is still in existence referring to this presentation, and severely did he reprehend it. Of the farce he wrote, "To keep up the character of these Generals, especially Prescot, they were obliged (I believe not to their sorrow) to indulge in very indecent and profane language." He states that many in the audience were much offended thereat, and says: "What adds to the illegality is that the actors not only were dressed agreeable to the characters they assumed as Men, but female apparell and ornaments were put on some contrary to an express statute. Besides it cost the lads £60." What this reverend complainer would have thought of the multitudinous exhibitions of masculine collegiate skirt-dancing of the present day is impossible to fathom.

There were circuses also in Connecticut. "Mr. Pool The first American Equestrian has erected a Menage at considerable Expence with seats Convenient. Mr. Pool beseeches the Ladies and Gentlemen who honour him with their Presence to bring no Dogs with them." As late as 1828 a bill prohibiting circus exhibitions passed both houses of the Connecticut Legislature, but was all in vain, for that State became the home of circuses and circus-makers.

During the seventeenth century and the first half of the eighteenth century there was little in New England that could properly receive the name of music. Musical instruments and books of musical instruction were rare. I have told the deplorable condition of church music in "The Sabbath in Puritan New England." A feeling of revolt rose in ministers and congregation. In 1712 Rev. Mr. Tuft's music-book appeared. The first organ came to Boston about 1711. The first concert of which I have read was advertised thus in the *New England Weekly Journal* of December 15, 1732:

"This is to inform the Publick That there will be a Consort of Music Perform'd by Sundry Instruments at the Court Room in Wings Lane near the Town Dock on the 28th of this Instant December; Tickets will be deliver'd at the Place of Performance at Five Shillings each Ticket. N.B. No Person will be admitted after Six."

In 1744 a concert was given in Faneuil Hall for the benefit of the poor, and after 1760 concerts were frequent. The universal time for beginning was six

o'clock, and the highest price of admission half a dollar, until after 1790.

Singing-schools, too, were formed, and the bands of
trained singers gave concerts. The story of the progress of New England concert-giving has been most
fully given by Henry M. Brooks, esq., in his delightful book, "Olden Time Music."

Lectures on pneumatics, electricity, and philosophy
were given in Boston as early as 1740, and soon acquired a popularity which they have retained to the
present day.

A very doubtful form of diversion was furnished
to New Englanders at the public expense and in the
performance of public duties. Not only were offend-
ers whipped, set in the stocks, bilboes, cage, or pillory on Lecture-day, but criminals were hung with
much parade before the eyes of the people, as a visi-
ble token of the punishment of evil living. In all
the civil and religious exercises previous to the execution of the sentence, publicity was given to the offender; petty and great malefactors were preached at
when sentenced, and after condemnation were made
public examples—were brought into church and made
the subject of discourse and even of objurgation from
the pulpit. Judge Sewall frequently refers to this
meretricious custom. Under date March 11, 1685,
he says: "Persons crowd much into the old Meeting House by reason of James Morgan (who was a
condemned murderer) and a very exciting and riot-
ous scene took place." This was at a Thursday
lecture, and in the gloomy winter twilight of the

same day the murderer was executed—"turn'd off" as Sewall said—after a parting prayer by Cotton Mather, who had preached over him in the morning. Cotton Mather's sermon and others on Morgan and his crimes, which were preached by Increase Mather and Joshua Moodey, were printed and sold in vast numbers, passing through several editions. Morgan's dying words and confessions were also printed and sold throughout New England by chapmen.

Captain Quelch and six other pirates were captured on June 11, 1704 ; were brought to Boston on the 17th, sentenced on the 19th, and, " the silver oar being carried before them to the place of execution," were hung on the 30th. An " extra " of the *News Letter* says that " Sermons were preached in their Hearing Every Day, And Prayers made daily with them. And they were Catechized and they had many Occasional exhortations ; " but the paper also states, " yet as they led a wicked and vitious life so to appearance they died very obdurately and impenitently hardened in their sin." Sewall gives this painfully particular account of the execution :

"After Dinner about 3 P.M. I went to see the Execution. Many were the people that saw upon Broughtons Hill But when I came to see how the River was covered with People I was amazed ; Some say there were 100 boats. 150 Boats & Canoes saith Cousin Moody of York. He Told them. Mr. Cotton Mather came with Captain Quelch & 6 others for Execution from the Prison to Scarletts Wharf and from thence in Boat to the place of Execution. When the Scaffold was hoisted to a due height the seven Malefactors went up. Mr. Mather pray'd for them standing upon the Boat. Ropes were all fastened to the Gallows save King who was Reprieved. When the Scaffold was let to sink there was such a Screech of the Women that my wife heard it sitting in our Entry next the Orchard and was much surprised at it, yet the wind was sou-west. Our house is a full mile from the place."

In another entry Sewall tells of brazen women jumping up on the cart with a condemned man.

A note was appended by Dr. Ephraim Eliot to the last page of a sermon delivered by his father, Dr. Andrew Eliot, on the Sunday before the execution of Levi Ames, who was hung for burglary October 21, 1773. Ames was present in church, and the sermon was preached at his request. The note runs thus :

"Levi Ames was a noted offender—though a young man, he had gone through all the routine of punishment, and there was now another indictment against him where there was positive proof, in addition to his own confession. He was tried and condemned. His condemnation excited extraordinary sympathy. He was every Sabbath carried through the streets with chains about his ankles, and handcuffed, in custody of the Sheriff officers and constables, to some public meeting, attended by an innumerable number of boys, women and men. Nothing was talked of but Levi Ames. The ministers were successively employed in delivering occasional discourses. Stillman improved the opportunity several times and absolutely persuaded the fellow that he was to step from the cart into Heaven."

One Worcester County murderess was hanged on Boston Common, and to the delight of beholders appeared in a beautiful white satin gown to be "turn'd off."

I think, in reading of the past, that next to executions the most vivid excitement, the most absorbing interest—indeed, the greatest amusement of New Englanders of the half century preceding and that succeeding the Revolutionary War—was found in the lottery. An act of Legislature in 1719 speaks of them as just introduced; but this licensed and highly approved form of gambling quickly had the sanction and participation of the entire community. The most esteemed citizens not only bought tickets, but sold them. Every scheme of public benefit, the raising of every fund for every purpose, was conducted and assisted through a lottery. Harvard, Rhode Island (now Brown University), and Dartmouth College thus increased their endowments. Towns and States thus raised money to pay the public debt. Congregational, Baptist, and Episcopal churches had lotteries "for promoting public worship and the advancement of religion." Canals, turnpikes, bridges, excavations, public buildings were brought to perfection by lotteries. Schools and academies were thus endowed; for instance, the Leicester Academy and the Williamstown Free School. In short, "the interests of literature were supported, the arts encouraged, the wastes of wars repaired, inundations prevented, the burthen of the taxes lessened" by lotteries. Private lotteries were also carried on in great number, as frequent advertisements show; pieces of furniture, wearing apparel, real estate, jewelry, and books being given as prizes. Much deception was practised in those private lotteries.

Though many lotteries were ostensibly for charitable, educational, or other beneficial purposes, the proportion of profit applied to such purposes was small. The Newbury Bridge Lottery sold ten thousand dollars' worth of tickets to raise one thousand dollars. The lottery to assist in rebuilding Faneuil Hall was to secure one-tenth of the value of tickets. Harvard College hoped to have twelve and a half per cent. The glowing advertisements of "Rich Wheels," "Real & Truly Fortunate Offices," "Lucky Numbers," "Full Drawings," appealed to every class; the poorest could buy a quarter of a ticket as a speculation. New England clergymen seemed specially to delight in this gambling excitement.

The evil of the system could not fail to be discovered by intelligent citizens. Judge Sewall, ever thoughtful, wrote his protest to friends when he found advertisements of four lotteries in one issue of the *Boston News Letter*. Though I have seen lottery tickets signed by John Hancock, he publicly expressed his aversion to the system, and Joel Barker and others wrote in condemnation. By 1830 the whole community seemed to have wakened to a sense of their pernicious and unprofitable effect, and laws were passed prohibiting them.

The sports and diversions herein named, of the first century of the Puritan commonwealth, were, after all, joined in by but a scanty handful of junketers. We see in our picture of the olden times no revellers, but a "crowd of sad-visaged people moving duskily through a dull gray atmosphere," who found, as Carlyle said, that work was enjoyment enough. The Pilgrim Fathers had been saddened with war and pestilence, with superstition, with exile, still they had as a contrast the keen novelty of life in the picturesque new land. The sons had lost all the romance and were more narrow, more intolerant. But we must not think them unhappy because they thought it no time for New England to dance. There be those nowadays who care not for dancing, nor for the playing of games, yet are not unhappy. There be, also, I trow, those who fare not at fairs, and show not at shows, and would fain read sober books or study their Bible as did the Puritans, and yet are cheerful. And perhaps also there is a singular little band of those who love not the play—a few such I wot of Puritan blood—yet are not sorrowful. Hawthorne said: "Happiness may walk soberly in dark attire as well as dance lightsomely in a gala-dress." And I cannot doubt that good Judge Sewall found as true and deep a pleasure—albeit a melancholy one—in slowly leading, sable-gloved and sable-cloaked, the funeral procession of one of the honored deputies through narrow Boston streets, as did roystering Morton in marshalling his drunken revellers at noisy Merrymount.

XI

BOOKS AND BOOK-MAKERS

THERE was no calling, no profession more reputable, more profitable in early colonial days than the trade of book-selling. President Dunster, of Harvard College, in his pursuance of that business, gave it the highest and best endorsement; and it must be remembered that all the book-sellers were publishers as well, books being printed for them at their expense. John Dunton, in his "Life and Errors," has given us a very distinct picture of Boston book-sellers and their trade toward the end of the seventeenth century. He landed at that port in 1686 with a large and expensive venture of books "suited to the genius of New England," and he says he was about as welcome to the resident book-sellers as "Sowr ale in Summer." Nevertheless they received him cordially and hospitably, and he in turn was an equally generous rival; for he drew eulogistically the picture of the four book-dealers which that city then boasted. Mr. Phillips was "very just, very thriving, young, witty, and the most Beautiful man in the town of Boston." Mr. Brunning, or Browning, was a "complete book-seller, generous and trustworthy." Dunton says:

"There are some men will run down the most elaborate peices only because they had none of their Midwifery to bring them into public View and yet shall give the greatest encomiums to the most Nauseous trash when they had the hap to be concerned in it."

But Browning would promote a good book whoever printed it. Mr. Cam bell, the third book-dealer, was "very industrious, dresses All-a-mode and I am told a young lady of Great Fortune is fallen in love with him." Of Mr. Usher, the remaining book-trader, Dunton asserts:

"He makes the best figure in Boston. He is very rich, adventures much to sea, but has got his Estate by Book selling."

Usher was a book-maker, undertaker, and adventurer, doubtfully attractive or desirable appellations nowadays; but what higher praise could have been given in colonial tongue? He would have angrily resented being dubbed a publisher; that name was assigned to and monopolized by the town-crier. Usher died worth £20,000, a tidy sum for those days.

Happy, indeed, were all the Boston book-sellers; blessed of the gods! rich, witty, modish, beloved, beautiful! The colony was sixty years old, opulent, prosperous, and fashionable; but a book-seller cut the best figure. Surely the book trade had in Boston a glorious ushering in, a golden promise which has not yet deserted it.

Book-printing, too, was a highly honored calling.

The first machine for the craft and mystery of printing was set up at Cambridge in 1639, and for twenty-
three years the president of Harvard College was responsible for its performances.   Then official licensers
were appointed to control its productions, and not till
a decade of years before the Declaration of Independence were legal restraints removed from the colonial
press.

The first printer in the colony, Steeven Daye, was
about as bad a printer as ever lived, as his work in
the Bay Psalm-Book proves; and he spent a term
in Cambridge jail, and was altogether rather trying in
his relations with the godly ministers who were associated with him in his printery.   The second printer
had to sleep in a cask after he landed, but he died
with a fortune, a true forerunner of the self-made men
of America.   The third printer, Johnson, having a
wife in England, was " brought up " and bound over
before the court not to seduce the affections of the
daughter of printer No. 2.   The next Bostonians who
tried their hands at the mechanical part of book-
making—the printing and binding—were two of the
most prominent citizens; Captain Green, a worthy
man, the father of nineteen children by one wife and
eleven by another, and rich, too, in spite of the thirty
Green olive-branches; and Judge Sewall, also, as
Cotton Mather said, " edified and beautified with
many children "—fourteen in all.   Truly, book-mak-
ing did prosper a man mightily both at home and
abroad in colonial days.

In a book-printer's wife, the mother of the nineteen children, did Dunton find his ideal New England wife; in a book-printer did he find his most agreeable companion.

"To name his trade will convince the world he was a man of good sense and understanding. He was so facetious and obliging and his conversation such that I took a great delight in his company."

So it may be seen that the book-sellers were rivalled by the book-printers—equally rich and witty though not so beautiful. To the credit of both callings, then and for a century to follow, redounds the fact that almost to a man they were deacons in the church. Mayhap their worldly and family prosperity was the reward of their piety. As nine-tenths of the authors were ministers, and the publishers all deacons, the church had at that time what might be called a monopoly of the book trade.

Dunton had a vast interest in the fair sex, owning plainly that he had a " heart of Wax, Soft, and Soon mellowing," though he was careful on every page to make everything seem perfectly straight and proper for the suspicious perusal of his English wife; but any nineteenth-century reader can read between the lines. His famous long-winded eulogies of the Boston virgin, the wife, the widow, "Madam Brick the flower of Boston," and the half widow "Parte per Pale, Madam Toy," whose husband was at sea; and his long rides with one or the other of them a-pillionback behind him, and his tedious conversations with them on platonics, the blisses of matrimony, and the chief causes of love, show plainly that he had a "wandering eye." He had a deal to say also of his lady customers (who were much the same in olden times as nowadays)—one simple soul who turned over his books rather vacantly till he asked her "in Joque" whether she wanted "Tom Thumb" (a penny chapbook). To his surprise she answered, "Yes;" and he said, still guying, "in Folio and with marginal notes?" and the dull creature replied, "Oh the best." Another hectored him by constantly changing her mind:

"Reach me that book, yet—let it alone; but let me see it however, and yet its no great matter either."

Another sedate Boston dame wished "The School of Venus," to which he reprovingly answered that he had best give her instead "The School of Virtue." Another, to whom he gave a sad setting off (more than hinting at a painted face, though she were a Puritan), wanted plays and romances and "Books of Gallantry." He adds:

"But she was a good Customer to me. Whilst I took her money I humoured her pride, and paid her (I blush to say it) a mighty observance."

He speaks plainly too of the men book-buyers. One Mr. Gouge, who was also "a Secret Friend to the Fair Sex," bought to give away two hundred copies of a book written by Parson Gouge, his father. Another "young beau who boasts more Villany than he ever committed bought a many of books;" hence

Dunton tolerated the "Young Spark's" demoralizing acquaintance. Mr. Thorncomb, another book-dealer from London, also bought of him, and, with the ever prevailing luck was "Acceptable to the Fair Sex, so extremely charming as makes 'em fond of being in his Company. However he is a virtuous person and deserved all the Respect they shewed him." Nor can I doubt, from the pervasive spirit of his books, that Dunton too found favor with the fair.

Though he spoke so warmly of individual purchasers and so positively of the wealth of his ilk in Boston, his own venture was not vastly prosperous. He took back to England but £400. He gave the Boston Yankees, too, rather a bad name in commercial transactions, saying :

"There is no trading for a stranger with them but with a Grecian Faith which is not to part with your own ware without ready Money ; for they are generally very backward in their payments ; great censors about other Mens manner but Extremely Careless about their own. When you are dealing with 'em you must look upon 'em as at cross purposes and read 'em like Hebrew backward ; for they seldom speak & mean the same thing but like the Watermen Look one way & row another."

Josselyn gave them no better name, saying :

"Their leading men are damnable rich, inexplicably covetous and proud ; like Ethiopians, white in the teeth only ; full of ludification and injurious dealing."

Of Dunton's patrons the majority were ministers, and I hope all the reverend gentlemen were as prompt payers as they were liberal purchasers. Since Dunton called ministers "the greatest benefactors to Booksellers," I think they were not included in his black list. Surely Cotton Mather was not, for he gave away one thousand books in one year, and I know he paid for them too. One Boston school-master, however, bought £200 worth of books, and when we consider the excessively small pay of members of that calling at that time, we feel that he showed a liberal interest in promoting in every manner the spread of learning, and only trust that he paid the bill promptly.

In 1719 there was but one book-shop in New York, but of cultured Boston Neal wrote at that date : "The Exchange is surrounded with booksellers' shops which have a good trade. There are five Printing Presses." Succeeding years did not change the luck of the craft in Boston, nor dim its honors, still wealth and love poured in on its members. The names of Henchman and Hancock show the opulence ; while Knox, in war and love alike prospered, winning the wealthy "belle of Massachusetts" for his bride, and winning equal glory with his sword in the Revolution. In other New England towns did book-publishing succeed, though Boston's earlier start, its leading position, and its more carefully preserved history give it place as a type of the whole province.

And now, what was the fruit of all this fairly garnished and richly nourished tree? What did these prosperous New England book-merchants bring forth in the first century of book-printing in the province?

What return did they make for all the romantic and material support given them? No love-poems or mild tales of gallantry, as you might expect from their alleged fascinating traits, but, instead, an almost unvaried production of dreary and dull funeral, execution, wedding, election, and baptismal sermons, and of psalm-books, with here and there a "two penny jeering gigge," or perhaps an anagram or acrostic or "pindarick," on some virtuous citizen or industrious dame, recently deceased. In business relations the deacon prevailed powerfully over the gallant. If, as Tyler says, the New England theocracy was a social structure resting on a book, that corner-stone was the Bay Psalm-Book and the walls above it were built of sermons. These sermons seem to us technical, sapless, and jejune, "as soporific as a bed of poppies," but they show the intelligence, energy, and assiduity of the writers just as plainly as they show the gloomy theology and sad earnestness of the time. And though no one now reads them, we profoundly respect them, for they have been conned by our honored forefathers with more studious and loving attention than falls to the lot of most modern books, no matter what their subject or who their author.

I have told at length the story of the publication of the Bay Psalm-Book and of other psalm-books printed and used in New England, in "The Sabbath in Puritan New England" and I need not dwell upon it here.

The first book or tract printed in Boston was in

1675—an execution sermon, by Increase Mather, "The Wicked Man's Portion." The first book printed in Connecticut was the "Saybrook Confession and Platform," in 1710. The first book of any considerable size printed in Rhode Island was "An Apology for the True Christian Divinity," issued in 1729.

There were a number of books for the Indians in the Indian tongue which no one but Hon. J. Hammond Trumbull could now read an he would; also a few histories of the Indian wars; and Thomas Prince published by subscription an exceedingly dull chronological History of New England. As he began his history with year 1, first month and sixth day—and Adam, he had tired out even pious Bostonians by the time he reached New England; and subscriptions and subscribers languished till the book died unmourned just when the year 1633 had been caught up with. The "Simple Cobler of Agawam" made a vast sensation with his scurrilous bombs. There were a few volumes of poems printed; one by "the Tenth Muse," Anne Bradstreet, of whose songs pious and cautious John Norton said (and evidently believed what he said too) that if Virgil could have read them he would have condemned his own work to the flames. Michael Wigglesworth's "Day of Doom," that epic of hell-fire and damnation which fairly chokes us with its sulphurous fumes, was widely read and deeply venerated; in fact it was a great popular success. Fifteen hundred copies were sold in the first year, one copy to each thirty-five inhabitants of New

England—a proportion showing a commercial success unsurpassed in modern times. It was printed also on broadsides, in a cheap form, and hawked over the country by chapmen in order to further spread its lurid and baleful shadow. The dull but sympathetic "Meat out of the Eater" by the same author quickly went through five editions. "New England's Crisis," "A Posie from Old Mr. Dods Garden," "A Looking Glasse for New England," and "The Origin of the Whalebone Petticoat—a Satyr," end the monotonous list of poetry. Fully three-quarters of the entire number of publications proceeded from the prolific Mather stock, and of course bore the pompous, verbose, Mather traits of authorship. Cotton Mather had the felicity of having published as his share of "New England's First Fruits" a list to make a modern author green with envy—three hundred and eighty-two different works; three hundred of these may be seen in the library of the American Antiquarian Society : not all were brought out in America, however. His "Magnalia" was printed in England, and the exigences and vicissitudes of publication at that time are fully told in his diary ; also the exalted and idealized view which he took of authorship. At the first definite plan which he formulated in his mind of his history of New England, he "cried mightily to God ; " and he went through a series of fasts and vigils at intervals until the book was completed, when he held extended exercises of secret thanksgiving. Prostrate on his study floor, in the dust, he joyfully received full assurance in his heart from God that his work would be successful. But writing the book is not all the work, as any author knows; and he then had much distress and many troubled fasts over the best way of printing it, of transporting it to England; and when at last he placed his "elaborate composures" on shipboard, he prayed an entire day. No ascetic Papist ever observed fast days more vigorously than did Cotton Mather while his book was on its long sea-voyage and in England. He sent it in June in the year 1700, and did not hear from it till December. What a thrill of sympathy one feels for him! Then he learned that the printers were cold; the expense of publication would be £600, a goodly sum to venture; it was "clogged by the dispositions" of the man to whom it was sent; it was delayed and obstructed; he was left strangely in the dark about it; months passed without any news. Still his faith in God supported him. At last a sainted Christian came forward in London, a stranger, and offered to print the book at his own expense and give the author as many copies as he wished. That was in what Carlyle called "the Day of Dedications and Patrons, not of Bargains with Booksellers." In October, 1702, after two and a half long years of waiting, one copy of the wished-for volume arrived, and the author and his dearest friend, Mr. Bromfield, piously greeted it with a day of solemn fasting and praise.

Can the contrast of that day with the present, can the character of Cotton Mather be more plainly shown than by this story of the publication of the "Magnalia?" Many anxious days did he pass over other manuscripts. Some were lost in London for seven years. One book disappeared entirely from his ken, but was recovered by his heirs. His most important and largest work, the six folio volumes of his "Biblia Americana," pursued by "Strange Frowns of Heaven" could not find a publisher and still is unprinted. Cotton Mather survived his own era, his congenial atmosphere, and, whether he was conscious of it or not, was indeed, as Dexter called him, a literary dodo, an isolated relic of early fantastic methods of composition. His work was not, as Prince said, "agreeable to the Gust of his Age." Even the name of Mather, all-powerful in New England, could not place the "Biblia Americana" in the press.

There were no American novels in those early days. The first book deserving the appellation that was printed in New England was "intituled" "The Power of Sympathy, or the Triumph of Nature—A Novel founded on truth and dedicated to the Young Ladies of America." It appeared in 1789. Four years later came "The Helpless Orphan, or The Innocent Victim of Revenge," and then "The Coquette, or the History of Eliza Wharton."

The only book that was written by a woman and published in New England during the first century of New England printing, was a collection of the poems of Anne Bradstreet. A few—very few—pamphlets by women authors of that date are also known : "The Confession of Faith—A Summary of Divinity drawn up by a young Gentlewoman in the 25th year of her Age ;" Mrs. Elizabeth Cotton's "Peculiar

Treasure of the Almighty King Opened;" Elizabeth White's "Experience;" Mary Rowlandson's pathetic account of her captivity—these are all. Hannah Adams was the first New England women to adopt literature as a profession.

Doubtless many Puritans shared Governor Winthrop's opinion of literary women, which that tolerant and gentle man expressed thus:

" The Governor of Hartford upon Connecticut came to Boston, and brought his wife with him (a godly young woman and of special parts) who was fallen into a sad infirmity, the loss of her understanding and reason which had been growing upon her divers years by occasion of her giving herself wholly to reading and writing, and had written many books. Her husband being very loving and tender of her, was loath to grieve her; but he saw his error when it was too late. For if she had attended her household affairs, and such things as belong to women, and not gone out of her way and calling to meddle in such things as are proper for men, whose minds are stronger, etc., she had kept her wits, and might have improved them usefully and honorably in the place God had set her."

I know of no illustrated books printed New England in the seventeenth century, nor any with frontispieces or portraits. In 1723 a yortrait of Increase Mather appeared in his Life, which was written by monopolizing Cotton Mather. It was a poor thing, being engraved in London by John Sturt. When Peter Pelham came to Boston about 1725 and started as a portrait engraver, and married the Widow Copley with her thriving tobacco shop, he engraved and published many likenesses of authors and ministers, some of which were bound with their books, others sold singly by subscription. The mezzotint of Cotton Mather, made in 1727, sold for two shillings. Hubbard's Narrative had a map in 1677 ; and in 1713 the lives of Dr. Faustus, Friar Bacon, Conjurors Bungay and Vanderwart were printed conjointly in a volume " with cuts "—perhaps the earliest illustrated New England book, unless we except the New England Primer. " The Prodigal Daughter, or the Disobedient Lady Reclaimed" had "curious cuts ; " so also did the " Parents Gift " in 1741, and " A Present for a Servant Maid." " Pilgrim's Progress " was printed in Boston in an illustrated edition in 1744. But for any handsomely illustrated books American readers sent, until Revolutionary times, to England.

There were, however, at a later date, some few books printed with special elegance, with broad margins. The " Discourse on the United Submission to Higher Powers" had some copies that were printed on pages ten inches by seven and a quarter inches in size, while the regular edition was only six by six and a half inches. A letter is in existence of Governor Trumbull's ordering that some copies of the funeral sermon preached at his wife's death be printed on heavy writing paper. Copies of the first edition of the " Magnalia " also were issued on large paper and owned in New England, but of course that work was done in London.

The printing of the earliest books was generally poor, showing the work of inexperienced and unaccustomed hands; but the paper was good, sometimes of fine quality, and always strong. The type was fairly good and clear until Revolutionary times, when paper, ink, and type, being made by new workmen out of the poorest materials, were bad beyond belief, producing, in fact, an almost unreadable page. Throughout the first half of the eighteenth century the books printed in New England compared favorably with the ones imported from England at that date, and in the special case of the "Poetical Oblation"—a fine quarto, offered by Harvard College to George III. on his accession to the throne, the typography is exquisite. For the early binding but one word can be said—that of praise. All these old books had Charles Lamb's desideratum of a volume, were "strong backed and neat bound." Well dressed was the morocco, the leather, the vellum, parchment, or basil, firmly was it glued in place, well-sewed were the leaves—loudly can we sing the goodness and true worth of colonial bookbinding.

In many New England libraries and collections may be seen specimens of colonial printing and binding; the library of the American Antiquarian Society is particularly rich in such ancient treasures. Some of the books from Cotton Mather's library may there be found, that library which Dunton called the glory of New England, and which he said was the largest privately owned collection of books that he had ever seen; but many of them were burned in the sacking of Boston by the British. It consisted of over seven thousand printed volumes and many manuscripts, and its estimated value was £8,000. The majority of these volumes was naturally upon divinity.

We can also form an idea of a New England library at a somewhat earlier date, for the list of books in Elder Brewster's library has been preserved. They numbered four hundred. Of these books, sixty-two were in Latin and three hundred in English. There were forty-eight folios and one hundred and twenty-one octavos. This was quite a bulky and heavy library for transportation to and through that new country. All were not imported at one time, as the succession of dates shows. Brewster purchased from time to time the best books brought out in England on subjects which interested him, until it was really a rich exegetical collection, and may possibly have been used as a circulating one. Nearly all the number were religious, theological, or historical books; fourteen were in rhyme. Among the poems were "A Turncoat of the Times," Spenser's "Prosopopeia," "The Scyrge of Drunkenness," a "Description of a Good Wife," the ballad of "The Maunding Soldier," and Wither's works. One might have been a tragedy, "Messalina," but there were no other dramatic works.

Other benefactors of booksellers had good libraries. Parson Hooker left behind him £300 worth of books in an estate of £1,336. Parson Wareham had £82 worth in an estate of £1,200. Rev. Ebenezer Pemberton left, in 1717, books which made one thousand lots in an auction, for which the first book catalogue

ever compiled in New England was printed.   Even
by 1723 the library of Harvard College contained
none of the works of Addison, Bolingbroke, Young,
Swift, Prior, Steele, Dryden, or Pope.   In 1734, the
catalogue of T. Cox, a prominent Boston bookseller,
did not contain the "Spectator" nor the works of
Shakespeare or Milton.   The literary revival of the
time of Queen Anne was evidently but little felt in
New England during its inception.   The facile and
constant quotation from the ancient classics show
how constantly and thoroughly the latter were studied.

Among early New England publications we must
not fail to speak of the omnipresent almanac.   Ere
there was a New England Psalm-Book there was a New
England Almanac, and succeeding years brought new
ones forth in flocks.   Though Charles Lamb included
almanacs in his catalogue of "books which are no
books," and the founder of the Bodleian Library
would not admit that they were books and excluded
them from the shelves of his library, when New England philomaths and philodespots numbered such
honored names as Mather, Dudley, Sewall, Chauncey,
Brattle, Ames, and Holyoke, New England Puritans
must have deemed almanacs to be books, and so do
we.   In many a colonial household where the Bible
and psalm-book formed the sole standing library, the
almanac was the only annual book-comer that crossed
the threshold and lodged under the roof-tree.   On
a nail by the side of the great fireplace hung proudly
and prominently the Family Almanac, the Ephemeris.

This Family Almanac was a guide, counsellor, and friend; a magazine, cyclopædia, and jest-book; was even a spelling-book. It was consulted by every member of the household on every subject, save possibly religion—for that they had the best of all books. The planters learned from it meteorological, astronomical, thaumaturgical, botanical, and agricultural facts—or rather what the editor stated as facts. Social customs and peculiarities and ethics were also touched upon in a manner suited to the requirements and capacity of the reader; medical and hygienic advice were given for man and beast, ending with the quaint warning to use before and after taking that unfashionable medicine, prayer. Wit, history, romance, poetry, all contributed to the almanac. The printer turned an extra penny by advertising various articles that he had for sale, from negro slaves to garden seeds. So, in addition to what the original readers learned, we now find an almanac a most suggestive record of the olden times.

As with many colonial books, the most attractive part of an almanac is not always the printed contents, but the interlined comments of the original owner. He kept frequently an account of his scanty and sparse purchases; from them we gain a knowledge of the price of commodities in his time. We learn also upon how little a New England planter could live, how little money he spent. He kept a record of the births, weights, and measures of his family; he entered the purchase and number of his lottery tickets (but I never found the proud and happy statement of a lottery prize). He wrote therein Greek verse, as did John Cotton. He entered wig-making and hair-dressing accounts, as did Thomas Prince. He kept the amount of beer and cider he made and drank, and the sad statement of deaths in the neighborhood; such grim entries are seen as these made by old Ezra Stiles: "This day Ethan Allen died and went to Hell." "This day died Joseph Bellamy and went to Heaven, where he can dictate and domineer no longer." President Stiles did not foresee that his great-grandson would be Joseph Bellamy's also, and would plan a social reform more vast in its changes than the really sensible scheme he thought out, of "uniting and cementing his offspring by transfusing to distant generations certain influential principles," and of benefiting the growing population of the New World by carefully planned and wide-spread marriages with virtuous and pious Stileses.

Of course the almanac-owner kept account of the weather—a brave record through January and February and March; then, lessening his zeal as spring-planting began, the hard-working summer months have clean pages; while a remorseful energy in November and December ofttimes made him renew in the smoke-dried almanac his crabbed entries. Hence from contemporary evidence does old New England life seem all winter, all bitter cold and fierce rains and harsh winds; yet there were surely some warm summer days and cheerful sunshine, so smoothly serene as to gain no record.

The relations between book-publishers and authors,

between book-publishers and the public, were from earliest days most friendly. There was much polite exchange of compliments; the intelligence of the public was always mightily flattered and shown up in a very civil fashion in such manner as this :

"A New Edition of the really beautiful & sentimental Novel Armine and Elvira Is this day published price 9d sewed in blue paper. To the Ladies in particular and others the lovers of Sentiment and Poetick Numbers this Novel is recommended, to them it will afford a delightful Repast. To others it is not an object."

"For the pleasing entertainment of the Polite Part of Mankind I have printed the most beautiful Poems of Mr. Stephen Duck the famous Wiltshire Poet. It is a full Demonstration to me that the People of New England have a fine Taste for good Sense and polite Learning having already sold 1200 of these Poems."

Though Stephen Duck appealed to polite and literate New Englanders just as he became the rage in old England, his name is now almost forgotten.

It must have inclined the public most favorably to a book to be told that the volume is "intended only for the highly virtuous ; " that "the glowing pen of the author brought this token into life solely from Admiration of a community fitted by amazing Intelligence to receive it : " that

" 'Tis said with truth by a secret but ingenious New England minister that no town is so worthy the vendue of this pleasing book as these polite gentlemen and gentlewomen to whom it will be on Friday offered."

Authors, if not authoresses, were treated with much respect and encouragement. Indeed, they were urged to write. Books printed by subscription were the rule, and, as an inducement, the names of subscribers were printed in a list at the end of the book, and an extra copy was given for every six numbers subscribed for. The "undertakers" did not always trouble themselves to deliver the book when printed. A notice was posted, or printed in a newspaper, advising subscribers pretty sharply that their copies (which had apparently been paid for in advance) must be sent for within a certain time or the books would be "sold to others desiring." One American poet, the author of "War—An Heroic Poem," a work which has been lost to us, threatened to prosecute his patrons for not taking his book. Sometimes the printer of the book also seized the opportunity of the large circulation to drum up delinquent citizens who had not paid him at previous dates for news letters, sermons, funeral verses, etc. One of the first books printed in Hartford was paid for largely by a man who ran a woollen mill in the vicinity. He took the convenient occasion to thriftily forward his own trade by having printed and bound with the poems, and thus distributing to sheep-farmers and farm-wives in the surrounding towns, full instructions about preparing the wool to be sent to him.

Frequently the notices in the newspapers bore, in quaint wording, warm testimony to the popularity of a book. "The above book is advertised by the desire of numbers who have read and admired it." "If to raise the soul to heights of honourable pride is not unworthy so great a mind, praise of this book may be given, though needless, since many request it." " Many curious gentlemen formerly buying their books in London now wish to buy only in New England where so acute a manner of composure is found." " For the polite and inquisitive part of Mankind in New England these poetick fancies are highly conformed as many residents testify by their frequent perusal and approval."

Public encouragement to aspiring authors was not lacking; this advertisement in the *New England Weekly Journal* of March, 1728, is indeed delightful :

" There is now preparing for the Press, and may upon Suitable Encouragement be communicated to the Publick, a Miscellany of Poems of Severall Hands and upon severall occasions some of which have already been Published and received the Approbation of the best Judges with many more very late performances of equal if not superior Beauty which have never yet seen the Light ; if therefore any Ingenious Gentlemen are disposed to contribute towards the erecting of a Poetickal Monument for the Honour of This Country Either by their Generous Subscriptions or Composures, they are desired to convey them to Mr. Daniel Henchman or the Publisher of this Paper by whom they will be received with Candour and Thankfulness."

Just fancy the effect of a similar advertisement in a prominent newspaper of to-day ! How composures would flow in from the ingenious gentlemen who love to see themselves in print! What a poetical monument could be reared—to the very sky! I have never seen in any colonial newspaper any subsequent references to this proposed collection or miscellany of composures, and I know of no book that was published at that time which could answer the description, so I suspect the well-laid plan came to naught. The specimens of local and ephemeral poetry that were printed in the colonial press in succeeding years make it easy to comprehend the failure of the project: the villanously rhymed effusions fairly imposthumate all the ribald vulgarity of the times; coarseness and dulness of subject and thought being rivalled only by the super-coarseness of the verbiage. I do not say that the newspapers provoked these stupid rhymes, which are about as much poetry as is a game of crambo; but I do not find them until "newspaper-time," and fear the extra circulation through the weekly press may be held partly responsible.

A book called "A Collection of Poems by Several Hands" apparently was gathered by methods similar to the one shown by the advertisement just quoted. It was printed in 1744, and was a puerile and banal collection containing but few good verses, and was apparently made expressly to show off the literary accomplishments of Mather Byles, who was what Carlyle would call an intellectual dapperling.

Book-auctions, held first in England in 1676, formed one of the rare diversions in the provinces, and were apparently largely attended by "sentimentalists," as one book-dealer called book-buyers. The business of book-auctioneering was called, in the bombastic language of the times, "the sublimest Auxiliary which Science Commerce and Arts either has or perhaps ever will possess," while the bookseller was called "Provedore to the Sentimentalists and Professor of Book Auctioneering." These sales or vendues were frequently held at taverns.

At a very early day intelligent and progressive Bostonians established a public library. By the year 1673 bequests had been made to such an institution, and consignments deemed suitable for it had been sent to Boston by London booksellers. All these books were properly sober and pious. The Prince library, that first large American book collection, which was conceived and started by Thomas Prince in 1703, was nobly planned and nobly carried out, and deserved more gratitude and more care than it received at modern hands.

But many towns had no public library, hence much friendly exchange and lending of books took place between book-owners and neighbors, sometimes apparently without the owner's consent or knowledge. The newspapers, among their sparse advertisements, have many such as this simply naïve one in the *Boston News Letter* of July 7, 1712:

"A certain Person having lent two Books viz; Rushworths Collections & Fullers Holy War & forgotten unto whom; These are desiring the Borrower to be so kind as to return said Books unto Owner."

Or this sarcastic request in the *Connecticut Courant*.

"The gentleman who took the second volume of Bacons Abridgment from Mr. David Balls bedroom on the 18th of November would do well to return it to the owner whose name he will find on the 15th Page. If he choose rather to keep it the owner wishes him to call and take the rest of the set."

Another Connecticut man is meekly asked to "return the 3rd Vol of Don Quixote & take the 4th instead if he chuse."

Connecticut folk seemed to be particularly given to this slipshod fashion of promiscuous and unlicensed book-borrowing, if we can trust the apparent proof given by Connecticut newspapers in their many advertisements of lost books. In some notices it is darkly hinted that "specifications of books long lent have been given" (to the sheriff perhaps); and again, a meek suggestion that the owner wishes to read a long missing volume and would be grateful for an opportunity to do so. One ungallant soul advertised for "the she-person that borrowed Mr. Thos. Browns Works from a gentleman she is well acquainted with."

There was not the redeeming excuse for non-return sometimes given by like "desuming deadheads" nowadays, that the owner's name had been forgotten, for the inscription "Perley Morse, His Book," or "Catey Bradford, Her Book," or whatever the name might be, was quickly and repeatedly written by

each colonial owner as soon as the book was acquired.

Frequently also the dates and places of residence
appear. Even the very dates of ownership and the
quaint old names are interesting. Bathsheba Spald-
ing, Noca Emmons, Elam Noyes, Titherming Layton,
Engrossed Bump, Sally Box, Tilly Minching, Zeru-
shaddi Key, Comfort Vine—these are a few of the
odd signatures I have found in old books.

Readers also had a pleasant habit of leaving a sign-
manual on the last page of a book, thus : "Timothy
Pitkin perlegit A.D. 1765," "Cotton Smith perlegit
1740." A clear-speaking lesson are such records to
this generation—a lesson of patience and diligence.
How we venerate, with what awe we regard the name
of Timothy Pitkin, and know that he lived to read
through that vast folio—the first ever printed in
America—the "Complete Body of Divinity," a folio
of over nine hundred double-columned, compactly
printed pages! And yet, why should not Timothy
Pitkin live through reading it when Samuel Willard
lived through writing it ? Entries of dates in old
Bibles frequently show that those sainted old Chris-
tians had read entirely through that holy book ten
times in regular order.

The handwriting in all these ancient books is very
different from our modern penmanship, invariably
bearing an appearance not exactly of much labor, but
of much care, as if the writer did not use a pen every
day—did not become too familiar with that weighty
implement, and hence had a vast respect for it when

he did take it in hand. Every *t* is crossed, every *i* is dotted, every *a* and *o* perfectly rounded, every tail of every *g* and *y* and *z* is precisely twisted in colonial script. I think the very trouble and preparation incident to writing conduced to the finish and elegance of the penmanship. No stylographic pens were used in those days, but instead, a carefully prepared quill; and the ink was made of ink-cake or ink-powder dissolved in water; or, more troublesome still, home-made ink, tediously prepared with nutgalls, walnut or swamp maple bark, or iron filings steeped in vinegar and water, or copperas.

Special pains were taken in writing a name in a book. Penmanship was almost a fine art in colonial days, the one indispensable accomplishment of a school teacher; and he was often hired to exercise it in writing a name "perspicuously" in a book. Sometimes the owner's name is seen drawn with much care in a little wreath or circle of ornamentation. This may be what Judge Sewall refers to with so much pride when he speaks of "writing a name" in a gift-book, or it may be what was known as "conceits" or "fine knotting."

The colonists had a very reprehensible habit, which (save for the pains taken in writing) might be called book-scribbling. Rude rhymes and sentiments are often found with the past owner's name, and form a title-page lore which, ill-spelt and simple as the verses are, have an interest to the antiquary of which the writer never dreamed. They consist chiefly of adjurations to honesty, specially with regard to the special volume thus inscribed :

> "Steal not this book my honest friend,
>   For fear the gallows will be your End."

> "If you dare to steal this Book
>   The Devil will catch you on his Hook."

This was accompanied by the outline of a very spirited "personal devil" with a pitchfork and an enormous gridiron.

Still another appealed to terrors :

> "This is Hanah Moxon Her book
>   You may just within it Look
>   You had better not do more
>   For old black Satan's at the Door
>   And will snatch at stealing hands
>   Look behind you!   There He Stands."

This had a tail-piece of an open door with a very black forked tail thrust out of it.

In a leather-bound Bible was seen this rhyme :

> "Evert Jonson His book
>   God Give him Grase thair in to look
>   not only to looke but to understand
>   that Larning is better than Hous or Land
>   When Land is Gon & Gold is spent
>   then larning is most Axelant
>   When I am dead & Rotton
>   If this you see Remember me
>   Though others is forgotton."

Different portions of this script have been seen in many books.

Four rhymes seem to be specially the property of schoolboys, being found in Accidences, Spellers, "Logick" Primers, and other school-books, down even to the present day.

> " This book is one thing, My fist's another,
>   If you touch the one thing, You'll feel the other."

>> " Hic liber est meus
>>   And that I will show
>> Si aliquis capit
>>   I'll give him a blow."

>> " This book is mine
>> By Law Divine
>>   And if it runs astray
>> I'll call you kind
>> My desk to find
>>   And put it safe away."

> " Hic liber est meus Deny it who can
>   Zenas Graves Junior An honest man."

There also appears a practical warning which may be read with attention and profit by the public now a days :

>> " If thou art borrowed by a friend
>>   Right welcome shall he be
>> To read, to study, *not* to lend
>>   But to *return* to me.

>> " Not that imparted knowledge doth
>>   Diminish Learnings Store
>> But books I find if often lent
>>   Return to me no more."

" Read *Slowly*—Pause *Frequently*—Think *Seriously*—Finger *Lightly*—Keep *Cleanly*—Return *Duly*—with the *Corners* of the *Leaves* NOT TURNED DOWN."

The fashion of using book-plates was by no means so general among New England Puritans as among rich Virginians and New Yorkers and Pennsylvanian Quakers. Mr. Lichtenstein, writing in the New England Historical and Genealogical Register in 1886, says he has seen no New England book-plates of earlier date than 1735. At later dates the Holyokes, Dudleys, Boylstons, and Phillips, all used book-plates. The plates most familiar to students in old libraries in New England are those of the Vaughans and of Isaiah Thomas.

Another, a living interest is found in these old, dusty, leather-bound volumes, which is not in the inscriptions and not, alas, in the printed words. They are the chosen home of a race of pigmy spiderlings who love musty theology with an affection found in no one else nowadays. In these dingy homes they live and rear their hideous little progeny : for in the cold light of a microscope these tiny brown book-dwellers are not beautiful ; they are flat, crab-like, goggle-eyed, hairy ; and they zigzag across the page on their ugly crooked legs in a sprawling, drunken fashion. They do not eat the books ; they live apparently on air ; yet if you crush them between the pages they leave a stain of vivid scarlet to reproach you in future readings for your needless cruelty. I cannot kill them ; though flaming is their blood's rebuke, it is aristocratically as well as theologically blue. In their veins runs the ichor—arachnidian though it be—that came over in the Mayflower; yes, doubly honored, came over in the special stateroom of an Ainsworth's Psalm-Book or a Genevan Bible. No degrading alliances, no admixtures through foreign emigration, have crossed that pure inbred strain ; my book-spiders are of real Pilgrim stock—they are true New England Brahmins.

Any one who turns over with attention the books of an old New England library must be struck with a sense of the affection with which these books have been treasured, the care with which they have been read, and, in case of accident, with which they have been repaired. One psalm-book, nibbled by mice, has had every page neatly mended by the insertion of thin sheets of paper to replace the lost bits ; and some painstaking and pious New Englander, with a pen and skill worthy the illuminating monks of another faith, has minutely printed the missing letters on both sides of the inserted slip in a text no larger than the surrounding print. Another book, a Bible, burnt in round holes by a slow-burning coal from the pipe of a sleepy reader, has been mended in the same careful manner. I have seen Bibles that have been read and turned over till the margins of the pages at the lower corner and outer edge were worn off down to the print by loving daily use. In one such the margins had been neatly replaced by pasted slips of paper. In more than one book I have found a minutely written home-made index on the blank pages at the end of the volume, showing a personal interest and love for a book which can hardly be equalled. Careful notes and references and postils also show a patient and appreciative perusal.

Though books were so closely cherished, so seemly bekept in colonial days, they were subject to one indignity with which now they are unmenaced and undegraded—they were sometimes sentenced to be burned by the public hangman. In 1654 the writings of John Reeves and Ludowick Muggleton, who set up to be prophets, were burned by that abhorred public functionary in Boston market-place; and two years later Quaker books were similarly destroyed. William Pyncheon's book was burned, in 1650, in Boston Market. In 1707 a "libel on the Governor" was hanged by the hangman. In 1754 a pamphlet called " The Monster of Monsters," a sharp political criticism on the Massachusetts Court, was thus burned in King Street, Boston. From the *Connecticut Gazette* of November 29th, 1755, we learn that another offending publication was sentenced to be "publickly whipt according to Moses Law with 40 stripes save one, then Burnt." How a true book-lover winces at the thought of the public hangman placing his blood-stained hand on any book, no matter how much a " monster."

XII

"ARTIFICES OF HANDSOMENESS"

FROM the earliest days the Puritan colonists fought stoutly, for the sake of St. Paul, against long hair. They proved themselves worthy the opprobrious name of Roundhead. Endicott's first act was to institute a solemn and insistent association against long hair. This wearing of long locks was one of the existing evils, a wile of the devil, which bade fair to creep into New England, and in its incipiency was proceeded against by the General Court, "that the men might not wear long hair like women's hair." The ministers preached bitterly and incessantly against the fashion; the Apostle Eliot, Parson Stoddard, Parson Rogers, President Chauncey, President Wigglesworth, all launched burning invective and skilful Biblical argument against the long-growing locks—"the disguisement of long Ruffianly hair" (or Russianly—whichever it may be). It was derisively suggested that long nails like Nebuchadnezzar's would next be in fashion. Men under sentence for offences were offered release from punishment if they would "cut off their long hair into a civil frame." Exact rules were given from the pulpit as to the properly Puritan length—that the hair should not lie over the neck, the band, or the doublet collar; in the winter it might be suffered to grow a little below the ear for warmth. Personal pride and dignity were appealed to, that no Christian gentleman would wish to look like "every Ruffian, every wild-Irish, every hang-man, every varlet and vagabond." By Sewall's time, however, Puritan though he were, we see his white locks flowing long over his doublet collar, and forming a fitting frame to his serene, benignant countenance.

Puritan woman also were not above reproach in regard to the fashion of extravagant hair-dressing; they also "showed the vile note of impudency." One parson thus severely addressed them from the pulpit: "The special sin of woman is pride and haughtiness, and that because they are generally more ignorant and worthless," and he added that this feminine pride vented itself in gesture, hair, behavior, and apparel. I fear all this was true, for the Court also complained of my ignorant and worthless sex for "cutting and curling and laying out of the hair, especially among the younger sort." Increase Mather gave them this thrust in his sermon on the comet, in 1683: " Will not the haughty daughters of Zion refrain their pride in apparell? Will they lay out their hair, and wear their false locks, their borders, and towers like comets about their heads? " And they were called " Apes of Fancy, friziling and curlying of their hayr."

I think the sober and decorous women settlers must have worn their hair cut straight across the forehead,

like our modern "bangs;" for Higginson, writing of
the Indians in 1692, says: "Their hair is generally
black and cut before like our gentlewomen." The
false locks denounced by Mather were doubtless "a
pair of Perukes which are pretty" of Pepys's time,
about 1656; or the "heart breakers" worn in 1670,
which set out like butterfly-wings over the ears, and
which were described thus: "False locks set on wyers
to make them stand at a distance from the head."

From a letter written by Knollys to Cecil we learn
that Mary Queen of Scots wore these perukes. He
says:

"Mary Seaton among other pretty devices yesterday
and this day, she did set such a curled hair upon the
Queen that was said to be a Peruke, that showed very
delicately, and every other day she hath a new device of
head dressing without any cost, and yet setteth forth a
woman gaylie well."

The "towers like comets" were doubtless commodes, which were in high fashion in Europe at the
beginning of the eighteenth century until about the
year 1711, though I have never found that the word
commode was used in America. These commodes
were enormously high frames of wire covered with
thin silk, or plaitings of muslin or lace, or frills of
ribbon—and sadly belied their name.

A simpler form of hair-dressing succeeded the
commode; portraits painted during the following
half-century, such as those of Copley, Smibert, and
Blackburn, show an elegant and graceful form of

coiffure, the hair brushed back and raised slightly from the forehead, and sometimes curled loosely behind the ears. At a later date the curls were almost universally surmounted by a lace cap. Pomatum began to be used by the middle of the century. In the *Boston News Letter* of 1768, we read of "Black White and Yellow Pomatum from six Coppers to Two Shillings per Roll." The hair was frequently powdered. Hair-dressers sold powdering puffs and powdering bags and powdering machines, and a dozen different varieties of hair-powder—brown, maréchal, scented, plain, and blue. By Revolutionary times a new tower, or "talematongue," had arisen; the front hair was pulled up over a stuffed cushion or roll, and mixed with powder and grease; the back hair was strained up in loops or short curls, surrounded and surmounted with ribbons, pompons, aigrettes, jewels, gauze, and flowers and feathers, till the structure was half a yard in height.. This fashion was much admired by some; a young lover of the day wrote thus sentimentally of a fair Hartford girl : "Her hair covered her cushion as a plate of the most beautiful enamel frosted with silver." A Revolutionary soldier wrote a poem, however, which regarded from a different point of view this elaborate headgear in such a time of national depression. His rhymes began thus :

> "Ladies you had better leave off your high rolls
> Lest by extravagance you lose your poor souls
> Then haul out the wool, and likewise the tow
> 'Twill clothe our whole army we very well know."

The " Dress-à-la-Independance " was a style of hair-dressing with thirteen curls at the neck, thus to honor the thirteen new States.

In the year 1771 Anna Green Winslow wrote in her diary an account of one of these elaborate hair-dressings which she then saw. She ends her description thus :

" How long she was under his opperation I know not. I saw him twist & tug & pick & cut off whole locks of gray hair at a slice, the lady telling him he would have no hair to dress next time, for a space of an hour and a half, when I left them he seeming not to be near done."

She also gives a most sprightly account of the manufacture of a roll for her own hair :

" I had my HEDDUS roll on. Aunt Storer said it ought to be made less, Aunt Deming said it ought not to be made at all. It makes my head ach and burn and itch like anything Mama. This famous Roll is not made wholly of a Red-Cow Tail but is a mixture of that & horsehair very coarse & a little human hair of a yellow hue that I suppose was taken out of the back part of an old wig. But D. (the barber) made it, all carded together and twisted up. When it first came home, Aunt put it on, and my new cap upon it ; she then took up her apron and measured me & from the roots of my hair on my forehead to the top of my notions I measured above an inch longer than I did downward from the roots of my hair to the end of my chin. Nothing renders a young person more amiable than Virtue and Modesty without the help of fals hair, Red-Cow tail or D. the barber."

The *Boston Gazette* had, in 1771, a ludicrous description of an accident to a young woman in the streets of that town. In an infaust moment she was thrown down by a runaway, and her tower received serious damage. It burst its thin outer wall of natural hair, and disgorged cotton and wool and tow stuffing, false hair, loops of ribbon and gauze. Ill-bred boys kicked off portions of the various excrescences, and the tower-wearer was jeered at until she was glad to escape with her own few natural locks.

A New England clergyman—Manasseh Cutler—wrote thus of the head-dress of Mrs. General Knox in 1787 :

"Her hair in front is craped at least a foot high much in the form of a churn bottom upward and topped off with a wire skeleton in the same form covered with black gauze which hangs in streamers down her back. Her hair behind is in a large braid turned up and confined with a monstrous large crooked comb. She reminded me of the monstrous cap worn by the Marquis of La Fayettes valet, commonly called on this account the Marquises devil."

Hair so elaborately arranged could not be dressed daily. Once a week was frequently thought sufficient; and some very disgusting accounts are given of methods to dress the hair so it would "keep safely" for a month. The Abbé Robin wrote of New England women in 1781 :

"The hair of the head is raised and supported upon cushions to an extravagant height somewhat resembling the manner in which the French ladies wore their hair some years ago. Instead of powdering they often wash the head, which answers the purpose well enough as their own hair is commonly of an agreeable light color, but the more fashionable among them begin to adopt the European fashion of setting off the head to the best advantage."

The fashion of the roll was of much importance, and various shaped rolls were advertised ; we find one of " a modish new roll weighing but 8 ounces when others weigh fourteen ounces." We can well believe that such a heavy roll made poor Anna Winslow's head " ach and itch like anything." A Salem hairdresser, who employed twelve barbers, advertised thus, in 1773 : " Ladies shall be attended to in the polite constructions of rolls such as may tend to raise their heads to any pitch they desire."

The grotesqueness of such adornment found frequent ridicule in prose and verse. One poet sang :

" Give Chloe a bushel of horsehair and wool,
    Of paste and pomatum a pound,
  Ten yards of gay ribbon to deck her sweet skull
    And gauze to encompass it round.

" Of all the gay colours the rainbow displays
    Be those ribbons which hang on her head,
  Be her flowers adapted to make the folks gaze,
    And about the whole work be they spread.

" Let her flaps fly behind for a yard at the least,
    Let her curls meet just under her chin,
  Let those curls be supported to keep up the list,
    With an hundred instead of one pin."

We can easily see that after such rough treatment the hair needed restoring waters; and indeed from earliest times hair-restorers and hair-dyes did these "vain ancients" use. "Women with juice of herbs gray locks disguised." In these days of manifold mysterious nostrums that gild the head of declining age and make glad the waste places on bald young masculine pates, let us read the simple receipts of the good old times:

"Take half a pound of Aqua Mellis in the Springtime of the Year, warm a little of it every morning when you rise in a Sawcer, and tie a little Spunge to a fine Box combe, and dip it in the water and therewith moisten the roots of the hair in Combing it, and it will grow long and thick and curled in a very short time."

"Take three spoonfuls of Honey and a good handful of Vine Twigs that twist like Wire, and beat them wel, and strain their Juyce into the Honey and anoynt the Bald Places therewith."

Here is what Captain Sam Ingersoll of Salem used, or at any rate had the formula of, in 1685:

"A Metson to make a mans heare groe when he is bald. Take sume fier flies & sum Redd wormes & black snayls and sum hume bees and dri them and pound them & mixt them in milk or water."

These washes were not so expensive as Hirsutus or Tricopherous, but quite as effective perhaps. There were hair-dyes, too, "to make hair grow black though any other color," and the leaf that holds this precious instruction is sadly worn and spotted with various tinted inks, as though the words had been often read and copied :

"Take a little Aqua Fortis, put therein a groat or six-pence, as to the quantity of the aforesaid water, then set both to dissolve before the fire, then dip a small Spunge in the said water, and wet your beard or hair therewith, but touch not the skin."

Hair-dressers also improved on nature. William Warden, a wig maker in King Street, Boston, re-spectfully informed the ladies of that town that he would " colour the hair on the head from a Red or any other Disagreable Colour to a Dark Brown or Black."

It did not matter long to our forefathers whether these hair-dyes dyed, or hair-restorers restored, for a fashion hated by some of the early Puritans as a choice device of Satan—the fashion of wig-wearing—was to revolutionize the matter of masculine hair. The question of wigs was a difficult one to settle, since the ministers themselves could not agree. John Wilson and Cotton Mather wore them, but Rev. Mr. Noyes launched denunciations at them from the pulpit and the Apostle Eliot delivered many a blast against " prolix locks with boiling zeal," and he stigmatized them as a " luxurious feminine protexity," but yielded sadly later in life to the fact that the " lust for wigs is become insuperable." The legislature of Massa-chusetts also denounced periwigs in 1675, but all in vain.

They were termed by one author "artificial deformed Maypowles fit to furnish her that in a Stage play should represent some Hagge of Hell," and other choice epithets were applied. To learn how these "Horrid Bushes of Vanity" could be hated, let us hear the pages of Judge Sewall's diary:

"1701. Having last night heard that Joshua Willard had cut off his hair (a very full head of hair) and put on a Wigg, I went to him this morning. Told his mother what I came about and she call'd him. I enquired of him what Extremity had forced him to put off his own Hair and put on a Wigg? He answered none at all. But said that his Hair was streight and that it parted behinde. Seem'd to argue that men might as well shave their hair off their head, as off their face. I answered men were men before they had any hair on their faces (half of mankind never have any). God seems to have ordain'd our Hair as a Test, to see whether we can bring out to be content at his finding: or whether we would be our own Carvers, Lords, and come no more at Him. If we disliked our Skin or Nails; tis no Thanks to us for all that we cut them not off. . . . He seem'd to say would leave off his Wigg when his hair was grown. I spake to his Father of it a day or two after. He thank'd me that had discoursed his Son, and told me when his Hair was grown to cover his ears he promised to leave off his Wigg. If he had known it would have forbidden him."

At a later day, though it was "gravaminous," Sewall would not go to hear the bewigged Joshua preach, but attended another meeting. The Judge frequently states his annoyance at the universally wigged condition of New England.

I never read of these wig-wearing times without fresh amaze at the manner in which our sensible ancestors disfigured themselves. We read such advertisements of mountebank head-gear as this, from the *Boston News Letter* of August 14, 1729 :

"Taken from the shop of Powers Mariott Barber, a light Flaxen Naturall Wigg Parted from the forehead to the Crown. The Narrow Ribband is of a Red Pinck Colour. The Caul is in Rows of Red Green & White."

Twenty shillings reward was offered for this gay wig, and " if it be offered for sale to any it is desired they wont stop it." Grafton Fevergrure, the peruke-maker at the sign of the Black Wigg, lost a " Light Flaxen Natural Wigg with a Peach-Blossom-coloured Ribband." In 1755 the house of barber Coes, of Marblehead, was broken into, and eight brown and three grizzle wigs were stolen ; some of these had " feathered tops," some were bordered with red ribbon, some with purple. In 1754 James Mitchel had white wigs and " grizzels." He asked £20 O. T. for the best. " Light Grizzels are £15, dark Grizzels are £12 10*s*." Under date of 1731 we read of the loss of "a horsehair bobwig," and another with crown hair, each with gray ribbon, an Indian hair bobwig with a light ribbon, and a goat's hair natural wig with red and white ribbons.

The " London Magazine " gave in 1753 a list of curious names of wigs : " The pigeons wing, the comet, the cauliflower, the royal bird, the staircase, the ladder, the brush, the wild boars back, the temple, the rhinoceros, the crutch, the negligent, the chancellor, the out-bob, the long-bob, the half-natural, the chain-buckle, the corded buckle, the detached buckle, the Jasenist bob, the drop wigg, the snail back, the spinage-seed, the artichoke."

Hawthorne's list of New England wigs was shorter: "The tie, the brigadier, the spencer, the albemarle, the major, the ramillies, the grave full-bottom, and the giddy feather-top." To these let me add the campaign, the neck-lock, the bob, the lavant, the vallaney, the drop-wig, the buckle-wig, the bag-wig, the Grecian fly, the peruke, the beau-peruke, the long-tail, the bob-tail, the fox-tail, the cut-wig, the tuck-wig, the twist-wig, the scratch. Sydney says the name campaign was applied to a wig which was imported from France in 1702, and was made very full and curled eighteen inches to the front. This date cannot be correct, when we find John Winthrop writing in 1695 for "two wiggs one a campane, the other short." The Ramillies wig had a long plaited tail, with a big bow at the top of the braid and a small one at the bottom. It would be idle to attempt to describe all these wigs, how they swelled at the sides, and turned under in rolls, and rose in puffs, and then shrank to a small close wig that vanished at Revolutionary times in powdered natural hair and a queue of ribbon, a bag, or an eel-skin, and finally gave way to cropped hair " à-la-Bru-

tus or à-la-Titus," as a Boston hair-dresser advertised in the year 1800.

Not only did gentlemen wear wigs, but children,
servants, prisoners, sailors, and soldiers also; as early
certainly as 1716 the fashion was universal. So great
was the demand for this false head-gear, that wigs
were made of goat-hair and horse-hair, as well as
human hair. The cost of dressing and caring for
wigs became a heavy item of expense to the wearer,
and income to the barber; often eight or ten pounds
a year were paid for the care of a single wig. Wig-
makers' materials were expensive also—" wig ribans,
cauls, curling pipes, sprigg wyers, and wigg steels;"
and were advertised in vast numbers that show the
universal prevalence of the fashion.

By the beginning of this century, women—having
powdered and greased and pulled their hair almost off
their heads—were glad to wear their remaining locks
à-la-Flora or à-la-Virginia, or to wear wigs to simulate
these styles. We find Eliza Southgate Bowne writing
thus to her mother from Boston in the year 1800 :

" . . . Now Mamma what do you think I am going to
ask for ?—A WIG. Eleanor Coffin has got a new one just
like my hair and only 5 dollars. I must either cut my hair
or have one. I cannot dress it at all *stylish*. Mrs. Coffin
bought Eleanor's and says that she will write to Mrs.
Sumner to get me one just like it. How much time it
will save—in one year! We could save it in pins and
paper, besides the *trouble*. At the Assembly I was quite
ashamed of my head, for nobody had long hair. If you
will consent to my having one do send me over a 5 dollar

bill by the post immediately after you receive this, for I am in hopes to have it for the next Assembly—do send me word immediately if you can let me have one."

This persuasive appeal was successful, for frequent references to the wig appear in later letters.

Though false teeth and the fashion of filling the teeth were known even by the ancient Egyptians, the science of dentistry is a modern one. But little care of the teeth was taken in early colonial days, and the advice given for their preservation was very simple :

"If you will keep your teeth from rot, plug, or aking, wash the mouth continually with Juyce of Lemons, and afterwards rub your teeth with a Sage Leaf and Wash your teeth after meat with faire water. To cure Tooth Ach. 1. Take Mastick and chew it in your mouth until it is as soft as VVax, then stop your teeth with it, if hollow, there remaining till it's consumed, and it wil certainly cure you. 2. The tooth of a dead man carried about a man presently suppresses the pains of the Teeth."

I suppose this latter ghoulish cure would not affect the teeth of a woman ; if, however, a seventeenth or eighteenth century dame could cure the tooth-ache simply with a plug of mastic, she was much to be envied by her degenerate nineteenth-century sister with her long dentist's bill.

If we can believe Josselyn, writing in 1684, New England women, then as now, lost their teeth at an early age. He speaks of them as "pitifully Tooth shaken." He recommended to relieve their misery

a compound of brimstone, gunpowder, and butter, to
be "rubbed on the mandible." This colonial remedy
is still employed on New England farms. Burnaby,
writing in 1759, said that New England dames had
universally and even proverbially very indifferent
teeth. The Abbé Robin says they were toothless at
eighteen or twenty years of age, and attributes this
premature disfigurement to tea-drinking and the eating of warm bread.

When we read the composition of the tooth-pow-
ders and dentifrices used in early colonial days, we
wonder that they had any teeth left to scour. Here
is Mr. Ferene's "rare Dentifrice : "

"First take eight ounces of Irios roots, also four ounces
of Pomistone, and eight ounces of Cutel Bone, also eight
ounces of Mother of Pearl, and eight ounces of Coral, and
a pound of Brown Sugar Candy, and a pound of Brick if
you desire to make them red; but he did oftener make
them white, and then instead of the Brick did take a
pound of fine Alabaster ; all this being thoroughly beaten
and sifted through a fine searse the powder is then ready
prepar'd to make up in a past which must be done as follows :

To make the Said Powders into a past.

Take a little Gum Dragant and lay it in steep twelve
hours, in Orange flower water or Damask Rose Water ;
and when it is dissolved take the sweet Gum and grind
it on a Marble Stone with the aforesaid Powder, and
mixing some crums of white bread it will come into a
past, the which you may make Dentifrices, of what shape

or fashion you please, but long rowles is the most commodious for your use."

Just fancy scouring your teeth with a commodious roll of cuttle-bone, brick-dust, and pumice-stone!

Another tooth-powder was composed of coral, Portugal snuff, Armenian bole, "ashes of good tobacco which has been burnt," and gum myrrh; and ground up "broken pans"—coarse earthenware—might be substituted for the coral.

A very popular and much advertised tooth-wash was called "Dentium Conservator." It was made and sold in New England by the manufacturer and vendor of Bryson's Famous Bug Liquid—not an alluring companionship. This person also " removed Stumps and unsound Teeth with a dexterity peculiar to Himself at the Sign on the Leapord." There were also rival Essences of Pearl advertised, each equally eulogized and disparaged; " Infallible Sivit rendering the teeth white as alabaster tho' they be black as Coal;" and " Very Neat Hawksbill and Key Draught Teeth Pullers." These key-draught teeth-pullers were one of the cruellest instruments of torture of the day, often breaking the jaw-bone, and always causing unutterable anguish. Old Zabdiel Boylston advertised in the *News Letter*, in 1712, " Powder to refresh the Gums & whiten the Teeth." There were also sold "tooth-sopes, tooth-blanchs, tooth-rakes."

I cannot find any notice of the sale of " teeth brushes" till nearly Revolutionary times. Perhaps the colonists used, as in old England, little brushes made of "dentissick root" or mallow, chewed into a fibrous swab.

I have seen no advertisements that strike a greater chill than the scanty notices of early dentists and dentistry that appear at the latter part of the past century. The glory of having a Revolutionary patriot for a workman cannot soften the hard plainness of speech of this advertisement in the *Boston Evening Post* of September 26, 1768 :

"Whereas many Persons are so unfortunate as to lose their Fore Teeth by Accident or Otherways to their great Detriment not only in looks but in speaking both in public and private. This is to inform all such that they may have them replaced with Artificial Ones that look as well as the Natural and answer the End of Speaking by Paul Revere Goldsmith near the head of Dr. Clarkes wharf. All Persons who have had false Teeth Fixed by Mr. Jos Baker Surgeon Dentist and They have got loose as they will in Time may have them fastened by above said Revere who learnt the method of fixing them from Mr. Baker."

It will be remarked that these teeth were only to display and talk with, and were but sorry helps in eating. This very appalling advertisement from the *Massachusetts Centinel* gives a clue to the way in which missing teeth were replaced : "Live Teeth. Those Persons inclined to dispose of Live Teeth may apply to Templeman." Or this from the *Connecticut Courant* of August 17, 1795 : "A generous price paid for Human Front Teeth perfectly sound, by Dr. Skinner." These "live teeth" were inserted in other and vainer, if not more squeamish persons' mouths, by a process of "ingrafting" which was much in vogue. There were few New England dentists *eo nomine* until well into this century—but three in Boston in 1816. As silversmith and engraver Revere also set teeth, so Isaac Greenwood, who waited at their houses on all who required his dental services, also made umbrellas, sold cane for hoop petticoats, and made dice and chessmen. Wm. Greenwood pulled teeth and sold pianos; and Dr. Flagg, a surgeon dentist, advertised in 1797 that he would get hand-organs in Europe suitable for church use. John Templeman, the live-teeth purchaser, was a broker as well as a dentist; and Whitlock, the actor, did a thriving dental business, and doubtless carried his "neat hawksbill or key-draught tooth-wrench" to the play-house, and used it, to his own profit and his fellow-townsmen's misery, between the acts.

Though the Pilgrim women were doubtless as simple at their toilet as they were in their dress, the sudden growth of the colony in wealth brought to their daughters, besides variety and richness of dress, a love of cosmetics. Dunton tells positively of one painted face in Boston in 1686. He said, "to hide her age she paints, and to hide her painting dares hardly laugh." One New England minister thus reproved and warned the women of his congregation: "At the resurrection of the Just there will no such sight be met as the Angels carrying Painted Ladies in their arms."

In the inventory of one of the early Cambridge settlers, Robert Daniel, is found the item "two Ceruse Jugs." Ceruse was a preparation of white lead with which women then painted their faces, and I think these ceruse jugs were part of the paraphernalia of my Lady Daniel's toilet-table.

With the advent of newspapers came various advertisements that showed the vanity of our forbears, the "collusions of women, their oyntments and potticary drugs, and all their slibber sawces."

" An Excellent Wash for the Skin which entirely taketh out all Freckles Moath & Sunburn from the Face Neck & Hands, which with Frequent Use adds a most Agreeable Lustre to the Complexion, softens & beautifies the Skin to Admiration And is generally used and approved of by most of the Gentry in London *of both Sexes.*"

" Best Face Powder which gives a fine Bloom to the Face which answers all the intents of White Paint without that Pernicious effect that attends Paint. Also a Composition to take off Superficious Hair."

The latter clause shows that our great-grandmothers were quite *au fait* with the nostrums of the present day, with "pargetting, painting, slicking, glazing, and renewing old rivelled faces."

Many pretty rules may be found in old books and diaries, that are of New England, rules "to make the face fair" and to " make sweet the mouth."

" Take the flowers of Rosemary and seeth them in VVhite VVine, with which wash your face, and if you drink thereof it wil make you have a sweet breath."

Maids were also told to gather the sweet May dew from the grass in the early morning to make a fair face, and like Sir Thomas Overbury's milkmaid, "put all face-physic out of countenance." And pretty it were to see Cicely, Peg, and Joan in petticoat and sack or smock, each with a " faire linnen cloath " a-dipping her rosy face in the fresh May dew. Could this have been but a sly trick to get the lasses from their beds betimes? We know the early hour at which Madam Pepys had to bathe her mighty handsome face in the beautifying spring dew.

Patches were worn as eagerly, apparently, by Boston as by London belles. Whitefield complained of the jewels, patches, and gay apparel donned in New England. In scores of old newspapars after 1760 appear notices of the sale of "Face Patches," " Patch for Ladies," " Gum Patches," etc., and the frequency of advertisement would indicate a popular and ready sale.

With regard to the bathing habits of our ancestors but little can be said, and but little had best be said. Charles Francis Adams writes, with witty plainness, " If among personal virtues cleanliness be indeed that which ranks next to godliness, then judged by the nineteenth century standards, it is well if those who lived in the eighteenth century had a sufficiency of the latter quality to make good what they lacked of the former." He says there was not a bath-room in the town of Quincy prior to the year 1820. And of what use would pitchers or tubs of water have been in bed-rooms in the winter time, when if exposed over night solid ice would be found therein in the morning? The washing of linen in New England homes was done monthly; it is to be hoped the personal baths were more frequent, even under the apparent difficulties of accomplishment. I must state, in truth, though with deep mortification, that I cannot find in inventories even of Revolutionary times the slightest sign of the presence of balneary appurtenances in bed-rooms; not even of ewers, lavers, and basins, nor of pails and tubs. As petty pieces of furniture, such as stools, besoms, framed pictures, and looking-glasses are enumerated, this conspicuous absence of what we deem an absolute necessity for decency speaks with a persistent and exceedingly disagreeable voice of the unwashed condition of our ancestors, a condition all the more mortifying when we consider their exceeding external elegance in dress. This total absence of toilet appliances does not of course render impossible a special lavatory or bath-room in the house, or the daily importation to the bed-rooms of hot-water cans, twiggen bottles, bath-tubs, and basins from other portions of the house; but even that equipment would show a lack of adequate bathing facilities. Nor do the tiny toilet jugs and basins of Staffordshire ware that date from the first part of this century point to any very elaborate ablutions.

But these be parlous words an we wish to honor the memory of our New England grandsires; and let us remember that these negative toilet traits were not peculiar to them, but dated from the fatherland.

A century ago the English were said to be the only European people that had the unenviable distinction of going to the dinner-table without previously washing or "dressing" the hands.

One very unpleasant cosmetic, or rather detergent, was in constant use, however, throughout colonial times—wash-balls. They were imported as early as 1693 in company with scented and plain hair-powder. In 1771, " Gentlemen's Fine Washballs " were advertised in Boston, and "Scented Marbled Washballs." Other varieties of these substitutes for soap were Chemical, Greek, Venice, Marseilles, camphor, ambergris, and Bologna wash-balls. This is a rule given in olden times for the "Composition for Best Wash Balls:"

"Take forty pounds of Rice in fine powder, twenty eight pounds of fine flour, twenty eight pounds of starch powder, twelve pounds of White Lead, and four pounds of Orris Root in fine powder but no Whitening. Mix the whole well together and pass it through a fine sieve, then place it in a dry place and keep it for use. Great care must be taken that the Flour be not musty, in which case the Balls will in time crack and fall to pieces. To this composition may be added Dutch pink or brown fine damask powder according to the colour required when the Wash Balls are quite dry."

The effect of so large an amount of white lead must have been felt and shown most deleteriously upon the complexion of the user of this disagreeable compound.

"Ipswitch balls"—also the mode—were more pleasing:

"Take a pound of fine White Castill Sope; shave it thin in a pinte of Rose water, and let it stand two or three dayes, then pour all the water from it, and put to it a halfe a pinte of fresh water, and so let it stand one whole day, then pour out that, and put to it halfe a pinte more and let it stand a night more, then put to it halfe an ounce of powder called sweet Marjoram, a quarter of an ounce of Winter Savory, two or three drops of the Oil of Spike and the Oil of Cloves, three grains of musk, and as much Ambergreese, work all these together in a fair Mortar with the powder of an Almond Cake dryed and beaten as small as fine flowre, so rowl it round in your hands in Rose water."

The favorite soap, if one can judge from importations, was "Brown or Gray Bristol Sope," but this was not used by many in the community. The manufacture of home-made soap, of soft soap, was one of the univeral, most important, and most trying of all the household industries. The refuse grease of the family cooking was stowed away in an unsavory mass till early spring, and the wood ashes from the fireplaces were also stored. When the soap-making took place, the ashes were placed in a leach tub out of doors. This tub was sometimes made from the section of the bark of a birch tree; it was set loosely in a circular groove in a base of wood, or preferably of stone. Water was poured on the ashes, and the lye trickled from an outlet cut in the groove. The boiling of the lye and grease was an ill-smelling process, which was also carried on out of doors, and required an enormous amount of labor and patience. It was judged that when the compound was strong enough to hold up an egg, the soap was done. This strong soft soap was kept in a wooden " soap box " in the kitchen, and used for toilet as well as household purposes.

Dearly did the English and the New English love perfumes. They made little rolls of sweet-scented powders and gums and oils, " as large as pease," that they placed between rose-leaves and burned on coals in skillets or in little perfume-holders to scent the room. They burned on their open hearths mint and rose-leaves with sugar. They took the "maste of sweet Apple trees gathered betwixt two Lady days," and with gums and perfumes made bracelets and pomanders, "to keep to one a sweet smell." They made cakes of damask rose-leaves and pulvilio, civit, and musk, of "linet and ambergreese," to perfume their linen chests, for lavender thrived not in New England. The duties of the still-room were the most luxury-bearing of all the old household industries. Its very name brings to us sweet scents of Araby, as it brought to our forbears the most charming and nice of all their domestic occupations. But these duties were not easy nor expeditious work, nor did all the work begin in the still-room. Faithfully did dames and maids gather in field and garden, from early spring to chilly autumn, precious stores for their stills and limbecks. In every garret, from every rafter, slowly swayed great susurrous bunches of withered herbs and simples awaiting expression and distillation, and dreaming perhaps of the summer breezes that had blown through them in the sunny days of their youth in their meadow homes. In many an old garret now bare of such stores "mints still perfume the air;" the very walls exhale "the homesick smell of dry forgotten herbs."

From these old stills, these retorts and mills, came not only perfumes and oils and beauty-waters, but half the medicines and diet-drinks, all the "kitchen-physicke" of the domestic and even the professional pharmacopæia.

Perfumes were also imported; we frequently find advertised "Royal Honey Water, an Excellent Perfume, good against Deafness, and to make the hair grow as the directions Sets forth. 1s 6d per bottle and proportionate by Ounce." Old Zabdiel Boylston had it in 1712. Spirit of Benjamin was also for toilet uses. This was the base of the well-known scent known as Queen Elizabeth's Perfume. It was combined with sweet marjoram. Lavender water was apparently a great favorite for importation, and we find notices of lavender bottles with shagreen cases.

We find in newspaper days many advertisements of other toilet articles such as nail-knippers, picktooth cases, silk and worsted powder-puffs, deerskin powder bags, lip-salve, ivory scratch-backs, flesh brushes, curling and pinching tongs, all showing a strongly crescent vanity and love of luxury.

XIII

RAIMENT AND VESTURE

WE know definitely the dress of the settlers of Massachusetts Bay, for the inventory of the "Apparell for 100 men" furnished by the Massachusetts Bay Company in 1628 is still in existence. From it we learn that enough clothing was provided to supply to each emigrant four "peare of shewes," four "peare of stockings," a "peare Norwich garters," four shirts, two "sutes dublet and hose of leather lynd with oil'd skyn leather, ye hose & dublett with hookes & eyes," a "sute of Norden dussens or hampshire kersies lynd, the hose with skins, dublets with lynen of gilford or gedlyman kerseys," four bands, two handkerchiefs, a " wastcoate of greene cotton bound about with red tape," a leather girdle, a Monmouth cap, a "black hatt lyned in the browes with lether," five "Red knit capps mill'd about 5d a piece," two pair of gloves, a mandillion "lyned with cotton," one pair of breeches and waistcoat, and a "lether sute of Dublett & breeches of oyled lether," and one pair of leather breeches and "drawers to serve to weare with both their other sutes."

This surely was a liberal outfit, save perhaps in the

matter of shirts and handkerchiefs, and doubtless intended to last many years. Though simple it was far from being a sombre one. Scarlet caps and green waistcoats bound with red made cheerful bits of color alongside the leather breeches and buff doublets on Salem shore.

The apparel of the Piscataquay planters, furnished in 1635, varied somewhat from that just enumerated. Their waistcoats were scarlet, and they had cassocks of cloth and canvas, instead of doublets. Though scarce more than a lustrum had passed since the settlement on the shores of the Bay, long hose like the Florentine hose had become entirely old-fashioned and breeches were the wear. Coats—"lynd coats, papous coats, and moose coats"—had also been invented, or at any rate dubbed with that name and assumed. Cassocks, doublets, and jerkins varied little in shape, and the names seem to have been interchangeable. Mandillions, said by some authorities to be cloaks, were in fact much like the doublets, and were worn apparently as an over-garment or greatcoat. The name appears not in inventories after the earliest years.

Though simplicity of dress was one of the cornerstones of the Puritan Church, the individual members did not yield their personal vanity without many struggles. As soon as the colonies rallied from the first years of poverty and, above all, of comparative isolation, and a sequent tide of prosperity and wealth came rolling in, the settlers began to pick up in dress, to bedeck themselves, to send eagerly to the mother country for new petticoats and doublets that, when proudly donned, did not seem simple and grave enough for the critical eyes of the omnipotent New England magistrates and ministers. Hence restraining and simplifying sumptuary laws were passed. In 1634, in view of some new fashions which were deemed by these autocrats to be immodest and extravagant, this order was sent forth by the General Court:

"That no person either man or woman shall hereafter make or buy any apparel, either woolen or silk or linen with any lace on it, silver, gold, or thread, under the penalty of forfeiture of said clothes. Also that no person either man or woman shall make or buy any slashed clothes other than one slash in each sleeve and another in the back; also all cut-works, embroideries, or needlework cap, bands, and rails are forbidden hereafter to be made and worn under the aforesaid penalty; also all gold or silver girdles, hatbands, belts, ruffs, beaverhats are prohibited to be bought and worn hereafter."

Liberty was thriftily given the planters, however, to " wear out such apparel as they are now provided of except the immoderate great sleeves, slashed apparel, immoderate great rails and long wings," which latter were apparently beyond Puritanical endurance.

In 1639 " immoderate great breeches, knots of ryban, broad shoulder bands and rayles, silk ruses, double ruffles and capes " were added to the list of tabooed garments.

In 1651 the General Court again expressed its

" utter detestation and dislike that men or women of meane condition, education and callings should take uppon them the garbe of gentlemen by the wearinge of gold or silver lace or buttons or poynts at their knees, to walke in great boots, or women of the same rank to wear silke or tiffany hoodes or scarfes."

Many persons were "presented" under this law; Puritan men were just as fond of finery as were Puritan women. Walking in great boots proved alluring to an illegal degree, just as did wearing silk and tiffany hoods. But Puritan women fought hard and fought well for their fine garments. In Northampton thirty-eight women were brought up at one time before the court in 1676 for their "wicked apparell." One young miss, Hannah Lyman, of Northampton, was prosecuted for "wearing silk in a fflaunting manner, in an offensive way and garb, not only before but when she stood presented, not only in Ordinary but Extraordinary times."

We can easily picture sixteen-year-old Hannah, in silk bedight, inwardly rejoicing at the unusual opportunity to fully and publicly display her rich attire, and we can easily read in her offensive flaunting in court a presage of the waning of magisterial power which proved a truthful omen, for in six years similar prosecutions in Northampton, for assumption of gay and expensive garments, were quashed. The ministers of the day note sadly the overwhelming love of fashion that was crescent throughout New England; a love of dress which neither the ban of religion, philosophy, nor law could expel; what Rev. Solomon Stoddard called, in 1675, "intolerable pride in clothes and hair." They were never weary of preaching about dress, of comparing the poor Puritan women to the haughty daughters of Judah and Jerusalem; saying threateningly to their parishioners, as did Isaiah to the daughters of Zion:

"The Lord will take away the bravery of their tinkling ornaments about their feet, and their cauls and their round tires like the moon.

"The chains and the bracelets and the mufflers.

"The bonnets and the ornaments of the legs and the head-bands and the tablets and the earrings.

"The rings and nose jewels.

"The changeable suits of apparel, and the mantles and the wimples and the crisping pins.

"The glasses and the fine linen and the hoods and the vails."

Every evil predicted by the prophet was laid at the door of these Boston and Plymouth dames; fire and war and poor harvests and caterpillars, and even baldness—but still they arrayed themselves in fine raiment, "drew iniquity with a cord of vanity and sin with a cart-rope," and "walked with outstretched necks and wanton eyes mincing as they go."

As an exposition of the possibilities, or rather the actual extensiveness, of a Puritanical feminine wardrobe at this date, let me name the articles of clothing bequeathed by the will of Jane Humphrey, who died in Dorchester, Mass., in 1668. I give them as they appear on the list, but with the names of her heirs omitted.

"Ye Jump. Best Red Kersey Petticoate, Sad Grey Kersey Wascote. My blemmish Searge Petticoate & my best hatt. My white Fustian Wascote. A black Silk neck cloath. A handkerchiefe. A blew Apron. A plain black Quoife without any lace. A white Holland Appron with a small lace at the bottom. Red Searge petticoat and a blackish Searge petticoat. Greene Searge Wascote & my hood & muffe. My Green Linsey Woolsey petticoate. My Whittle that is fringed & my Jump & my blew Short Coate. A handkerchief. A blew Apron. My best Quife with a Lace. A black Stuffe Neck Cloath. A White Holland apron with two breadths in it. Six yards of Redd Cloth. A greene Vnder Coate. Staning Kersey Coate. My murry Wascote. My Cloake & my blew Wascote. My best White Apron, my best Shifts. One of my best Neck Cloaths, & one of my plain Qnieus. One Callico Vnder Neck Cloath. My fine thine Neck Cloath. My next best Neck Cloath. A square Cloath with a little lace on it. My greene Apron."

It is pleasing to note in this list that not only the garments and stuffs, but the very colors named, have an antique sound; and we read in other inventories of such tints as philomot (feuillemort), gridolin (gris-de-lin or flax blossom), puce color, grain color (which was scarlet), foulding color, Kendal green, Lincoln green, watchet blue, barry, milly, tuly, stammel red, Bristol red, sad color—and a score of other and more fanciful names whose signification and identification were lost with the death of the century. In later days Congress brown, Federal blue, and Independence green show our new nation.

This wardrobe of Jane Humphrey's was certainly a very pretty and a very liberal outfit for a woman of no other fortune. But to have all one's possessions in the shape of raiment did not in her day bear quite the same aspect as it would at the present day. Many persons, men and women, preferred to keep their property in the form of what they quaintly called " duds." The fashion did not, in New England, wear out more apparel than the man, for clothing, no matter what its cut, was worn as long as it lasted, doing service frequently through three generations. For instance, we find Mrs. Epes, of Ipswich, when she was over fifty years old, receiving this bequest by will : "If she desire to have the suit of damask which was the Lady Cheynies her grandmother, let her have it upon appraisement." Hence we cannot wonder at clothing forming so large a proportion of the articles bequeathed by will and named in inventories ; for all the colonists

> " . . . studied after nyce array,
> And made greet cost in clothing."

Nor can we help feeling that any woman should have been permitted to have plenty of gowns in those days without being thought extravagant, since a mantua-maker's charge for making a gown was but eight shillings.

Though the shops were full of rich stuffs, there was no ready-made clothing for women for sale either in outside garments or in under-linen. Occasionally, by the latter part of the eighteenth century, we read the advertisement of a " vandoo " of " full-made gowns, petticoats and sacs of a genteel lady of highest fashion "—a notice which reads uncommonly like the " forced sales " of the present day of mock-outfits of various kinds.

About the middle of the century there began to appear " ready-made clothes for men." Jolley Allen advertised such, and under that name, in 1768, " Coats, Silk Jackets, Shapes and Cloth Ditto; Stocking Breeches of all sizes & most colours. Velvet Cotton Thickset Duroy Everlasting & Plush Breeches. Sailors Great Coats, outside & inside Jackets, Check Shirts, Frocks, long and wide Trowzers, Scotch bonnets & Blue mill'd Shirts." But women's clothes were made to order in the town by mantua makers, and in the country by travelling tailoresses and sempstresses, or by the deft-fingered wearers.

New England dames had no mode-books nor fashion-plates to tell to them the varying modes. Some sent to the fatherland for " fire-new fashions in sleeves and slops," for garments and head-gear made in the prevailing court style ; and the lucky possessors lent these new-fashioned caps and gowns and cloaks as models to their poorer or less fortunate neighbors. A very taking way of introducing new styles and shapes to the new land was through the importation by milliners and mantua-makers of dressed dolls, or "babys" as they were called, that displayed in careful miniature the fashions and follies of the English court. In the *New England Weekly Journal* of July 2, 1733, appears this notice:

"To be seen at Mrs. Hannah Teatts Mantua Maker at the Head of Summer Street Boston a Baby drest after the Newest Fashion of Mantues and Night Gowns & everything belonging to a dress. Latilly arrived on Capt. White from London, any Ladies that desire to see it may either come or send, she will be ready to wait on 'em, if they come to the House it is Five Shilling & if she waits on 'em it is Seven Shilling."

We can fancy the group of modish Boston belles and dames each paying Hannah Teatts her five shillings, and like overgrown children eagerly dressing and undressing the London doll and carefully examining and noting her various diminutive garments.

These fashion models in miniature effigy obtained until after Revolutionary times. Sally McKean wrote to the sister of Dolly Madison, in June, 1796: " I went yesterday to see a doll which has come from England dressed to show the fashion"—and she then proceeds to describe the modes thus introduced.

We can gain some notion of the general shape of the dress of our forbears at various periods from the portraits of the times. Those of Madam Shrimpton and of Rebecca Rawson are among the earliest. They were painted during the last quarter of the seventeenth century. The dress is not very graceful, but far from plain, showing no trace of Puritanical simplicity; in fact, it is precisely that seen in portraits of English well-to-do folk of the same date. Both have strings of beads around the neck and no other jewels; both wear loosely tied and rather shapeless flat hoods concealing the hair, Madam Shrimpton's having an embroidered edge about two inches wide. Similar hoods are shown in Romain de Rooge's prints of the landing of King William, on the women in the coronation procession. They were like the Nithesdale hoods of Hogarth's prints, but smaller. Both New English dames have also broad collars, stiff and ugly, with uncurved horizontal lower edge, apparently trimmed with embroidery or cut-work. Both show the wooden contour of figure, which was either the fault of the artist's brush or of the iron busk of the wearer's stays. The bodies are stiffly pointed, and the most noticeable feature of the gown is the sleeve, consisting of a double puff drawn in just above the elbow and confined by knots of ribbon; in one case with very narrow ribbon loops. Randle Holme says that a sleeve thus tied in at the elbow was called a virago sleeve. Madam Shrimpton's sleeve has also a falling frill of embroidery and lace and a ruffle around the armsize. The question of sleeves sorely vexed the colonial magistrates. Men and women were forbidden to have but one slash or opening in each sleeve. Then the inordinate width of sleeves became equally trying, and all were ordered to restrain themselves to sleeves half an ell wide. Worse modes were to come; " short sleeves whereby

the nakedness of the arm may be discovered " had to
be prohibited ; and if any such ill-fashioned gowns
came over from London, the owners were enjoined to
wear thick linen to cover the arms to the wrist.   Existing portraits show how futile were these precau-
tions, how inoperative these laws; arms were bared
with impunity, with complacency, and the present-
ment of Governor Wentworth shows three slashes in
his sleeve.

Not only were the arms of New England women
bared to an immodest degree, but their necks also,
calling forth many a " just and seasonable reprehen-
sion of naked breasts."   Though gowns thus cut in
the pink of the English mode proved too scanty to
suit Puritan ministers, the fair wearers wore them
as long as they were in vogue.

It is curious to note in the oldest gowns I have
seen, that the method of cutting and shaping the
waist or body is precisely the same as at the present
day.   The outlines of the shoulder and back-seams,
of the bust forms, are the same, though not so grace-
fully curved ; and the number of pieces is usually
the same.   Very good examples to study are the
gorgeous brocaded gowns of Peter Faneuil's sister,
perfectly preserved and now exhibited in the Boston
Art Museum.

Nor have we to-day any richer or more beautiful
stuffs for gowns than had our far-away grandmothers.
The silks, satins, velvets, and brocades which wealthy
colonists imported for the adornment of their wives
and daughters, and for themselves, cannot be excelled

by the work of modern looms; and the laces were equally beautiful. Whitefield complained justly and more than once of the "foolish virgins of New England covered all over with the Pride of Life;" especially of their gaudy dress in church, which the Abbé Robin also remarked, saying it was the only theatre New England women had for the display of their finery. Other clergymen, as Manasseh Cutler, noted with satisfaction that "the congregation was dressed in a very tasty manner."

In old New England families many scraps of these rich stuffs of colonial days are preserved; some still possess ancient gowns, or coats, or waistcoats of velvet and brocade. In old work-bags, bed-quilts, and cushions rich pieces may be found. When we see their quality, color, and design we fully believe Hawthorne's statement that the "gaudiest dress permissible by modern taste fades into a Quakerlike sobriety when compared with the rich glowing splendor of our ancestors."

The royal governor and his attendants formed in each capital town a small but very dignified circle, glittering with a carefully studied reflection of the fashionable life of the English Court, and closely aping English richness of dress. The large landed proprietors, such as the opulent Narragansett planters, and the rich merchants of Newport, Salem, and Boston, spent large sums annually in rich attire. In every newspaper printed a century or a century and a quarter ago, we find proof of this luxury and magnificence in dress; in the lists of the property of deceased persons, in the long advertisements of milliners and mercers, in the many notices of "vandoos." And the impression must be given to every reader of letters and diaries of the times, of the vast vanity not only of our grandmothers, but of our grandfathers. They did indeed "walk in brave aguise." The pains these good, serious gentlemen took with their garments, the long minute lists they sent to European tailors, their loudly expressed discontent over petty disappointments as to the fashion and color of their attire, their evident satisfaction at becoming and rich clothing, all point to their wonderful love of ostentation and their vanity—a vanity which fairly shines with smirking radiance out of some of the masculine faces in the "bedizened and brocaded" portraits of dignified Bostonians in Harvard Memorial Hall, and from many of the portraits of Copley, Smibert, and Blackburn.

Here is a portion of a letter written by Governor Belcher to a London tailor in 1733 :

"I have desired my brother, Mr. Partridge to get me some cloaths made, and that you should make them, and have sent him the yellow grogram suit you made me at London ; but those you make now must be two or three inches longer and as much bigger. Let 'em be workt strong, as well as neat and curious. I believe Mr. Harris in Spittlefields (of whom I had the last) will let you have the grogram as good and cheap as anybody. The other suit to be of a very good silk, such as may be the Queens birthday fashion, but I don't like padisway. It must be a substantial silk, because you'll see I have ordered it to be trimm'd rich, and I think a very good white shagrine will be the best lining. I say let it be a handsome compleat suit, and two pair of breeches to each suit."

Picture to yourself the garb in which the patriot John Hancock appeared one noonday in 1782:

"He wore a red velvet cap within which was one of fine linen, the last turned up two or three inches over the lower edge of the velvet. He also wore a blue damask gown lined with velvet, a white stock, a white satin embroidered waistcoat, black satin small-clothes, white silk stockings and red morocco slippers."

What gay peacock was this strutting all point-device in scarlet slippers and satin and damask, spreading his gaudy feathers at high noon in sober Boston streets!—was this our boasted Republican simplicity? And what "fop-tackle" did the dignified Judge of the Supreme Court wear in Boston at that date? He walked home from the bench in the winter time clad in a magnificent white corduroy surtout lined with fur, with his judicial hands thrust in a great fur muff.

Fancy a Boston publisher going about his business tricked up in this dandified dress—a true New England jessamy.

"He wore a pea-green coat, white vest, nankeen small-clothes, white silk stockings and pumps fastened with silver buckles which covered at least half the foot from instep to toe. His small-clothes were tied at the knees with riband of the same color in double bows the ends reaching down to the ancles. His hair in front was well loaded with pomatum, frizzled or creped, and powdered; the ear locks had undergone the same process. Behind his natural hair was augmented by the addition of a large queue, called vulgarly the false tail, which, enrolled in some yards of black riband, hung halfway down his back."

We must believe that the richest brocades, the finest lawn, the choicest laces, the heaviest gold and silver buckles, did not adorn the persons of New England dames and belles only; the gaudiest inflorescence of color and stuffs shone resplendent on the manly figures of their husbands and brothers. And yet these men were no " lisping hawthorn buds," their souls were not in their clothes, or we had not the signers of the Declaration of Independence and the heroes of the Revolution.

The domination of French ideas in America after the Revolution found one form of expression in French fashions of dress; and where New England women had formerly followed English models and English reproductions of French fashions, they now copied the French fashions direct, to the improvement, I fancy, of their modes. Too many accounts and representations exist of these comparatively recent styles to make it of value to enter into any detail of them here. But another influence on the dress of the times should be recorded.

The sudden and vast development of the Oriental

trade by New England ship-owners is plainly marked by many changes in the stuffs imported and in the dress of both men and women. Nankeens became at once one of the chief articles of sale in drygoods shops. Though Fairholt says they were not exported to America till 1825, I find them advertised in the *Boston Evening Post* of 1761. Shawls appeared in shopkeepers' lists. The first notice that I have seen is in the *Salem Gazette* of 1784—" a rich sortment of shawls." This was at the very time when Elias Haskett Derby—the father of the East India trade—was building and launching his stout ships for Canton. We have a vast variety of stuffs nowadays, but the list seems narrow and small when compared with the record of Indian stuffs that came in such numbers a hundred years ago to Boston and Salem markets. The names of these Oriental materials are nearly all obsolete, and where the material is still manufactured it bears a different appellation. A list of them will preserve their names and show their number. Some may prove not to have been Indian, but were so called in the days of their importation.

Alrabads.	Bengals.	Betelles.
Anjungoes.	Briampaux.	Byrampauts.
Allejars.	Bagatapaux.	Cushlas.
Atlasses.	Bumrums.	Coffies.
Addaties.	Bulschauls.	Chinachurry
Allibanies.	Brawls.	Cherrydarry.
Anbraeahs.	Bafraes.	Chilloes.
Arradahs.	Bejauraupauts.	Chints.
Budoys.	Bafts.	Cutthees.
Boglipores.	Baguzzees.	Cossas.

Chenarize.
Chittabullus.
Coopees.
Callowaypoose.
Cuttanees.
Carradaries.
Cheaconies.
Chucklaes.
Cadies.
Chowtahs.
Culgees.
Chaffelaes.
Corottas.
Doreas.
Deribands.
Doorguzzees.
Doodanies.
Dorsatees.
Danadars.
Elatchies.
Emertees.
Gurrahs.
Guzzinahs.
Goaconcheleras.
Gurraes.
Gelongs.
Ginghams.
Gunieas.
Humhums.

Humadies.
Izzarees.
Jollopours.
Jandannies.
Januwars.
Luckhouris.
Lemmones.
Lungees.
Mamoodies.
Mahmudihiaties.
Mugga-Mamoo-
chis.
Mickbannies.
Masaicks.
Moorees.
Mowsannas.
Mulmouls.
Mulye-Gungee.
Nicanees.
Nillaes.
Neganepauts.
Nenapees.
Nagurapaux.
Oringals.
Paunchees.
Patnas.
Pallampores.
Ponabaguzzies.
Persias.

Peniascoes.
Pagnas.
Poppolis.
Photaes.
Pelongs.
Quilts.
Romalls.
Rehings.
Seersuckers.
Sallampores.
Soraguzzes.
Soofeys.
Seerbettees.
Sannoes.
Seerindams.
Shalbafts.
Seerbands.
Succatums.
Starrets.
Terindams.
Tapseils.
Tanjeebs.
Tepoys.
Tainsooks.
Taffatties.
Tapis.
Tarnatams.
Taundah-Khassah.
Tandarees.

XIV

DOCTORS AND PATIENTS

THERE lies before me a leather-bound, time-stained, dingy little quarto of four hundred and fifty pages that was printed in the year 1656. Its contents comprise three parts or books. First, "The Queens Closet Opened, or The Pearl of Practise: Accurate, Physical, and Chirurgical Receipts." Second, "A Queens Delight, or The Art of Preserving, Conserving, and Candying, as also a Right Knowledge of Making Perfumes and Distilling the most Excellent Waters." Third, "The Compleat Cook, Expertly Prescribing the most ready wayes, whether Italian, Spanish, or French, For Dressing of Flesh and Fish, Ordering of Sauces, or Making of PASTRY "—pastry in capitals, as is due so distinguished an article and art.

This conjunction of leechcraft and cooking was in early days far from being considered demeaning to the healing art. A great number of the cook-books of the seventeenth and eighteenth centuries were written by physicians. Dr. Lister, physician to Queen Anne, wrote plainly, "I do not consider myself as hazarding anything when I say no man can be a good physician who has not a competent knowledge of cookery."

The book contains a long, pompous preface, in which it is asserted that these receipts were collected originally for her " distress'd Soveraigne Majesty the Queen"—Henrietta Maria; that they had been "laid at her feet by Persons of Honour and Quality;" and that since false and poor copies had been circulated during her banishment, and the compiler, who fell with the court, was not able to render his beloved queen any further service, he felt that he could at least " prevent all disservices" by giving in print to her friends these true rules. Thus could he keep the absent queen in their minds; and also he could give a fair copy to her, since she had lost her receipts in her flight.

Though Agnes Strickland stated that copies of this Queens Closet Opened are exceedingly rare in England, several are preserved in old New England families, some of them the descendants of colonial physicians; and the book may be shown as a fair example of the methods of practice and composition of prescriptions in colonial and provincial days.

This volume of mine was one of those which were not fated to dwell among " Persons of Honour and Quality " in old England; it crossed the waters to the new land with simpler folk, and was for many years the pocket-companion of an old New England doctor. Two names are carefully written on the inside of the cover of my book, names of past owners: " Edward Talbot, His Book," is in the most faded ink, and " William Morse, His Book, in the y'r 1710, Boston." A musty, leathery smell pervades and exhales from the pages, and is mingled with whiffs of an equally ancient and more penetrating odor, that of old drugs and medicines ; for many a journey over bleak hills and lonely dales has the book made, safely reposing at the bottom of its owner's pocket, or lying cheek by jowl with the box of drugs and medicines, and case of lancets in his ample saddlebags.

This country doctor, like others of his profession at the same date, had not studied deeply in college and hospital; nor had he taken any long course of instruction in foreign schools and universities. When he had decided to become a doctor, he had simply ridden with an old, established physician—ridden literally—in a half-menial, half-medical capacity. He had cared for the doctor's horse, swept the doctor's office, run the doctor's errands, pounded drugs, gathered herbs, and mixed plasters, until he was fitted to ride for himself. Then he had applied to the court and received a license to practise—that was all. I doubt not that this book of mine, and perhaps a manuscript collection of recipes and prescriptions, and a few Latin treatises that he could hardly decipher, formed his entire pharmacopœia. As he had chanced to inherit a small fortune from a relative, he became a physician of some note ; for in colonial days wealth and position were as essential as were learning and experience, to enable one to become a good doctor.

I like to think of the rich and pompous old doctor a-riding out to see his patients, clad in his suit of sober brown or claret color with shining buttons made of silver coins. The full-skirted coat had great pockets and flaps, as had the long waistcoat that reached well over the hips. Knee-breeches dressed his shapely legs, while fine silk stockings and buckled shoes displayed his well-turned calves and ankles. On his head he wore a cocked hat and wig. He owned and wore in turn wigs of different sizes and dignity—ties, periwigs, bags, and bobs. His portrait was painted in a full-bottomed wig that rivalled the Lord Chancellor's in size; but his every-day riding-wig was a rather commonplace horsehair affair with a stiff eel-skin cue. One wig he lost by a mysterious accident while attending a patient who was lying ill of a fever, of which the crisis seemed at hand. The doctor decided to remain all night, and sat down by a table in the sick man's room. The hours passed slowly away. Physician and nurse and goodwife talked and droned on; the sick man moaned and tossed in his bed, and begged fruitlessly for water. At last the room grew silent, the tired watchers dozed in their chairs, the doctor nodded and nodded, bringing his eel-skin cue dangerously near the flame of the candle that stood on the table. Suddenly there was heard a sharp explosion, a hiss, a sizzle; and when the smoke cleared, and the terrified occupants of the room collected their senses, the watcher and wife were discovered under the valance of the bed; the doctor stood scorched and bareheaded, looking around for his wig; while the sick man, who had jumped out of bed in the confusion and captured a pitcher of water, drunk half the contents, and thrown the remainder over the doctor's head, was lying behind the bed curtains laughing hysterically at the ridiculous appearance of the man of medicine. Instant death was predicted for the invalid, who, strange to say, either from the laughter or the water, began to recover from that moment. The terrified physician was uncertain whether he ought to attribute the conflagration of his wig to a violent demonstration of the devil in his effort to obtain possession of the sick man's soul, or to the powerful influence of some conjunction of the planets, or to the new-fangled power of electricity which Dr. Franklin had just discovered and was making so much talk about, and was so recklessly tinkering with in Philadelphia at that very time. The doctor had strongly disapproved of Franklin's reprehensible and meddlesome boldness, but he felt that it was best, nevertheless, to write and obtain the philosopher's advice as to the feasibility, advisability, and the best convenience of having one of the new lightning-rods rigged upon his medical back, and running thence up through his wig, thus warding off further alarming demonstration. Ere this was done the mystery of the explosion was solved. When the doctor's new wig arrived from Boston, he ordered his newly purchased negro servant to powder it well ere it was worn. He was horrified to see Pompey give the wig a liberal sprinkling of gunpowder from the powder-horn, instead of starch from the dredging-box; and the explosion of the old wig was no longer assigned to diabolical, thaumaturgical, or meteorological influences.

Let us turn from the doctor and the wig to the book ; let us see what he did when he singed his head and burnt his face. He whipped my little book out of his pocket and turned to page 77 ; there he was told to make " Oyl of Eggs. Take twelve yolks of eggs and put them in a pot over the fire, and let them stand until you perceive them to turn black ; then put them in a press and press out the Oyl." Or he could make "Oyl of Fennel" if he preferred it. But probably the New England goodwife had on hand one of the dozen astounding salves described in the book, that the doctor had ere this instructed her to make, and in which I trust he found due relief.

One cannot wonder that the sick man craved water, when we read what he had had to drink. He had been given, a spoonful at a time, this " Comfortable Juleb for a Feaver," made of " Barley Water & White Wine each one pint, Whey one quart, two ounces of Conserves of Barberries, and the Juyces of two limmons and 2 Oranges." The doctor had also taken (if he had followed his Pearl of Practice) " two Salt white herrings & slit them down the back and bound them to the soles of the feet" of his patient ; and I doubt not he had bled the sufferer at once, for he always bled and purged on every possible occasion.

The Water of Life was also given for fevers, a few drops at a time, and also as a tonic in health.

"Take Balm leaves and stalks, Betony leaves and flowers, Rosemary, red sage, Taragon, Tormentil leaves, Rossolis and Roses, Carnation, Hyssop, Thyme, red strings that grow upon Savory, red Fennel leaves and root, red Mints, of each a handful; bruise these hearbs and put them in a great earthern pot, & pour on them enough White Wine as will cover them, stop them close, and let them steep for eight or nine days; then put to it Cinnamon, Ginger, Angelica-seeds, Cloves, and Nuttmegs, of each an ounce, a little Saffron, Sugar one pound, Raysins solis stoned one pound, the loyns and legs of an old Coney, a fleshy running Capon, the red flesh of the sinews of a leg of Mutton, four young Chickens, twelve larks, the yolks of twelve Eggs, a loaf of White-bread cut in sops, and two or three ounces of Mithridate or Treacle, & as much Muscadine as will cover them all. Distil al with a moderate fire, and keep the first and second waters by themselves; and when there comes no more by Distilling put more Wine into the pot upon the same stuffe and distil it again, and you shal have another good water. This water strengtheneth the Spirit, Brain, Heart, Liver, and Stomack. Take when need is by itself, or with Ale, Beer, or Wine mingled with Sugar."

Who could doubt that it strengthened the spirit, especially when taken with ale or wine? Plainly here do we see the need of a doctor being a good cook. But what pot would hold all that flesh and fowl, that blooming flower-garden of herbs and posies, that assorted lot of fruits and spices, to say nothing of the muscadine?

Our ancestors spared no pains in preparing these

medicines. They did not, shifting all responsibility, run to a chemist or apothecary with a little slip of paper; with their own hands they picked, pulled, pounded, stamped, shredded, dropped, powdered, and distilled, regardless of expense, or trouble, or hard work. Truly they deserved to be cured. They did not measure the drugs with precision in preparing their medicines, as do our chemists nowadays, nor were their prescriptions written in Latin nor with cabalistic marks—the asbestos stomachs and colossal minds of our forefathers were much above such petty minuteness; nor did they administer the doses with exactness. "The bigth of a walnut," "enough to lie on a pen knifes point," "the weight of a shilling," "enough to cover a French crown," "as bigg as a haslenut," "as great as a charger," "the bigth of a Turkeys Egg," "a pretty draught," "a pretty bunch of herbs," "take a little handful," "take a pretty quantity as often as you please"—such are the lax directions that accompany these old prescriptions.

Of course, the remedies given in this book were largely for the diseases of the day. Physicians and parsons, lords and ladies, combined to furnish complex and elaborate prescriptions and perfumes to cure and avert the plague; and the list includes one plague-cure that the Lord Mayor had from the Queen, and I may add that it is a particularly unpleasant and revolting one. A plague swept through New England and decimated the Indian tribes; and though it was not at all like the great plague that devastated London, I doubt not red man and white man took confidingly and faithfully medicines such as are given in this little book of mine : the king's feeble and much-vaunted dose of " White Wine, Ginger, Treacle, and Sage ; " Dr. Atkinson's excellent perfume against the Plague, of "Angelica roots and Wine Vinegar, that if taken fasting, your breath would kill the Plague " (it must have been a fearful dose) ; " Mr. Fenton's the Chirurgeon's Posset and his Sedour Root."

Cures for small-pox and for gout are many. Varied are the lotions for the " pin and web in the eye ; " so many are there of these that it makes me suspect that our forefathers were sadly sore-eyed.

One very prevalent ail that our ancestors had to endure (if we can judge from the number of prescriptions for its relief) was a " cold stomack ; " literally cold, one might think, since most of the cures were by external application. Lady Spencer used a plebeian "greene turfe of grasse" to warm her stomach, with the green side, not the dirt side, placed next the skin. She could scarcely have worn this turf when she was up and around the house, could she ? She must have had it placed upon her while she was in bed. Josselyn said in his "New England Rarities" that, " to wear the skin of a Gripe dressed with the doun on " would cure pain and coldness of the stomach. Thus did like cure like. A " Restorative Bag " of herbs and spices heated in " boyl'd Vinegar " is asserted to be " comfortable." " It must be as hot as can be endured, and keep yourself from studying and musing and it will comfort you much." So it seems you ought not to study nor to muse if your stomach be cold.

Many and manifold are the remedies to "chear the heart," to "drive melancholy," to " cure one pensive," "for the megrums," "for a grief ; " and without doubt the lonely colonists often needed them. We know, too, that "things ill for the heart were beans, pease, sadness, onions, anger, evil tidings, and loss of friends," —a very arbitrary and unjust classification. Melancholy was evidently regarded as a disease, and a much-to-be-lamented one. External applications were made to "drive the worms out of the Brain as well as Dross out of the Stomack." Here is " A pretious water to revive the Spirits : "

"Take four gallons of strong Ale, five ounces of Aniseeds, Liquorish scraped half a pound, Sweet Mints, Angelica, Eccony, Cowslip flowers, Sage & Rosemary Flowers, sweet Marjoram, of each three handfuls, Palitory of the VVal one handful. After it is fermented two or three dayes, distil it in a Limbeck, and in the water infuse one handful of the flowers aforesaid, Cinnamon and Fennel-seed of each half an ounce, Juniper berries bruised one dram, red Rosebuds, roasted Apples & dates sliced and stoned, of each half a pound ; distil it again and sweeten it with some Sugarcandy, and take of Ambergreese, Pearl, Red Coral, Hartshorn pounded, and leaf Gold, of each half a Dram, put them in a fine Linnen bag, and hang them by a thread in a Glasse."

Think of taking all that trouble to make something to cheer the spirits, when the four gallons of strong ale with spices would have fully answered the purpose, without bothering with the herbs and fruits. I suppose the gold and jewels were particularly cheering ingredients, and perhaps entitled the drink to its name of precious water. Indeed, it would be cheering to the spirits nowadays to have the precious metals and gems that were so lavishly used in these ancient medicines.

Full jewelled were the works of English persons of quality in the time of the Merry Monarch and his sire. The gold and gems were not always hung in bags in the medicines ; frequently they were powdered and dissolved, and formed a large portion of the dose. Like Chaucer's Doctour, they believed that "gold in phisike is a cordial." Dr. Gifford's " Amber Pils for Consumption " contained a large quantity of pearls, white amber, and coral, as did also Lady Kent's powder. Sir Edward Spencer's eye-salve was rich in powdered pearls. The Bishop of Worcester's "admirable curing powder " was composed largely of "ten skins of snakes or adders or Slow worms " mixed with "Magistery of Pearls." The latter was a common ingredient, and under the head of " Choice Secrets Made Known " we are told how to manufacture it :

" Dissolve two or three ounces of fine seed Pearl in distill'd Vinegar, and when it's perfectly dissolved and all taken up, pour the Vinegar into a clean glasse Bason ; then drop some few drops of oyl of Tartar upon it, and it will call down the Pearl into the powder ; then pour the Vinegar clean off softly ; then put to the Pearl clear

Conduit or Spring water ; pour that off, and do so often until the taste of the Vinegar and Tartar be clean gone ; then dry the powder of Pearl upon warm embers and keep for your use."

Gold and precious stones were specially necessary "to ease the passion of the Heart," as indeed they are nowadays. In that century, however, they applied the mercenary cure inwardly, and prepared it thus :

"Take Damask Roses half-blown, cut off thier whites, and stamp them very fine, and straine out the Juyce very strong ; moisten it in the stamping with a little Damask Rose water ; then put thereto fine powder Sugar, and boyl it gently to a fine Syrup ; then take the Powders of Amber, Pearl, Rubies, of each half a dram, Ambergreese one scruple, and mingle them with the said syrup till it be somewhat thick, and take a little thereof on a knifes point morning and evening."

I can now understand the reason for the unceasing, the incurable melancholy that hung like a heavy black shadow over so many Puritan divines in the early days of New England, as their gloomy sermons, their sad diaries and letters, plainly show. Those poor ministers had no chance to use these receipts and thus get cured of " worms in the brain," with annual salaries of only £60, which they had to take in corn, wheat, codfish, or bearskins, in any kind of "country pay," or even in wampum, in order to get it at all. Rubies and pearls and gold and coral were scarce drugs in clerical circles in Massachusetts Bay and Plymouth plantations. Even amber and ivory were far from plentiful. We find John Winthrop writing in 1682, "I am straitened, having no ivory beaten, neither any pearle nor corall." Cleopatra drinks were out of fashion in the New World. So Mather and Hooker and Warham were condemned to die with uncheered spirits and unjewelled stomachs.

Another ingredient, unicorns' horns, which were ground and used in powders, must have been difficult to obtain in New England, although I believe Governor Winthrop had one sent to him as a gift from England; and John Endicott, writing to him in 1634, said: "I have sent you Mrs Beggarly her Vnicorns horne & beza stone." Both the unicorn's horn and the bezoar stone were sovereign antidotes against poison. At another time Winthrop had sent to him " bezoar stone, mugwort, orgaine, and galingall root." Ambergris was also too rare and costly for American Puritans to use, though we find Hull writing for golden ambergroose.

Insomnia is not a bane of our modern civilization alone. This little book shows that our ancestors craved and sought sleep just as we do. Here is a prescription to cure sleeplessness, which might be tried by any wakeful soul of modern times, since it requires neither rubies, pearls, nor gold for its manufacture :

"Bruise a handful of Anis-seeds, and steep them in Red Rose Water, & make it up in little bags, & binde one of them to each Nostrill, and it will cause sleep."

So aniseed bags were used in earlier days for a purpose very different from our modern one ; if your nineteenth century nose should refuse to accustom itself to having bags hung on it, you can " Chop Chammomile & crumbs of Brown Bread smal and boyl them with White Wine Vinegar, stir it wel and spred it on a cloth & binde it to the soles of the feet as hot as you can suffer it." And if that should not make you sleepy, there are frankincense-perfumed paper bags for your head, and some very pleasant things made of rose-leaves for your temples, and hard-boiled eggs for the nape of your neck—you can choose from all of these.

They had abounding faith in those days. Several of the prescriptions in "The Queen's Closet " are to cure people at a remote distance, by applying the nostrums to a linen cloth previously wet with the patient's blood. They had plasters of power to put on the back of the head to draw the palate into place ; and wonderful elixirs that would keep a dying man alive five years ; and herb-juices to make a dumb man speak. The following suggestion shows plainly their confiding spirit :

"To Cure Deafnesse.—Take the Garden Dasie roots and make juyce thereof, and lay the worst side of the head low upon the bolster & drop three or four drops thereof into the better Ear ; this do three or four dayes together."

"Simpatheticall " medicines had a special charm for all the Winthrops, and that delightful but gullible old English alchemist, Sir Kenelm Digby, kept them well posted in all the newest nonsense.

In a medical dispensatory of the times the different varieties of medicines used in New England are enumerated. They are leaves, herbs, roots, barks, seeds, flowers, juices, distilled waters, syrups, juleps, decoctions, oils, electuaries, conserves, preserves, lohocks, ointments, plasters, poultices, troches, and pills. These words and articles are all used nowadays, except the lohock, which was to be *licked up*, and in consistency stood in the intermediate ground between an electuary and a syrup. These terms, of course, were in the Galenic practice. In "The Queen's Closet" all the physic was found afield, with the exception of the precious metals and one compound, rubila, which was made of antimony and nitre, and which was in special favor in the Winthrop family—as many of their letters show. They sent it and recommended it to their friends—and better still, they took it faithfully themselves, and with most satisfactory results.

There was also one mineral "oyntment" made of quicksilver, verdigris, and brimstone mixed with "barrows grease," which was good for "horse, man, or other beast." Alum and copperas were once recommended for external use. The powerful "plaister of Paracelsus," also beloved of the Winthrops, was not composed of mineral drugs, as might be supposed, but was made of herbs, and from the ingredients named must have been particularly nasty smelling as well as powerful.

The medicine mithridate forms a part of many of

these prescriptions; it does not seem to be regarded as an alexipharmic, but as a soporific. It is said to have been the cure-all of King Mithridates. I will not give an account of the process of its manufacture; it would fill about three pages of this book, and I should think it would take about six weeks to compound a good dose of it. There are forty-five different articles used, each to be prepared by slow degrees and introduced with great care; some of them (such as the rape of storax, camel's hay, and bellies of skinks) must have been inconvenient to procure in New England. Mithridates would hardly recognize his own medicine in this conglomeration, for when Pompey found his precious receipt it was simple enough: "Pound with care two walnuts, two dried figs, twenty pounds of rice, and a grain of salt." I think we might take this *cum grano salis*.

Queer were the names of some of the herbs; alehoof, which was ground-ivy, or gill-go-by-ground, or haymaids, or twinhoof, or gill-creep-by-ground, and was an herb of Venus, and thus in special use for "passions of the heart," for "amorous cups," which few Puritans dared to meddle with. The blessed thistle, of which one scandalized old writer says, "I suppose the name was put upon it by them that had little holiness themselves." Clary, or cleareye, or Christ's-eye, which latter name makes the same writer indignantly say, "I could wish from my soul that blasphemy and ignorance were ceased among physicians"—as if the poor doctors gave these folknames! The crab-claws so often mentioned was also an herb, otherwise known as knight's-pond water and freshwater-soldier. The mints to flavor were horsemint, spearmint, peppermint, catmint, and heartmint.

The earliest New England colonists did not discover in the new country all the herbs and simples of their native land, but the Indian powwows knew of others that answered every purpose—very healing herbs too, as Wood in his " New England's Prospects " unwillingly acknowledges and thus explains : " Sometimes the devill for requitall of their worship recovers the partie to nuzzle them up in thier devilish Religion." The planters sent to England for herbs and drugs, as existing inventories show ; and they planted seeds and soon had plenty of home herbs that grew apace in every dooryard. The New Haven colony passed a law at an early date to force the destruction of a " great stinking poisonous weed," which is said to have been the *Datura stramonium*, a medicinal herb. It had been brought over by the Jamestown colonists, and had spread miraculously, and was known as " Jimson " or Jamestown weed.

Josselyn gives in his " New England's Rarities " an interesting list of the herbs known and used by the colonists. Cotton Mather said the most useful and favorite medicinal plants were alehoof, garlick, elder, sage, rue, and saffron. Saffron has never lost its popularity. To this day " saffern tea " is a standing country dose in New England, especially for the " jarnders." Elder, rue, and saffron were English herbs that were made settlers here and carefully cultivated ; so also were sage, hyssop, tansy, wormwood,

celandine, comfrey, mallows, mayweed, yarrow, cham-
omile, dandelion, shepherd's-purse, bloody dock, elecampane, motherwort, burdock, plantain, catnip, mint,
fennel, and dill—all now flaunting weeds.   Dunton
wrote with praise of a Dr. Bullivant, in Boston, in
1686, " He does not direct his patients to the East
Indies to look for drugs when they may have far
better out of their gardens."

There is a charm in these medical rules in my old
book, in spite of the earth-worms and wood-lice and
adders and vipers in which some of them abound (to
say nothing of other and more shocking ingredients).
In surprising and unpleasant compounds they do not
excel the prescriptions in a serious medical book published in Exeter, New Hampshire, as late as 1835.
Nor is Cotton Mather's favorite and much-vaunted
ingredient *millepedes*, or sowbugs, once mentioned
within.   All are not vile in my Queen's Closet—far
from it.   Medicines composed of Canary wine or
sack, with rose-water, juice of oranges and lemons,
syrup of clove-gillyflower, loaf sugar, " Mallago raisins," nutmegs, cloves, cinnamon, mace, remind me
strongly of Josselyn's New England Nectar, and render me quite dissatisfied with our modern innovations
of quinine, antipyrine, and phenacetin, and even
make only passively welcome the innocuous and un-
interesting homœopathic pellet and drop.

Many other dispensatories, guides, collections, and
records of medical customs and concoctions, remain
to us even of the earliest days.   We have the private
receipt-book of John Winthrop, a gathering of choice

receipts given to him in manuscript by one Stafford, of England. These receipts have been printed in the Collections of the Massachusetts Historical Society for the year 1862, with delightful notes by Dr. Oliver Wendell Holmes, and are of the same nature as those in the Queen's Closet. Here is one, which was venomous, yet harmless enough :

"My black powder against ye plague, small-pox, purples, all sorts of feavers, Poyson ; either by way of prevention or after Infection. In the Moneth of March take Toades, as many as you will, alive; putt them into an Earthen pott, so yt it be halfe full ; Cover it with a broad tyle or Iron plate, then overwhelme the pott, so yt ye bottome may be uppermost; putt charcoals round about it and over it and in the open ayre not in an house ; sett it on fire and lett it burne out and extinguish of itself ; when it is cold take out the toades ; and in an Iron morter pound them very well ; and searce them ; then in a Crucible calcine them ; So againe ; pound them & searce them again. The first time they will be a brown powder, the next time blacke. Of this you may give a dragme in a Vehiculum or drinke Inwardly in any Infection taken : and let them sweat upon it in their bedds : but let them not cover their heads ; especially in the Small-Pox. For prevention half a dragme will suffice."

I do not know what meteorological influence was assigned to the month of March ; perhaps it was chosen because toads would be uncommonly hard to get in New England during that month.

All the medicines in Dr. Stafford's little collection

were not, however, so unalluring, and were, on the
whole, very healing and respectable.   He prescribed
nitre, antimony, rhubarb, jalap, and spermaceti, "the
sovereignest thing on earth—for an inward bruise;"
and he also culled herbs and simples in vast variety.
He gave some very good advice regarding the con-
duct of a physician, the latter clause of which might
well be heeded to-day.

" Nota bene.   No man can with a good Conscience take
a fee or Reward before ye partie receive benefit apparent
and then he is not to demand anything but what God
shall putt it into the heart of the partie to give him.   A
man is not to neglect that partie to whom he had once
administered but to visit him at least once a day & to
medle with no more than he can well attend."

The account books of other old New England physicians, and other medical books such as " A Treatise
of Choice Spagyrical Preparations," show to us that
the seventeenth and eighteenth century medicines,
though disgusting, were not deadly.   We know what
medicines were given the colonists on their sea
journey hither: " Oil of Cloves, Origanum, Purging
Pills, and Ressin of Jalap " for the toothache ; a Dia-
phoretic Bolus for an "Extream Cold;" Spirits of
Castor and Oil of Amber for "Histericall Fitts;"
"Seaurell Emplaisters for a broken Shin;" and for
other afflictions, "Gascons Powder, Liquorish, Car-
minative Seeds, Syrup of Saffron, Pectoral Syrups
and Somniferous Boluses."

Cod livers were given then as cod-liver oil is given now, "to restore them that have melted their Grease." A favorite prescription was "Rulandus, his Balsam which tho' it smel not wel" was properly powerful, and could be gotten down if carefully hidden in "poudered shuger."

Cotton Mather, who tried his skilful hand at writing upon almost every grave and weighty subject, composed a book of medical advice called the "Angel of Bethesda." It was written when he was sixty years of age, but was never printed; the manuscript is preserved in the library of the American Antiquarian Society at Worcester. It begins characteristically with a sermon, and is fantastically peppered with pompous scriptural and classical quotations, as was the Mather wont. The ingredients of the prescriptions are vile beyond belief, though, as Mather said in one of his letters, they are "powerful and parable physicks," which are two desirable qualities or attributes of any physic. The book gives an interesting account of Mather's share in that great colonial revolution in medicine—the introduction of the custom of inoculation for the small-pox. His friend, Dr. Zabdiel Boylston, of Boston, was the first physician to inaugurate this great step by inoculating his own son—a child six years old. Deep was the horror and aversion felt by the colonial public toward both the practice and practitioners of this daring innovation, and fiercely and malignantly was it opposed; but its success soon conquered opposition, and also that fell disease, which six times within a hundred years had

devastated New England, bringing death, disfigurement, and business misfortunes to the colonists. So
universal was the branding produced by this scourge
that scarcely an advertisement containing any personal description appears in any colonial print, without containing the words, pock-fretten, pock-marked,
pock-pitted, or pock-broken.

Through the possibility of having the small-pox to
order, arose the necessity of small-pox hospitals, to
which whole families or parties resorted to pass
through the ordeal in concert. Small-pox parties
were made the occasion of much friendly intercourse ; they were called classes. Thus in the *Salem
Gazette* of April 22, 1784, after Point Shirley was set
aside as a small-pox retreat, it was advertised that
" Classes will be admitted for Small pox." These
classes were real country outings, having an additional zest of novelty since one could fully partici-
pate in the pleasures, profits, and pains of a small-
pox party but once in a lifetime. Much etiquette
and deference was shown over these " physical gatherings," formal invitations were sometimes sent to join
the function at a private house. Here is an extract
from a letter written July 8, 1775, by Joseph Bar-
rell, a Boston merchant, to Colonel Wentworth : " Mr.
Storer has invited Mrs. Martin to take the small-pox
in her house ; if Mrs. Wentworth desires to get rid of
her fears in the same way we will accomodate her in
the best way we can. I've several friends that I've
invited, and none of them will be more welcome than
Mrs. Wentworth." These brave classes took their

various purifying and sudorific medicines in cheerful concert, were "grafted" together, "broke out" together, were feverish together, sweat together, scaled off together, and convalesced together. Not a very prepossessing conjoining medium would inoculation appear to have been, but many a pretty and sentimental love affair sprang up between mutually "pock-fretten" New Englanders.

The small-pox hospitals were of various degrees of elegance and comfort, and were widely advertised. I have found four separate announcements in one of the small sheets of a Federal newspaper. From the luxurious high-priced retreat "without Mercury" were grades descending to the Suttonian, Brunonian, Pincherian, Dimsdalian, and other plebeian establishments, in which the patient paid from fifteen to as low as three dollars per week for lodging, food, medicine, care, and inoculation. At the latter cheap establishment each person was obliged to furnish for his individual use one sheet and one pillow-case— apparently a meagre outfit for sickness, but possibly merely a supplemental one.

This is a fair example of the prevailing advertisement of small-pox hospitals, from the *Connecticut Courant* of November 30, 1767 :

"Dr. Uriah Rogers, Jr., of Norwalk County of Fairfield takes this method to acquaint the Publick & particularly such as are desirous of taking the Small Pox by way of Inoculation, that having had Considerable Experience in that Branch of Practice and carried on the same the last season with great Success ; has lately erected a convenient Hospital for that purpose just within the Jurisdiction Line of the Province of New York about nine miles distant from N. Y. Harbour, where he intends to carry said Branch of Practice from the first of October next to the first of May next.   And that all such as are disposed to favour him with their Custom may depend upon being well provided with all necessary accomodations, Provisions & the best Attendance at the moderate Expence of Four Pounds Lawful Money to Each Patient. That after the first Sett or Class he purposes to give no Occasion for waiting to go in Particular Setts but to admit Parties singly, just as it suits them.   As he has another Good House provided near Said Hospital where his family are to live, and where all that come after the first Sett that go into the Hospital are to remain with his Family until they are sufficiently Prepared & Inoculated & Until it is apparent that they haven taken the infection."

Of all the advertisements of small-pox hospitals, inoculation, etc., which appear in the newspapers through the eighteenth century, none is more curious, more comic than this from a Boston paper of 1772:

"Ibrahim Mustapha Inoculator to his Sublime Highness & the Janissaries : original Inventor and sole Proprietor of that Inestimable Instrument, the Circassian Needle, begs leave to acquaint the Nobility & Gentry of this City and its Environs that he is just arrived from Constantinople where he has inoculated about 50,000 Persons without losing a Single Patient.   He requires not the least Preparation Regimen or Confinement.

Ladies and Gentlemen who wish to be inoculated only acquaint him with how many Pimples they choose and he makes the exact number of Punctures with his Needle which Produces the Eruptions in the very Picquers. Ladies who fancy a favorite Pitt may have it put in any Spot they please, and of any size : not the Slightest Fever or Pain attends the Eruption ; much less any of those frightful Convulsions so usual in all the vulgar methods of Inoculation, even in the famous Peter Puffs. This amazing Needle more truly astonishing and not less useful than the Magnetic one, has this property in common with the latter, that by touching the point of a common needle it communicates its wonderful Virtues to it in the same manner that Loadstone does to Iron. And that no part of this extensive Continent may want the Benefit of this Superlatively excellent Method, Ibrahim Mustapha proposes to touch several Needles in order to have them distributed to different Colonies by which means the Small Pocks may be entirely eradicated as it has been in the Turkish Empire."

Generous Ibrahim Mustapha! despite the testimony of the Janissaries and the entire Turkish Empire, I cannot doubt that in your early youth you frequently kissed the Blarney Stone, hence your fluent tongue and your gallant proposition to becomingly decorate with pits the ladies.

Besides the scourge of small-pox, the colonists were afflicted grievously with other malignant distempers —fatal throat diseases, epidemic influenzas, putrid fevers, terrible fluxes; and as the art of sanitation was absolutely disregarded and almost unknown, as drainage there was none, and the notion of disinfection was in feeble infancy, we cannot wonder that the death-rates were high. Well might the New Englander say with Sir Thomas Browne: "Considering the thousand doors that lead to death, I do thank my God that we can die but once."

Cotton Mather was not the only kind-hearted New England minister who set up to heal the body as well as the soul of the entire town. All the early parsons seem to have turned eagerly to medicine. The Wigglesworths were famous doctors. President Hoar, of Harvard College, President Rogers, President Chauncey, all practised medicine. The latter's six sons were all ministers, and all good doctors, too. It was a parson, Thomas Thatcher, who wrote the first medical treatise published in America, a set of "Brief Rules for the Care of the Small Pocks," printed as a broadside in 1677. Many of the early parsons played also the part of apothecary, buying drugs at wholesale and compounding and selling medicines to their parishioners. Small wonder that Cotton Mather called the union of physic and piety an "Angelical Conjunction."

Other professions and callings joined hands with chirurgy and medicine. Innkeepers, magistrates, grocers, and schoolmasters were doctors. One surgeon was a butcher—sadly similar callings in those days. This butcher-surgeon was not Mr. Pighogg, the Plymouth "churregein," whose unpleasant name was, I trust, only the cacographical rendering of the good old English name Peacock.

With all these amateur and semi-professional rivals, it is no wonder that Giles Firmin, who knew how to pull teeth and bleed and sweat in a truly professional manner, complained that he found physic but a " meene helpe " in the new land.

So vast was the confidence of the community in some or any kind of a doctor, and in self-doctoring, that as late as the year 1721 there was but one regularly graduated physician in Boston — Dr. Samuel Douglas; and it may be noted that he was one of the most decided opponents of inoculation for small-pox.

Colonial dames also boldly tried their hand at the healing art; the first two, Anne Hutchinson and Margaret Jones, did not thrive very well at the trade. The banishment of the former has oft been told. The latter was hung as a witch, and the worst evidence against her character, the positive proof of her diabolical power was, that her medicines being so simple, they worked such wonderful cures. At the close of King Philip's War the Council of Connecticut paid Mrs. Allyn £20 for her services to the sick, and Mistress Sarah Sands doctored on Block Island. Sarah Alcock, the wife of a chirurgeon, was also " active in physick ;" and Mistress Whitman, the Marlborough midwife, visited her patients on snow-shoes, and lived to be seventy-eight years old, too. In the Phipps Street Burying Ground in Charlestown is the tombstone of a Boston midwife who died in 1761, aged seventy-six years, and who, could we believe the record on the gravestone, "by ye blessing of God has brought into this world above 130,000 children." But a close

examination shows that the number on the ancient
headstone, through the mischievous manipulation of
modern hands, has received a figure at either end, and
the good old lady can only be charged with three
thousand additions to wretched humanity.

Negroes, and illiterate persons of all complex-
ions, set up as doctors. Old Joe Pye and Sabbatus
were famous Indian healers. Indian squaws, such as
Molly Orcutt, sold many a decoction of leaves and
barks to the planters, and, like Hiawatha,

> " Wandered eastward, wandered westward,
>   Teaching men the use of simples,
>   And the antidotes for poisons,
>   And the cure of all diseases."

A good old Connecticut doctor had a negro servant,
Primus, who rode with him and helped him in his
surgery and shop. When the master died, Doctor
Primus started in to practise medicine himself, and
proved extraordinarily successful throughout the
county; even his master's patients did not disdain
to employ the black successor, wishing no doubt their
wonted bolus and draught.

In spite of the fact that everyone and anyone
seemed to be permitted, and was considered fitted to
prescribe medicine, the colonists were sharp enough
on the venders of quack medicines—or, perhaps I
should say, of powerless medicines—on "runnagate
chyrurgeons and physickemongers, saltimbancoes,
quacksalvers, charlatans, and all impostourous empi-
ricks." As early as 1631, one Nicholas Knapp was

fined and whipped for pretending " to cure the scur-
vey by a water of noe worth nor value which he sold
att a very deare rate." The planters were terribly
prostrated by scurvy, and doubtless were specially
indignant at this heartless cheat.

Tides of absurd attempts at medicine, or rather at
healing, swept over the scantily settled New England
villages in colonial days, just as we have seen in our
own day, in our great cities, the abounding success—
financially—of the blue-glass cure, the faith cure, and
of science healing. The Rain Water Doctor worked
wondrous miracles, and did a vast and lucrative business until he was unluckily drowned in a hogshead of
his own medicine at his own door. Bishop Berkeley,
in his pamphlet Siris, started a flourishing tar-water
craze, which lived long and died slowly. This cure-
all, like the preceding aquatic physic, had the merit
of being cheap. A quart of tar steeped for forty-eight
hours in a gallon of water, tainted the water enough
to make it fit for dosing. Perhaps the most expansive
swindle was that of Dr. Perkins, with his Metallic
Tractors. He was born in Norwich, Conn., in 1740,
and found fortune and fame in his native land. Still
he was expelled from the association of physicians in
his own country, but managed to establish a Perkinean
Institution in London with a fine, imposing list of officers and managers, of whom Benjamin Franklin's son
was one. He had poems and essays and eulogies and
books written about him, and it was claimed by his
followers that he cured one million and a half of suf-
ferers. At any rate, he managed to carry off £10,000

of good English money to New England. His wonderful Metallic Tractors were little slips of iron and brass three inches long, blunt at one end, and pointed at the other, and said to be of opposite electrical conditions. They cost five guineas a pair. When drawn or trailed for several minutes over a painful or diseased spot on the human frame, they positively removed and cured all ache, smart, or soreness. I have never doubted they worked wonderful cures ; so did bits of wood, of lead, of stone, of earthenware, in the hands of scoffers, when the tractorated patients did not see the bits, and fancied that the manipulator held Metallic Tractors.

As years passed on various useful medicines became too much the vogue, and were used to too vast and too deleterious an extent, particularly mercury. Many a poor salivated patient sacrificed his teeth to his doctor's mercurial doses. One such toothless sufferer, a carpenter, having little ready money, offered to pay his physician in hay-rakes ; and he took a revengeful delight in manufacturing the rakes of green, unseasoned wood. After a few days' use in the sunny fields, the doctor's rakes were as toothless as their maker.

Physicians' fees were " meene " enough in olden times ; but sixpence a visit in Hadley and Northampton in 1730, and only eightpence in Revolutionary times. A blood-letting, or a jaw-splitting tooth-drawing cost the sufferer eightpence extra. No wonder the doctor cupped and bled on every occasion. In extravagant Hartford the opulent doctor got a shilling a visit. Naturally all the chirurgeons eked out and augmented their scanty fees by compounding and selling their own medicines, and dosed often and dosed deeply, since by their doses they lived. In many communities a bone-setter had to be paid a salary by the town in order to keep him, so few and slight were his private emoluments, even as a physic-monger.

The science of nursing the sick was, in early days, unknown; there were but few who made a profession of nursing, and those few were deeply to be dreaded. In taking care of the sick, as in other kindnesses, the neighborly instinct, ever so keen, so living in New England, showed no lagging part. For it is plain to any student of early colonial days that, if the chief foundation of the New England commonwealth was religion, the second certainly was neighborliness. There was a constant exchange of kindly and loving attentions between families and individuals. It showed itself in all the petty details of daily life, in assistance in housework and in the field, in house-raising. Did a man build a barn, his neighbors flocked to drive a pin, to lay a stone, to stand forever in the edifice as token of their friendly goodwill. The most eminent, as well as the poorest neighbors, thus assisted. In nothing was this neighborly feeling more constantly shown than in the friendly custom of visiting and watching with the sick; and it was the only available assistance. Men and women in this care and attention took equal part. As in all other neighborly duties, good Judge Sewall was never remiss in the sick-room. He was generous with his gifts and generous with his time, even to those humble in the community. Such entries as this abound in his diary : " Oct. 26th 1702. Visited languishing Mr. Sam Whiting. I gave him 2 Balls of Chockalett and a pound of Figgs." And when Mr. Bayley lay ill of a fever, he prayed with him and took care of him through many a long night, and wrote:

" When I came away call'd his wife into the Next Chamber and gave her Two Five Shilling Bits. She very modestly and kindly accepted them and said I had done too much already. I told her if the State of my family would have born it I ought to have watched with Mr. Bayley as much as that came to."

To others he gave China oranges, dishes of marmalet, Meers Cakes, Banberry Cakes ; and even to well-to-do people gave gifts of money, sometimes specifying for what purpose he wished the gift to be applied.

The universal custom of praying at inordinate length and frequency with sick persons was of more doubtful benefit, though of equally kind intent. One cannot but be amazed to find how many persons— ministers, elders, deacons, and laymen were allowed to enter the sick-room and pray by the bedside of the invalid, thus indeed giving him, as Sewall said, "a lift Heavenward." Sometimes a succession of prayers filled the entire day.

Judge Sewall's friendly prayers and visits were not always welcome. After visiting sick Mr. Brattle the Judge writes, but without any resentment, " he plainly told me that frequent visits were prejudicial to him, it provok'd him to speak more than his strength would bear, would have me come seldom." And on September 20, 1690, he met with this reception:

"Mr. Moody and I went before the others came to neighbor Hurd who lay dying where also Mr. Allen came in. Nurse Hurd told her husband who was there and what he had to say; whether he desir'd them to pray with him; He said with some earnestness, Hold your tongue, which was repeated three times to his wives repeated entreaties; once he said Let me alone or Be quiet (whether that made a fourth or was one of the three do not remember) and, My Spirits are gon. At last Mr. Moody took him up pretty roundly and told him he might with some labour have given a pertinent answer. When we were ready to come away Mr. Moody bid him put forth a little Breath to ask prayer, and said twas the last time had to speak to him; At last ask'd him, doe you desire prayer, shall I pray with you. He answered, Ay for Gods sake and thank'd Mr. Moody when had done. His former carriage was very startling and amazing to us. About one at night he died. About 11 o'clock I supposed to hear neighbor Mason at prayer with him just as my wife and I were going to bed."

One cannot but feel a thrill of sympathy for poor, dying Hurd on that hot September night, fairly hectored by pious, loud-voiced neighbors into eternity; and can well believe that many a colonial invalid who lived through mithridate and rubila, through sweating and blood-letting, died of the kindly and godly-intentioned praying of his neighbors.

XV

FUNERAL AND BURIAL CUSTOMS

THE earliest New Englanders had no religious services at a funeral. Not wishing to "confirm the popish error that prayer is to be used for the dead or over the dead," they said no words, either of grief, resignation, or faith, but followed the coffin and filled the grave in silence. Lechford has given us a picture of a funeral in New England in the seventeenth century, which is full of simple dignity, if not of sympathy:

"At Burials nothing is read, nor any funeral sermon made, but all the neighborhood or a goodly company of them come together by tolling of the bell, and carry the dead solemnly to his grave, and then stand by him while he is buried. The ministers are most commonly present."

As was the fashion in England at that date, laudatory verses and sentences were fastened to the bier or herse. The name herse was then applied to the draped catafalque or platform upon which the candles stood and the coffin rested, not as now the word

hearse to a carriage for the conveyance of the dead.
Sewall says of the funeral of the Rev. Thomas Shepherd : " There were some verses, but none pinned on
the Herse." These verses were often printed after
the funeral. The publication of mourning broadsides
and pamphlets, black-bordered and dismal, was a
large duty of the early colonial press. They were
often decorated gruesomely with skull and crossbones, scythes, coffins, and hour-glasses, all-seeing
eyes with rakish squints, bow-legged skeletons, and
miserable little rosetted winding-sheets.

A writer in the *New England Courant* of November
12, 1722, says :

Of all the different species of poetry now in use I find
the Funeral Elegy to be most universally admired and
used in New England. There is scarce a plough jogger
or country cobler that has read our Psalms and can make
two lines jingle, who has not once in his life at least exercised his talent in this way. Nor is there one country
house in fifty which has not its walls garnished with half
a Score of these sort of Poems which praise the Dead to
the Life."

When a Puritan died his friends conspired in
mournful concert, or labored individually and painfully, to bring forth as tributes of grief and respect,
rhymed elegies, anagrams, epitaphs, acrostics, epicediums, and threnodies ; and singularly enough,
seemed to reserve for these gloomy tributes their
sole attempt at facetiousness. Ingenious quirks and
puns, painful and complicate jokes (printed in italics

that you may not escape nor mistake them) bestrew these funeral verses. If a man chanced to have a name of any possible twist of signification, such as Green, Stone, Blackman, in doleful puns did he posthumously suffer; and his friends and relatives endured vicariously also, for to them these grinning death's-heads of rhymes were widely distributed.

It was with a keen sense of that humor which comes, as Sydney Smith says, from sudden and unexpected contrast, that I read a heavily bordered sheet entitled in large letters, "A Grammarian's Funeral." It was printed at the death of Schoolmaster Woodmancey, and was so much admired that it was brought forth again at the demise of Ezekiel Cheever, who died in 1708 after no less than seventy years of school-teaching. I think we may truly say of him, teaching at ninety-three years of age,

> " With throttling hands of death at strife,
> Ground he at grammar."

For the consideration and investigation of Browning Societies, I give a few lines from this New England conception of a Grammarian's Funeral.

> " Eight parts of Speech This Day wear Mourning Gowns,
> *Declin'd* Verbs, Pronouns, Participles, and Nouns.
> The Substantive seeming the limbed best
> Would set an hand to bear him to his *Rest*
> The Adjective with very grief did say
> Hold me by Strength or I shall faint away.

Great Honour was conferred on *Conjugations*
They were to follow next to the *Relations*

.   .   .   .

But Lego said, by me his got his Skill
And therefore next the Herse I follow will
A Doleful Day for *Verbs* they look so *Moody*
They drove Spectators to a mournful Study."

I have a strong suspicion that this funeral poem
may have been learned by heart by succeeding generations of Boston scholars, as a sort of grammatical
memory-rhyme—a mournful study, indeed.

Funeral sermons were also printed, with trappings
of sombreness, black-bordered, with death's-heads and
crossbones on the covers. These sermons were not,
however, preached at the time of the funeral, save
in exceptional cases. It is said that one was delivered at the funeral of President Chauncey in 1671.
Cotton Mather preached one at the funeral of Fitz-
John Winthrop in 1707, and another at the funeral
of Waitstill Winthrop in 1717. Gradually there crept
in the custom of having suitable prayers at the house
before the burial procession formed, the first instance
being probably at the funeral of Pastor Adams, of Roxbury, in 1683. Sometimes a short address was given
at the grave, as when Jonathan Alden was buried at
Duxbury, in 1697. The *Boston News Letter* of December 31, 1730, notes a prayer at a funeral, and says:
" Tho' a custom in the Country-Towns 'tis a Singular
instance in this Place, but it's wish'd may prove a
Leading Example to the General Practice of so
Christian and Decent a Custom." Whitefield wrote

disparagingly of the custom of not speaking at the grave.

We see Judge Sewall mastering his grief at his mother's burial, delaying for a few moments the filling of the grave, and speaking some very proper words of eulogy "with passion and tears." He jealously notes, however, when the Episcopal burial service is given in Boston, saying : "The Office for the dead is a Lying bad office, makes no difference between the precious and the Vile."

There were, as a rule, two sets of bearers appointed ; under-bearers, usually young men, who carried the coffin on a bier ; and pall-bearers, men of age, dignity, or consanguinity, who held the corners of the pall which was spread over the coffin and hung down over the heads and bodies of the under-bearers. As the coffin was sometimes carried for a long distance, there were frequently appointed a double set of under-bearers, to share the burden. I have been told that mort-stones were set by the wayside in some towns, upon which the bearers could rest the heavy coffin for a short time on their way to the burial-place ; but I find no record or proof of this statement. The pall, or bier-cloth, or mort-cloth, as it was called, was usually bought and owned by the town, and was of heavy purple, or black broadcloth, or velvet. It often was kept with the bier in the porch of the meeting-house ; but in some communities the bier, a simple shelf or table of wood on four legs about a foot and a half long, was placed over the freshly filled-in grave and left sombrely waiting till it was needed to carry another coffin to the burial-place. In many towns there were no gravediggers; sympathizing friends made the simple coffin and dug the grave.

In Londonderry, N. H., and neighboring towns that had been settled by Scotch-Irish planters, the announcement of a death was a signal for cessation of daily work throughout the neighborhood. Kindly assistance was at once given at the house of mourning. Women flocked to do the household work and to prepare the funeral feast. Men brought gifts of food, or household necessities, and rendered all the advice and help that was needed. A gathering was held the night before the funeral, which in feasting and drinking partook somewhat of the nature of an Irish wake. Much New England rum was consumed at this gathering, and also before the procession to the grave, and after the interment the whole party returned to the house for an " arval," and drank again. The funeral rum-bill was often an embarrassing and hampering expense to a bereaved family for years.

This liberal serving of intoxicating liquor at a funeral was not peculiar to these New Hampshire towns, nor to the Scotch-Irish, but prevailed in every settlement in the colonies until the temperance-awakening days of this century. Throughout New England bills for funeral baked meats were large in items of rum, cider, whiskey, lemons, sugar, spices.

To show how universally liquor was served to all who had to do with a funeral, let me give the bill for the mortuary expenses of David Porter, of Hartford, who was drowned in 1678.

" By a pint of liquor for those who dived for him..   1s.
By a quart of liquor for those who bro't him home.   2s.
By two quarts of wine & 1 gallon of cyder to jury
    of inquest..................................   5s.
By 8 gallons & 3 qts. wine for funeral............   £1 15s.
By Barrel cyder for funeral....................   16s.
1 Coffin......................................   12s.
Windeing sheet...............................   18s."

Even town paupers had two or three gallons of rum or a barrel of cider given by the town to serve as speeding libations at their unmourned funerals. The liquor at the funeral of a minister was usually paid for by the church or town—often interchangeable terms for the same body. The parish frequently gave, also, as in the case of the death of Rev. Job Strong, of Portsmouth, in 1751, " the widow of our deceased pasture a full suit of mourning."

A careful, and above all an experienced committee was appointed to superintend the mixing of the funeral grog or punch, and to attend to the liberal and frequent dispensing thereof.

Hawthorne was so impressed with the enjoyable reunion New Englanders found in funerals that he wrote of them :

"They were the only class of scenes, so far as my investigation has taught me, in which our ancestors were wont to steep their tough old hearts in wine and strong drink and indulge in an outbreak of grisly jollity.

Look back through all the social customs of New England in the first century of her existence and read all her traits of character, and find one occasion other than a funeral feast where jollity was sanctioned by universal practice. . . . Well, old friends! Pass on with your burden of mortality and lay it in the tomb with jolly hearts. People should be permitted to enjoy themselves in their own fashion ; every man to his taste—but New England must have been a dismal abode for the man of pleasure when the only boon-companion was Death."

This picture has been given by Sargent of country funerals in the days of his youth :

" When I was a boy, and was at an academy in the country, everybody went to everybody's funeral in the village. The population was small, funerals rare ; the preceptor's absence would have excited remark, and the boys were dismissed for the funeral. A table with liquors was always provided. Every one, as he entered, took off his hat with his left hand, smoothed down his hair with his right, walked up to the coffin, gazed upon the corpse, made a crooked face, passed on to the table, took a glass of his favorite liquor, went forth upon the plat before the house and talked politics, or of the new road, or compared crops, or swapped heifers or horses until it was time to *lift*. A clergyman told me that when settled at Concord, N. H., he officiated at the funeral of a little boy. The body was borne in a chaise, and six little nominal pall-bearers, the oldest not thirteen, walked by the side of the vehicle. Before they left the house a sort of master of ceremonies took them to the table and mixed a tumbler of gin, water, and sugar for each."

It was a hard struggle against established customs and ideas of hospitality, and even of health, when the use of liquor at funerals was abolished. Old people sadly deplored the present and regretted the past. One worthy old gentleman said, with much bitterness: "Temperance has done for funerals."

As soon as the larger cities began to accrue wealth, the parentations of men and women of high station were celebrated with much pomp and dignity, if not with religious exercises. Volleys were fired over the freshly made grave—even of a woman. A barrel and a half of powder was consumed to do proper honor to Winthrop, the chief founder of Massachusetts. At the funeral of Deputy-Governor Francis Willoughby eleven companies of militia were in attendance, and "with the doleful noise of trumpets and drums, in their mourning posture, three thundering volleys of shot were discharged, answered with the loud roarings of great guns rending the heavens with noise at the loss of so great a man." When Governor Leverett died, in 1679, the bearers carried banners. The principal men of the town bore the armor of the deceased, from helmet to spur, and the Governor's horse was led with banners. The funeral-recording Sewall has left us many a picture of the pomp of burial. Colonel Samuel Shrimpton was buried "with Arms" in 1697, "Ten Companies, No Herse nor Trumpet but a horse Led. Mourning Coach also & Horses in Mourning, Scutcheons on their sides and Deaths Heads on their foreheads." Fancy those coach-horses with gloomy death's-heads on their foreheads. At the funeral of Lady Andros, which was held in church, six " mourning women " sat in front of the draped pulpit, and the hearse was drawn by six horses. This English fashion of paid mourners was not common among sincere New Englanders; Lady Andros was a Church of England woman, not a Puritan. The cloth from the pulpit was usually given, after the burial, to the minister. In 1736 the *Boston News Letter* tells of the pulpit and the pew of the deceased being richly draped and adorned with escutcheons at a funeral. Thus were New England men, to quote Sir Thomas Browne, " splendid in ashes, and pompous in the grave."

Many local customs prevailed. In Hartford and neighboring towns all ornaments, mirrors, and pictures were muffled with napkins and cloths at the time of the funerals, and sometimes the window-shutters were kept closed in the front of the house and tied together with black for a year, as was the fashion in Philadelphia.

Hawthorne tells us that at the death of Sir William Pepperell the entire house was hung with black, and all the family portraits were covered with black crape.

The order of procession to the grave was a matter of much etiquette. High respect and equally deep slights might be rendered to mourners in the place assigned. Usually some magistrate or person of dignity walked with the widow. Judge Sewall often speaks of " leading the widow in a mourning cloak."

One great expense of a funeral was the gloves. In

some communities these were sent as an approved
and elegant form of invitation to relatives and friends
and dignitaries, whose presence was desired. Occasionally, a printed " invitation to follow the corps "
was also sent. One for the funeral of Sir William
Phipps is still in existence—a fantastically gloomy
document. In the case of a funeral of any person
prominent in State, Church, or society, vast numbers
of gloves were disbursed; " none of 'em of any figure but what had gloves sent to 'em." At the funeral
of the wife of Governor Belcher, in 1736, over one
thousand pairs of gloves were given away; at the
funeral of Andrew Faneuil three thousand pairs; the
number frequently ran up to several hundred. Different qualities of gloves were presented at the same
funeral to persons of different social circles, or of
varied degrees of consanguinity or acquaintance.
Frequently the orders for these *vales* were given in
wills. As early as 1633 Samuel Fuller, of Plymouth,
directed in his will that his sister was to have gloves
worth twelve shillings; Governor Winthrop and his
children each " a paire of gloves of five shilling; "
while plebeian Rebecca Prime had to be contented
with a cheap pair worth two shillings and sixpence.
The under-bearers who carried the coffin were usually
given different and cheaper gloves from the pall-
bearers. We find seven pairs of gloves given at a
pauper's funeral, and not under the head of " Ex-
trodny Chearges " either.

Of course the minister was always given gloves.
They were showered on him at weddings, christen-

ings, funerals.   Andrew Eliot, of the North Church,
in Boston, kept a record of the gloves and rings
which he received ; and, incredible as it may seem,
in thirty-two years he was given two thousand nine
hundred and forty pairs of gloves.   Though he had
eleven children, he and his family could scarcely
wear them all, so he sold them through kindly Boston
milliners, and kept a careful account of the transac-
tion, of the lamb's-wool gloves, the kid gloves, the
long gloves—which were probably Madam Eliot's.
He received between six and seven hundred dollars
for the gloves, and a goodly sum also for funeral
rings.

Various kinds of gloves are specified as suitable
for mourning ; for instance, in the *Boston Independent Advertiser* in 1749, " Black Shammy Gloves and
White Glazed Lambs Wool Gloves suitable for Funerals."   White gloves were as often given as black,
and purple gloves also.   Good specimens of old
mourning gloves have been preserved in the cabinets
of the Worcester Society of Antiquity.

At the funeral of Thomas Thornhill " 17 pair of
White Gloves at £1 15s. 6d., 31½ yard Corle for Scarfs
£3 10s. 10½d., and Black and White Ribbin " were
paid for.   In 1737 Sir William Pepperell sent to
England for " 4 pieces Hat mourning and 2 pieces
of Cyprus or Hood mourning."   This hat mourning
took the form of long weepers, which were worn on
the hat at the funeral, and as a token of respect afterward by persons who were not relatives of the deceased.   Judge Sewall was always punctilious in

thus honoring the dead in his community. On May 2, 1709, he writes thus :

" Being artillery day and Mr. Higginson dead I put on my mourning Rapier and put a mourning ribbon in my little Cane."

Rings were given at funerals, especially in wealthy families, to near relatives and persons of note in the community. Sewall records in his diary, in the years from 1687 to 1725, the receiving of no less than fifty-seven mourning rings. We can well believe the story told of Doctor Samuel Buxton, of Salem, who died in 1758, aged eighty-one years, that he left to his heirs a quart tankard full of mourning rings which he had received at funerals ; and that Rev. Andrew Eliot had a mugful. At one Boston funeral, in 1738, over two hundred rings were given away. At Wait-still Winthrop's funeral sixty rings, worth over a pound apiece, were given to friends. The entire expense of the latter-named funeral—scutcheons, hatchments, scarves, gloves, rings, bell-tolling, tailor's bills, etc., was over six hundred pounds. This amounted to one-fifth of the entire estate of the deceased gentleman.

These mourning rings were of gold, usually enamelled in black, or black and white. They were frequently decorated with a death's-head, or with a coffin with a full-length skeleton lying in it, or with a winged skull. Sometimes they held a framed lock of hair of the deceased friend. Sometimes the ring was shaped like a serpent with his tail in his mouth.

Many bore a posy. In the *Boston News Letter* of October 30, 1742, was advertised: "Mourning Ring lost with the Posy Virtue & Love is From Above." Here is another advertisement from the *Boston Evening Post:*

> " Escaped unluckily from me
>   A Large Gold Ring, a Little Key ;
>   The Ring had Death engraved upon it ;
>   The Owners Name inscribed within it ;
>   Who finds and brings the same to me
>   Shall generously rewarded be."

A favorite motto for these rings was : "Death parts United Hearts." Another was the legend : "Death conquers all ; " another, " Prepare for Death ; " still another, " Prepared be To follow me." Other funeral rings bore a family crest in black enamel.

Goldsmiths kept these mourning rings constantly on hand. " Deaths Heads Rings " and "Burying Rings " appear in many newspaper advertisements. When bought for use the name or initials of the dead person, and the date of his death, were engraved upon the ring. This was called fashioning. It is also evident from existing letters and bills that orders were sent by bereaved ones to friends residing at a distance to purchase and wear mourning rings in memory of the dead, and send the bills to the heirs or the principals of the mourning family. Thus, after the death of Andrew, son of Sir William Pepperell, Mr. Kilby, of London, wrote to the father that he accepted " that melancholy token of y'r regard to Mrs. K. and myself at the expense of four guineas in the whole. But, as is not unusual here on such occasions, Mrs. K. has, at her own expense, added some sparks of diamonds to some other mournful ornaments to the ring, which she intends to wear."

It is very evident that old New Englanders looked with much eagerness to receiving a funeral ring at the death of a friend, and in old diaries, almanacs, and note-books such entries as this are often seen: "Made a ring at the funeral," "A death's-head ring made at the funeral of so and so;" or, as Judge Sewall wrote, "Lost a ring" by not attending the funeral. The will of Abigail Ropes, in 1775, gives to her grandson "a gold ring I made at his father's death;" and again, "a gold ring made when my bro. died."

As with gloves, rings of different values were given to relatives of different degrees of consanguinity, and to friends of different stations in life; much tact had to be shown, else much offence might be taken.

I do not know how long the custom of giving mourning rings obtained in New England. Some are in existence dated 1812, but were given at the funeral of aged persons who may have left orders to their descendants to cling to the fashion of their youth.

A·very good collection of mourning rings may be seen at the rooms of the Essex Institute in Salem, and that society has also published a pamphlet giving a list of such rings known to be in existence in Salem.

As years passed on a strong feeling sprang up

against these gifts and against the excessive wearing of mourning garments because burdensome in expense. Judge Sewall notes, in 1721, the first public funeral "without scarfs." In 1741 it was ordered by Massachusetts Provincial Enactment that "no Scarves, Gloves (except six pair to the bearers and one pair to each minister of the church or congregation where any deceased person belongs), Wine, Rum, or rings be allowed to be given at any funeral upon the penalty of fifty pounds." The *Connecticut Courant* of October 24, 1764, has a letter from a Boston correspondent which says, "It is now out of fashion to put on mourning for nearest relatives, which will make a saving to this town of £20,000 per annum." It also states that a funeral had been held at Charlestown at which no mourning had been worn. At that of Ellis Callender in the same year, the chief mourner wore in black only bonnet, gloves, ribbons, and handkerchief. Letters are in existence from Boston merchants to English agents rebuking the latter for sending mourning goods, such as crapes, "which are not worn." A newly born and fast-growing spirit of patriotic revolt gave added force to the reform. Boston voted, in October, 1767, " not to use any mourning gloves but what are manufactured here," and other towns passed similar resolutions. It was also suggested that American mourning gloves be stamped with a patriotic emblem. In 1788 a fine of twenty shillings was imposed on any person who gave scarfs, gloves, rings, wine, or rum at a funeral; who bought any new mourning apparel to wear at or after a funeral, save a crape arm-band if a masculine mourner, or black bonnet, fan, gloves, and ribbons if a woman. This law could never have been rigidly enforced, for much gloomy and ostentatious pomp obtained in the larger towns even to our own day. "From the tombs a mournful sound " seemed to be fairly a popular sound, and the long funeral processions, always taking care to pass the Town House, churches, and other public buildings, obstructed travel, and men were appointed in each town by the selectmen to see that " free passage in the streets be kept open." Funerals were forbidden to be held on the Lord's Day, because it profaned the sacred day, through the vast concourse of children and servants that followed the coffin through the streets.

Some attempt was made to regulate funeral expenses. In Salem a tolling of the bell could cost but eightpence, and "the sextons are desired to toll the bells but four strokes in a minute." The undertakers could charge but eight shillings for borrowing chairs, waiting on the pall-holders, and notifying relatives to attend.

The early graves were frequently clustered, were even crowded in irregular groups in the churchyard; and in larger towns, the dead—especially persons of dignity — were buried, as in England, under the church. Sargent, in his "Dealings with the Dead," speaks at length of the latter custom, which prevailed to an inordinate extent in Boston. In smaller settlements some out-of-the-way spot was chosen for a common burial-place, in barren pasture or on lonely hillside, thus forcibly proving the well-known lines of Whittier,

> " Our vales are sweet with fern and rose,
>   Our hills are maple crowned,
> But not from them our fathers chose
>   The village burial ground.

> " The dreariest spot in all the land
>   To Death they set apart ;
> With scanty grace from Nature's hand
>   And none from that of Art."

To the natural loneliness of the country burial-place and to its inevitable sadness, is now too frequently added the gloomy and depressing evidence of human neglect. Briers and weeds grow in tangled thickets over the forgotten graves; birch-trees and barberry bushes spring up unchecked. In one a thriving grove of lilac bushes spreads its dusty shade from wall to wall. Winter-killed shrubs of flowering almond or snowballs, planted in tender memory, stand now withered and unheeded, and the few straggling garden flowers—crimson phlox or single hollyhocks—that still live only painfully accent the loneliness by showing that this now forgotten spot was once loved, visited, and cared for.

In many cases the worn gravestone lies forlornly face downward ; sometimes,

> " The slab has sunk ; the head declined,
>   And left the rails a wreck behind.
> No names ; you trace a ' 6 '—a ' 7,'
>   Part of ' affliction ' and of ' Heaven.'

And then in letters sharp and clear,
You read—O Irony austere!—
'Tho' lost to Sight, to Memory dear.'"

"Truly our fathers find their graves in our short
memories, and sadly show us how we may be buried
in our survivors.'"   Still, this neglect and oblivion is
just as satisfactory as was the officious "deed without a name" done in orderly Boston, where, in the
first half of this century, a precise Superintendent
of Graveyards and his army of assistants—what
Charles Lamb called "sapient trouble-tombs"—
straightened out mathematically all the old burial-
places, levelled the earth, and set in trim military
rows the old slate headstones, regardless of the
irregular clusters of graves and their occupants.

And there in Boston the falsifying old headstones
still stand, fixed in new places, but marking no coffins
or honored bones beneath; the only true words of
their inscriptions being the opening ones "Here
lies," and the motto that they repeat derisively to
each other—"As you are now so once was I."

In many communities each family had its own burying-place in some corner of the home farm, sometimes at the foot of garden or orchard. Such is no-
ticeably the case throughout Narragansett; almost
every farm has a grave-yard, now generally unused and
deserted. Sometimes the burying-place is enclosed
by a high mossy stone wall, often it is overgrown with
dense sombre firs or hemlocks, or half shaded with
airy locust-trees. Beautifully ideal and touching is

the thought of these old Narragansett planters resting with their wives and children in the ground they
so dearly loved and so faithfully worked for.

A vast similarity of design existed in the early
gravestones. Originality of inscription, carving, size,
or material was evidently frowned upon as frivolous,
undignified, and eccentric — even disrespectful. A
few of the early settlers used freestone or sienite, or a
native porphyritic green stone called beech-bowlder.
Sandstone was rarely employed, for though easily
carved, it as easily yielded to New England frosts
and storms. A hard, dark, flinty slate-stone from
North Wales was commonly used, a stone so hard
and so enduring that when our modern granite and
marble monuments are crumbled in the dust I believe these old slate headstones still will speak their
warning words of many centuries.

> " As I am now so you shall be,
>   Prepare for Death & follow me."

These stones were imported from England ready
carved. A high duty was placed on them, and a
Boston sea captain endeavored and was caught in the
attempt to bring into port, free of duty, for one of
his friends, one of these carved slate gravestones, by
entering it as a winding-sheet. It is one of the curiosities of New England commercial enterprises, that
for many years gravestones should have been imported to New England, a land that fairly bristles
with stone and rock thrusting itself through the earth
and waiting to be carved.

The Welsh stones were made of a universal pattern—a carved top with a space enclosing a miserable death's or winged cherub's head as a heading, a border of scrolls down either side of the inscription, and rarely a design at the base. Weeping willows and urns did not appear in the carving at the top until the middle of the eighteenth century, and fought hard with the grinning cherub's head until this century, when both were supplanted by a variety of designs— a clock-face, hour-glass, etc. Capital letters were used wholly in the inscriptions until Revolutionary times, and even after were mixed with Roman text with so little regard for any printer's law that, at a little distance, many a New England tombstone of the latter part of the past century seems to be carven in hieroglyphics.

Special families in New England seem to have appropriated special verses as epitaphs, evidently because of the rhyme with the surname. Thus the Jones family were properly proud of this family rhyme:

> " Beneath this Ston's
> Int'r'd the Bon's
> Ah Frail Remains
> Of Lieut Noah Jones "—

or Mary Jones or William Jones, as the case might be.

The Noyes family delighted in these lines:

> " You children of the name of Noyes
> Make Jesus Christ yo'r only choyse."

The Tutes and Shutes and Roots began their epitaphs thus:

> " Here lies cut down like unripe fruit
> The wife of Deacon Amos Shute."

Gershom Root was " cut down like unripe fruit " at the fully mellowed age of seventy-three.

A curiously incomprehensible epitaph is this, which always strikes me afresh, upon each perusal, as a sort of mortuary conundrum :

> " O ! Happy Probationer !
> Accepted without being Exercised."

Sometimes an old epitaph will be found of such impressive though simple language that it clings long in the memory. Such is this verse of gentle quaintness over the grave of a tender Puritan blossom, the child of an early settler :

> " Submit Submitted to her heavenly Kinge
> Being a flower of that Aeternal Spring
> She died at laste in Heaven to waite
> The Yeare was sixteen hundred 48."

Another of unusual beauty and sentiment is this :

> " I came in the morning—it was Spring
>   And I smiled.
> I walked out at noon—it was Summer
>   And I was glad.

I sat me down at even—it was Autumn
And I was sad.
I laid me down at night—it was Winter
And I slept."

Collections of curious old epitaphs have been made and printed, but seem dull and colorless on the printed page, and the warning words seem to lose their power unless seen in the sad graveyard, where, "silently expressing old mortality," the hackneyed rhymes and tender words are touching from their very simplicity and the loneliness which surrounds them, and for their calm repetition, on stone after stone, of an undying faith in a future life.

One cannot help being impressed, when studying the almanacs, diaries, and letters of the time, with the strange exaltation of spirit with which the New England Puritan regarded death. To him thoughts of mortality were indeed cordial to the soul. Death was the event, the condition, which brought him near to God and that unknown world, that "life elysian" of which he constantly spoke, dreamed and thought; and he rejoiced mightily in that close approach, in that sense of touch with the spiritual world. With unaffected cheerfulness he yielded himself to his own fate, with unforced resignation he bore the loss of dearly loved ones, and with eagerness and almost affection he regarded all the gloomy attributes and surroundings of death. Sewall could find in a visit to his family tomb, and in the heart-rending sight of the coffins therein, an "awfull yet pleasing Treat;" while Mr. Joseph

Eliot said ' " that the two days wherein he buried his wife and son were the best he ever had in the world." The accounts of the wondrous and almost inspired calm which settled on those afflicted hearts, bearing steadfastly the Christian belief as taught by the Puritan church, make us long for the simplicity of faith, and the certainty of heaven and happy reunion with loved ones which they felt so triumphantly, so gloriously.